THE HONEYMOONERS LOST EPISODES

THE HONEYMOONERS LOST EPISODES

by Donna McCrohan
and Peter Crescenti

Workman Publishing, New York

Library of Congress Cataloging-in-Publication Data
McCrohan, Donna.
The Honeymooners' lost episodes.
1. Honeymooners (Television program) I. Crescenti,
Peter. II. Title.
PN1992.77.H623M33   1986   791.43'72   86-40203
ISBN 0-80480-157-0 (pbk.)

The Sheaffer magazine ads on page 176 are reproduced by
permission of Sheaffer Eaton Division of Textron, Inc. The Nescafé
instant coffee promotion on page 176 is used with permission of the
copyright owner Nestlé Foods Corporation.

Cover photograph courtesy
Personality Photos, Inc.

Cover design: Charles Kreloff
Book design: Linda Peterson

Workman Publishing
1 West 39 Street
New York, New York 10018

Manufactured in the United States of America
First printing October 1986
10 9 8 7 6 5 4 3 2 1

*To Jackie Gleason
and his air-conditioned vault.*

ACKNOWLEDGMENTS

Very special thanks to Jackie Gleason, whom we have long known to be a Great One and a good guy, and who continues to come up with ways to remind us that he is both.

Special thanks, too, to Richard Green, Esquire, truly one of nature's noblemen, and to Jaffer Ali, Ethel Owen Almy, Bart Andrews, Boris Aplon, Howard Bender, Louise Bender, Bruce Bennett, Howard Berk, Joan Reichman Canale, Art Carney, Brian Carney, Joe Cates, Frances Tannehill Clark, Sara Cole, Bob Columbe, Harry Crane, Dawn Crescenti, Phil Cuoco, Virginia (Gingr Jones) Damon, Frank Davis, Humphrey Davis, Bullets Durgom, Tamara Ehlin, Liz Evans, Ken Farrell, Lynn Fero, Herb Finn, Alexander Frank, Howard Frank, Michael Gerber, Stu Ginsberg, Marilyn Gleason, Eddie Hanley, Val Irving, Coleman Jacoby, Just Kids, Jay Larkin, Philip M. Levine, Joe Lewinger, Denise Marcil, Bill Mark, Frank Marth, Doreen Marx, Mary Helen McMahon, Audrey Meadows, James Oliver, George Petrie, Patti Petrie, Jack Philbin, Rosalie Poznachowski, Joyce Randolph, Sandy Renda, Freda Rosen, A.J. Russell, Frank Satenstein, Herb Scannell, Anne Seymour, Ron Simon, Sydell Spear, Frederica Stalter, Leonard Stern, Walter Stone, Phil Tantillo, June Taylor, Betsy Vorce, Cora Zelinka, Bill Zuckert, and our much-beleaguered editor, Sally Kovalchick.

Thanks also to Viacom, Showtime, and Maljack Productions, Inc. for allowing us to view episodes of the "Lost Honeymooners."

CONTENTS

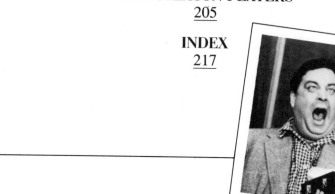

INTRODUCTION

"The Honeymooners" merits the kind of respect
accorded "Playhouse 90" and "Kraft Television Theater."
THE WASHINGTON POST (1985)

Nobody knew. Nobody could have known. Nor would anyone in the '50s have believed that, despite its enormous popularity, *The Honeymooners* was destined to gather steam with the decades. Other phenomena of its vintage might, with reason, have been trusted to endure—The Mouseketeers, the annual election of Miss Rheingold, that dropping ball in Times Square to signal the arrival of the New Year. But *The Honeymooners*? *The Honeymooners* was a weekly burst of excitement, just like the fireworks in its opening credits. It was a shooting star, and we all know what happens to shooting stars.

Or, we thought we did. It took *The Honeymooners* to prove us wrong.

*Perhaps no other TV program of the '50s—not even
the great "I Love Lucy"—has become as firmly
ingrained in the national consciousness as "The Honeymooners."*
THE NEW YORK POST (1985)

*There is still a pervasive purity to it. "The
Honeymooners" has not become camp, the way
"Leave It to Beaver" has, or the way "Dynasty" instantly is.*
THE WASHINGTON POST (1985)

*So, in Brooklyn, in the Fifties, we watched "The
Honeymooners".... We didn't imagine in those days
that "The Honeymooners" would be with us the rest of
our lives.... Ralph and Norton remain the same, and
we know them better now than we did then.*
PETE HAMILL, NEW YORK MAGAZINE (1985)

So? Thirty-plus years ago, we guessed wrong. That's old news. At least we've got our perspectives straight now.

No, we haven't. Rather, we haven't, yet we have. That's the new news—for which we have the "Lost Episodes" to thank. These recently unearthed treasures reveal long-forgotten sides of the Kramdens and Nortons. Inconsistencies too. They leave us questioning not the greatness of the show—which they resoundingly confirm—but how well we really know these people we claim to know completely.

For what we've been watching all these years—the long syndicated "Classic Thirty-nine" episodes—was an end product from the 1955–56 season. The Lost Episodes were made, for the most part, earlier. Seeing them is like watching home movies taken years *before* we knew good friends. Our friends are the same people they were yesterday, but now we see them through different eyes.

The Lost Episodes challenge our perspectives along with our eyeballs. Even the seemingly dated details are ultimately profound. Take another look at Ralph's bang-zoom threats, his crazy harebrained schemes, his poverty. You're not just seeing superb cast chemistry and jokes against a backdrop. You're seeing a man at war with his emotions, whose whole personality alternately screams and moans, "Gimme a break." And all the while, he is, and his team is, and the show is, monumentally funny.

Oh, Ralph Kramden is the same man he was yesterday. But wait till you see his home movies!

What you thought Ralph couldn't do, wouldn't do, never did—like shove Alice when his heart is breaking with jealous pain—maybe he did after all.

And just when you thought you knew every last thing about Ralph and Alice and Ed and Trixie, you discover you've only just met.

LOST SHOWS FOUND

The Honeymooners *has the strangest history of any*
sitcom ever.
The New York Daily News

For as long as fans have known that not all *Honeymooners* episodes
were in the regular rerun packages, fans have asked for redress.
Invariably they were told that (1) the episodes were lost, and (2) the
technical quality would be so poor that they wouldn't be fit to watch if
they were found. As recently as 1982, one New Jersey fan asked the
local *Honeymooners* station whether the *Honeymooners* kinescopes could be
found and somehow rejuvenated for broadcast. Since the station had just presented a movie in 3-D, it seemed like a good time to raise the question.
"Unfortunately," came the reply, "the technical quality of a kinescope is
impossible to broadcast without substantial expense. Although we don't see this
happening in the near future, with increasing technological advances, the possibility of cost reduction for this type of process is not incomprehensible."

The only thing that seems incomprehensible today is how sensible the answer
seemed then. *Revenge of the Creature* in 3-D swimming around in your living
room? A mere bag of shells. But *The Honeymooners* kinescopes found and fixed
for broadcast? Ask again in a hundred years.

The scene shifts to Florida, to Jackie Gleason. Blissfully unaware of this
exchange. Playing golf. Sitting on a secret. Biding his time. Unfindable kinescopes? Unfixable kinescopes? Har-har-HAR-dee-har-har.

To fans in Jersey, maybe you say "incomprehensible" and "impossible." To
Jackie Gleason, you say, apparently, "Open sesame." Jackie, you see, is one
sharp guy. He didn't just fall off the turnip truck, nor did he find the Lost
Episodes in one. He never lost several million dollars worth of *Honeymooners*
episodes in the first place. Quite the contrary. "Nobody asked about them," is his
simple explanation for their disappearance and subsequent rediscovery. "They
were nicely stacked, waiting for the phone to ring."

They were in storage—while a handful of other *Honeymooners* episodes had
been playing in almost seamless syndication since October 1956—because *The*

Honeymooners occupies a unique position in television history. Its Lost Episodes were created for and originally seen as sketches of varying lengths in the early '50s as part of the live, hourlong Jackie Gleason variety show. Though these *Jackie Gleason Shows* were live and seen only once, cameras were pointed at television monitors to film them for prime time airing an hour later in the Midwest and three hours later on the West Coast. Films of this sort, called *kinescopes,* were not in themselves unique. They were made not only for the Gleason program, but for most live, prime-time network offerings of the period.

What sets *The Honeymooners* apart from its contemporaries is *one* 1955–56 season, when thirty-nine live sketches were produced as half-hour sitcoms and recorded by Electronicam, a more advanced technology than kinescopes, with a view toward rerunning them. The reruns gave Gleason a decided edge over '50s comedy giants such as Sid Caesar and Milton Berle, who had tremendous sway over their audiences but no ''repeats'' to keep them in the public eye. Now, the Lost Episodes give *The Honeymooners* the advantage over Golden Age reruns like *I Love Lucy* and *Sergeant Bilko,* of which every available episode long since went into syndication.

As RALPH (Royal Association for the Longevity and Preservation of *The Honeymooners*) co-founder Bob Columbe sums up the situation, ''It's like finding records the Beatles made twenty-five years ago that were never released.'' Better yet—it's like finding twice as many as the Beatles ever released, since the Lost Episodes virtually treble the footage of *Honeymooners* material available to fans.

Nor is their impact diminished by the fact that Gleason had them all along, since most people genuinely believed they were lost, as so many Golden Age kinescopes had been. ''All of us relied on the networks to store our shows,'' reflects producer Joe Cates, who was assistant producer when *The Honeymooners* was first created for *The Cavalcade of Stars.* ''I discovered in 1969 that all the shows I did in the '50s and '60s were lost. The networks had destroyed them all, to clear space on their shelves.''

Up until early 1984, fans had been emphatically assured that the *Honeymooners* kinescopes were no more. But in March of that year, at RALPH's first convention, *Honeymooners* director Frank Satenstein dropped the bombshell. He said there were kinescopes galore in CBS vaults. He suggested that fans write and call CBS asking for their release.

Meanwhile, the Museum of Broadcasting in New York latched onto the idea. ''The assumption was that they were lost, missing,'' says Ron Simon, the museum's curator of television. ''No one—two or three years ago—would have guessed that Gleason had seventy-odd programs in his collection, nor did we know that CBS kept complete records of these variety shows. We always assumed that they didn't exist. But there was something in the back of my mind saying that it was something I would like to work on. The time came when we wanted to start our 'Discovery Series,' where we would just devote time to discovering lost material. *The Honeymooners* was at the top of our list.

"I spoke to RALPH, and learned that they were aware of the existence of some of these episodes. I decided to take one last look at the CBS vaults, and I worked with the person in charge of the film library in Fort Lee, New Jersey. We worked from a list of dates we had of shows that might possibly represent lost *Honeymooners*, and turned up four.

"During the summer, two years ago, we showed them. It really was a successful event. The first or second day we were running them, we were contacted by two or three cable systems, including Showtime. They were very interested and wanted to know how we got them and if more were available. Later, CBS pursued the matter with Gleason's lawyer.

"We've run *The Honeymooners* in the context of the whole variety show whenever we were able. I always prefer a show that's complete. I think it's almost essential, in anything, to see how it develops, how it evolved. These are part and parcel of the show—the Lescoulie introduction, the commercials . . . you get a much better feel of the rhythm of it. Later, we discovered one of the DuMont shows. We screened it, along with other routines from Gleason that we discovered from that time. They really put Gleason himself into context, and you get a sense of the interrelationship between it and other things."

By August, four of the Lost Episodes were being screened at the museum. Public response was overwhelming, with lines wrapping around the block, and hundreds of would-be viewers unable to get in. "Four rare art treasures went on display," enthused Marvin Kitman in *Newsday.* "Museum land is not used to the kind of density per square inch that will occur when all the members of RALPH discover the Museum of Broadcasting."

Among witnesses to the congestion was Michael Gerber, senior vice president of Viacom Enterprises. Viacom, which has long held syndication rights

Kramden's classic "pain bit."

to the Classic Thirty-nine, was already investigating possible acquisition of the properties. "We had heard over the years that there existed *Honeymooners* material that hadn't been seen since its original airing, but people were vague about the nature of the programming," explains Gerber. "So, for me, for Viacom, from the day that these episodes played at the Museum of Broadcasting, it was a go. I'm telling you, that created it all. We knew there was oil in the ground. We went after it."

Gleason owned the segments as well as the rights, having never sold CBS more than one-time live-broadcast use. Gerber got in touch with Rob Scheidlinger, Gleason's business representative. Then, with Viacom's vice president of program development and production, Toby Martin, he was on his way to Florida and Jackie Gleason: "There were a lot of complicated issues, not just in putting the deal together, but the issue of the guilds and the copyrights, all of these issues came up. Throughout these negotiations, I was most concerned with the technical quality. The material hadn't been seen in thirty years. We were lucky it hadn't decayed.

"Going down to Florida, to see them for the first time, was one of the most interesting things I've ever done in this business, because we were in Jackie's house, which is an interesting house to begin with, and he hadn't seen this material himself in over thirty years. So there we were, Toby, myself, Jackie, and Marilyn, the four of us, watching Jackie watch himself. It was as interesting watching his face as it was watching the monitor."

"We sat," says Toby Martin, "in Gleason's rather enormous game room. It was quite extraordinary to sit there and watch Mr. Gleason chuckling, and kind of doing body English, along with the characters we were watching. And of course, the things we were screening turned out to be absolutely hilarious."

The net result was nearly one hundred and twenty hours of *The Jackie Gleason Show*, containing *Honeymooners* sketches ranging in length from seven minutes to nearly an hour. Found! As to the second aspect of the find-and-fix dilemma, says Gerber, "We saw superb vintage comedic material which far exceeded acceptable technical standards."

Toby Martin, who would have the responsibility of restoring, editing, and transferring the material, was relieved. Many months later, when he'd gone through every inch of film, he was delighted that, "Out of all of it, I saw maybe two hours we couldn't use. For the rest, what we had to do was very interesting. On much of the film was a scratch line down the left side of the screen. There's an electronic device called an *ADO* which, basically, enables us to enlarge the images, putting the scratch mark all the way to the left of the screen. That way, when we use only the television-sized portion of the material, the scratch line is out of the picture entirely. Had we not been able to do this, we probably would have a quarter of the film we have now."

In the end, according to Michael Gerber, "Everyone involved in the project had spent endless hours putting it together. But for all of us it was a labor of love. Without exception, everyone said they never enjoyed working on a project more, and couldn't get enough of it.''

Gleason and Viacom struck the deal. Viacom computers began applying the latest in frame-by-frame technology to bring the films to peak restored quality. Now a press conference had to be called. The first two procedures took place behind closed doors. Actually, the third did too, but at New York City's fabulous 21 Club.

February 6, 1985: The press conference begins. Pandemonium. At least three hundred reporters, photographers, Viacom executives, Showtime executives, and others pack a room that would not otherwise seem small. Take one step to the left and someone accuses you of trying to kick a camera. Step to the right and hors d'oeuvres cascade down your neck. Stay right where you are, and you're still in everyone's way. Enter Joyce Randolph, who is instantly ringed by media people with cameras and mikes. Enter Audrey Meadows, just as quickly surrounded. Art Carney doesn't enter, since he's too sick at home with the flu.

Enter Gleason and wife Marilyn—they've been cautioned not to panic,

Gleason mobbed at Lost Episodes press conference.

though they're sure to be engulfed—and the crowds magically part. Gleason strides as if his shoes are flying carpets. "Just a shade aghast," Ron Powers described him in *GQ*, "at encountering a press contingent the size and intensity of a CIA–backed counterrevolutionary force." Aghast nothing. Standing imperturbably behind a lectern, sporting his signature red carnation, he's king of all he surveys.

The announcement is made that the Lost Episodes will premiere on Showtime cable, beginning later in the year, then go to noncable television the following year. Jackie Gleason reveals that he never merely relied on CBS to store his kinescopes; he's had his own set carefully squirreled away in an air-conditioned vault.

Asked why he chose this moment to unveil them, he jokes, "I think it's certainly the right time. I'm sick of watching those other ones." Then he confides. "You don't need the money, but you sure need the praise." To another query—does he think he was funny?—he allows, "I guess I was pretty funny, but I feel like I'm watching someone else." A voice calls out, "Where's Norton?" Gleason says, "He's sick." "No, not Art Carney," the voice clarifies. "I mean the character, Ed Norton." "Oh," says Gleason, smiling. "He's still in the sewer." Where's Kramden? "He's just driving a smaller bus and he's making the same salary. And the truth is, he's still around."

And where were the kinescopes, really? Replies Gleason, "Ralph found them on the backseat of a bus."

A sampling of Lost Episode tidbits, shown on monitors around the room, follows the interrogation. Funny moves and fat jokes elicit howls of laughter. Jackie goes downstairs to tape a few minutes of *Good Morning America* with David Hartman. Don't anyone else go downstairs. It's land-mined down there with more cameras, more hors d'oeuvres.

The following morning, it's TV history. While the occasional hit series has attempted a reunion special, or even tried to resume a weekly spot after a hiatus, no other show in the career of television has ever emerged—particularly not in its ninety-third rerun cycle—with unseen episodes.

At last, officially as well as in fact, the ball is rolling.

On May 13, NBC presents an hourlong special of Lost Episodes snippets, grouped by theme. Ralph bellowing in pain, for instance, is a theme. The hour is introduced by Jackie Gleason and Audrey Meadows from a replica of the original set, this one constructed by NBC and flown down to Miami for the momentous occasion. Its dimensions aren't quite identical to the original's. But most of the props *are* the originals.

From May through September, the Museum of Broadcasting presents "Discovery: Lost *Honeymooners*." The twenty-week exhibition offers seventeen *Honeymooners* sketches, plus one so rare it isn't even in the Lost Episodes bundle. Made when Gleason was out of action with a broken leg, this one has Art

Audrey Meadows, Jackie Gleason, and Joyce Randolph at Showtime press conference, 1986.

Carney playing Ed Norton's father in a *Person to Person* parody called "People to People." As before, the series is shown in a representative *Jackie Gleason Show* context with commercials, June Taylor Dancers, and Gleason monologue.

Meanwhile, Showtime is mounting the largest promotional campaign in its history to be based on a single program. Among its components are a "premium-driven subscriber-acquisition campaign, a year-long retention campaign, and a national awareness campaign featuring a nationwide tour of the *Honeymooners* fan club RALPH." Translated, this means local promotions like bowling parties; Ralph- and Alice-imitation competitions; "Bus-Driver-of-the-Month" contests; a "Racoon Entrance Exam" trivia test; bowling shirts; T-shirts; wristwatches; mugs; lunch bags; a *Honeymooners* day at Shea Stadium (July 26—fantastic turnout. Then it rains); and a cross-country junket by RALPH co-founders Bob Columbe and Pete Crescenti previewing film clips.

On August 1, Showtime announces its most extensive closed-caption effort to date: the Lost Episodes with closed captions for the hearing-impaired. Comments Gleason, "I am delighted that through the involvement of the National Captioning Institute *The Honeymooners* will be reaching, for the first time, a very special audience. It gives me great pleasure to now be able to share the unique talents of the entire cast and crew of *The Honeymooners* with the hearing-impaired community."

Also in August, for just under a million dollars, MPI seals its own deal for Lost Episodes rights—the right to release them to the home videotape market. MPI lables them the "Hidden Episodes," imparting a certain mystical connotation that just naturally attends secret rituals, sacred ceremonies, and occult lore hidden in plain sight, which only the pure in heart can see. All told, MPI acquires some 115 hours of *Jackie Gleason Show* footage, which would yield more than thirty one-hour *Honeymooners* cassettes compiled from the original skits of varying lengths. "They're real collectibles," notes MPI sales director Jaffer Ali. "They sell much better than they rent through video stores. The first went gold last week. That's thirty thousand cassettes sold. At least three others will be going gold soon. Of course, when you think about great television, you've got to think about *The Honeymooners*. We're big fans here, we always have been. We watched those thirty-nine episodes so many times we memorized the dialogue, and we went after the hidden *Honeymooners* episodes, which we've got now. So it's no surprise to us that they're in such high demand."

By August 19, Showtime is giving the cable-television public its first prolonged glimpses of the Lost Episodes. In *Jackie Gleason's Second Honeymoon,* Jackie, Audrey Meadows, Art Carney, and Joyce Randolph are finally reunited on the TV screen to reminisce about life as the Kramdens and Nortons. The footage, including much more than snippets, is further enhanced by newsreel footage from the '50s and shots of Jackie's old neighborhood in Brooklyn.

On September 2, Showtime airs a three-and-a-half-hour Labor Day marathon of Lost Episodes: "Alice's Aunt Ethel," "Ralph's Sweet Tooth," "Suspense," "Cold," "The Hypnotist," "Glow Worm Cleaning," "Ralph's Diet," "Battle of the Sexes," "Pickles," and "Kramden vs. Norton." On September 5, Showtime commences its regular run of Lost Episodes—like "Masterpiece Theatre," airing each week's offering three separate times in the week. On Showtime. Showtime *cable.*

Not everyone has cable. Suddenly there are *Honeymooners* haves and *Honeymooners* have-nots. Noncable TV enters the playoffs with a pair of two-hour specials from Viacom. The first, Honeymooners *Anniversary Celebration,* includes the memorable "Adoption" episode and, as an added bonus, a computer-colorized "Glow Worm Cleaning." The second noncable special, *Season's Greetings from The Honeymooners*, sweetens the pot with a Kramden Christmas openhouse, and the Kramdens and Nortons on New Year's Eve with Tommy and Jimmy Dorsey.

But the cable haves are getting, weekly, what the noncable have-nots get only in controlled doses. The cable haves are absorbing whole new levels of trivia. The noncable have-nots are still thinking of Herman Gruber as a Racoon bowler and pizza connoisseur, and ''Trixie'' as the given name of Norton's wife. Little do they know . . .

Now, with the full-fledged arrival of the Lost Episodes to *all* television, the smoke of confusion is clearing, but the fireworks have only begun.

''I was talking to Joyce Randolph,'' said Audrey Meadows after the 21 Club press conference, ''and she said, 'Do you remember the one where we bought a hotel?' I said, *'Bought a hotel?'*''

If Audrey forgot, think of fans not yet old enough to remember. Not just ''Ralph's Sweet Tooth'' and ''The Hypnotist,'' but ''Two Men on a Horse,'' ''Stars over Flatbush,'' and ''Letter to the Boss.'' And more. And more. And more. Once there were the Classic Thirty-nine. Now the lump sum exceeds one hundred.

Hello out there in television land.
There's a lot of catching up to do. . . .

The Showtime mementos— catalogue, tote bag, watch, T-shirt, program guide (a.k.a. Gotham Bus Schedule).

EXCERPTS FROM THE 21 CLUB PRESS CONFERENCE

REPORTER: Why were they in the vault so long?

GLEASON: No one asked for anything. And we had them there, nice, stacked up, in an air-conditioned room...waiting for the phone to ring. And, finally, it rang, and... that's why we're here tonight.

REPORTER: How did you like seeing yourself? (i.e., in the Lost Episodes segments just shown.)

GLEASON: Well, I guess I was pretty funny, then. *(Laughter)*

REPORTER: Are you funny? Were you funny?

GLEASON: Yeah! *(Laughter)* Except Art might have been a little funnier. *(Laughter)* And Audrey got a couple of laughs there that I didn't remember. *(Laughter)*

REPORTER: Mr. Gleason, was it routine procedure to do kinescopes on all these, or did you have some personal involvement in preserving these films?

GLEASON: No. They made kinescopes because an hour later they showed in Chicago, and they had to use kinescopes. And, of course, three hours later in California.

REPORTER: Well, how did the shows get into someone's vault, and whose vault was it?

At the press conference, Gleason quips that the Lost Episodes were "found on the back seat of a bus."

GLEASON: Well, we always received a copy of the show. That was in my contract.

REPORTER: Were these your personal copies?

GLEASON: These are my personal copies.

REPORTER: You knew they were there all along, didn't you?

GLEASON: Yes. *(Laughter)* I certainly did.

REPORTER: Did you expect to wait thirty years, though, to release them?

GLEASON: I don't know. We really didn't think about it . . . until Ralph found them on the back seat of the bus. *(Laughter)*

REPORTER: Why has *The Honeymooners* remained so popular all these years?

GLEASON: I don't know. I could give you a couple of academic reasons, but the real reason is they're funny. And that people liked the people in the show. And that's the main thing. If you've got the people liking you, you're home.

REPORTER: Back in the '60s, you did a reunion of *The Honeymooners*. Would you consider doing another reunion show?

GLEASON: Oh, sure. If we get a good script and there's a reason to do . . . an hour *Honeymooners*, we'll . . . I'm sure we'll do it.

REPORTER: Really? And you would have the original cast?

GLEASON: Yes.

REPORTER: With Joyce?

GLEASON: I believe so.

REPORTER: Has television comedy lost something since the days of *The Honeymooners*? I mean, people seem to be more interested in what you did thirty years ago than they are in what's going on today.

GLEASON: Well, isn't that nice. *(Laughter)* I don't know why. I think the shows now are, usually, indulged in sexual innuendo and . . . very few real funny moves. There's nobody in television, now, like Art Carney. That's a cinch. And . . . they're taking actors, now, and making comedians out of actors. Which is a strange thing. I know of several comedians who became good actors. But I never heard of a good actor becoming a good comedian.

REPORTER: How did Ralph develop? Was he within yourself?

GLEASON: Well, there were a thousand Ralphs living in my neighborhood when I was a kid. *(Laughter)* And a couple of hundred Nortons. *(Laughter)* So it wasn't difficult.

REPORTER: Is this a different Ralph in these earlier episodes?

GLEASON: No, it's the same . . . the same poor soul.

Gleason in All Through the Night, *1942.* Left to right: *William Demarest, Wally Ford, and Frank McHugh.*

WORKS IN PROGRESS

Jackie Gleason is a cinch for stardom.
NEW YORK DAILY MIRROR (**1944**)

A mong works in progress in the 1930s and '40s was television, its development severely restricted by the need to channel the nation's technology into the war effort.

Another work in progress was Herbert John Gleason, whose mother called him "Jackie." When he was a boy, Saturday movie matinees were his chief recreation. From the first time his father took him to a vaudeville show, from the first intermission when the house lights went on and Jackie turned to see the audience seated behind him, he realized his true calling was to face the audience, not the actors. "I wouldn't be afraid up there," he chirped. He left the theater a stage-struck kid, and returned home a fledgling ham.

A protected only child whose older brother had died when Jackie was three, he'd often entertain himself and his parents at home by doing Charlie Chaplin and Buster Keaton routines. When his mother wouldn't let him out to play with other children—which was most of the time—he'd watch through the window, observing human nature in action. These observations would serve him handsomely, years later, on stage.

His premier public laugh came in school, when the principal dropped, then picked up, a microphone and Jackie quipped, "That's the first thing you've ever done for us kids."

At age fifteen, Jackie broke into the world of bright lights and tinsel with victory in an amateur-night contest at Brooklyn's Halsey Theater. For ever after, he was some way or another performing for pay. He tried his hand at prizefighting and exhibition diving. He was an emcee and a disc jockey and a comic. He did burlesque comedy and night-club acts. Along the way, he picked up the style, the timing, and the knowhow that would one day merge with his own innate gifts to produce the inimitable Great One.

One Gleason friend who recalls his work-in-progress days is Eddie Hanley. Eddie, a vaudeville star when Gleason came on the scene, later became a

Gleason with Bullets Durgom.

Honeymooners regular. "Jackie's act," says Eddie, "was a mixed bag that was largely determined by the crowd. Partly it was an insult act. When I say 'insult act,' it wasn't as bad as Don Rickles. It was—for example, a movie star comes in, and Jackie says, 'I saw your last picture. I think it *is* your last picture.' Or like when Hollywood's skating sweetheart, Sonja Henie, came to Club 18. He accosted her with an ice cube and said, 'Do something.' Or a woman would get up from her table and take a walk to the ladies' room, and he'd sing, 'I know where you're go-iiing.' The minute she'd get inside, he'd rap on the door with a cane. 'Come on out. You've had enough time in there.' Then there'd maybe be a drum roll. He also played a bum trumpet, and he did imitations. Just a few words. They weren't sustained imitations by a long shot. Peter Lorre, that sort of thing. It wasn't a set act you could sell. But he was perfect for cafés, because he could ad-lib."

Jackie, on a 1986 Johnny Carson *Tonight* show, was even harder on himself. "I had the worst act in show business. It was horrible. It was six minutes of absolute boredom. And on my TV show one night, the curtain got stuck, so I did my old act, and it was a riot. I can't understand it. When I needed it, it didn't work. At Club 18, the greatest night club in the world, you weren't allowed to *do* an act. It was all ad lib. And every night there were big stars, Robert Taylor, Jimmy Cagney, and they'd come in and we'd make fun of them."

A chance acquaintance from Jackie's early years, Bullets Durgom, later became his manager: "I'll tell you where I first saw Gleason. It was Singac, New Jersey. I was working for Tommy Dorsey then, and he was looking for a little gal singer. He had Jo Stafford and the Pied Pipers and he had Sinatra, but Tommy wanted somebody to do the cute stuff. I went to Singac, which wasn't far from Meadowbrook, where I hung out. There was Connie Haines, who was just right for Tommy, and there was Jackie, the comic, the opening act. It was a little joint. The place was so small, every table was ringside. I don't think there were more than six or eight people in that front area. Out came this comic, this fat guy, and I'm sitting, waiting for Connie to come on, and this fat guy started picking on me. I was bald *then*. He made cracks. I was chewing a Chiclet or something. He made cracks. I came back at him. Then we started going back and forth. I was just kibitzing with him. People laughed, I suppose, but it was over and that was the end of it.

"When the show was finished, I was waiting for Connie. I spoke to her. And then Gleason came over to me and said, 'How'd you like to be in my act?' I said, 'What?' He said, 'Why don't we team up? We could have some laughs.' Now he didn't know me from anyone, didn't know if I was a customer there or what. I declined. I said, 'No, Jackie, it's not for me. I'm not in that end of the business. I'm a manager.' He said, 'Oh?' But we didn't pursue it."

In 1940, Gleason appeared on Broadway in *Keep Off the Grass*. Frances Tannehill Clark, who was in it too, recalls, "It had everybody in the world in it. It had Ray Bolger, Jimmy Durante, Jane Froman, Ilka Chase, Jackie Gleason, José Limón as a featured dancer, and Jerome Robbins was in the chorus. It was a revue, and revues were sort of a thing of the past, because apparently there was no future in a Broadway show if you couldn't sell it to the movies, and Hollywood wasn't interested in acquiring rights to Broadway revues. So even with that stellar lineup, it only ran six weeks. While he was in this, Gleason was working in that enormous night club in Flushing, Queens, which was equivalent to the Stork Club

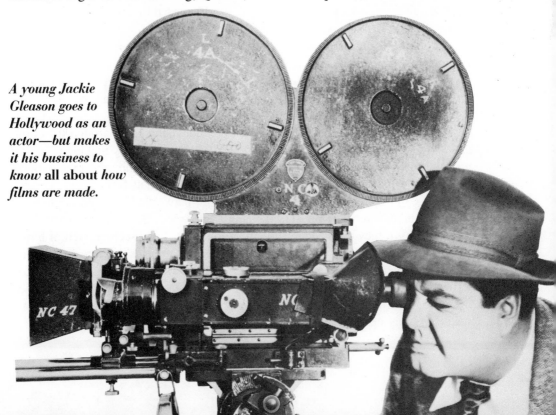

A young Jackie Gleason goes to Hollywood as an actor—but makes it his business to know all about *how films are made.*

of Flushing. He was working there at night, and rehearsing with us during the day. It was kind of a drag for him, to put it mildly. It was grueling, getting done at four A.M. or whenever, and having to be at our rehearsal at ten A.M.

Also in 1940, movie producer Jack Warner saw Jackie perform at Club 18 in New York, was successfully insulted by him, and immediately signed him to a Hollywood contract. Though signed to be funny, he found himself cast in a series of roles (as Jackie C. Gleason) that were lifelessly bland. In one film, *Orchestra Wives,* he played a guy in the orchestra—quickly forgettable—but the starring orchestra was the Glenn Miller Orchestra, the singer was Connie Haines, and Miller's road manager was Bullets Durgom.

"The first time I can say that I got to know Gleason was when he was making *Orchestra Wives* for 20th Century-Fox," says Durgom. "He played bass in the picture. He was a bit player then, in a sense, a character actor. He'd come out to the West Coast and brought his family, but he had no car. I'd give him rides back and forth to the set every day because I was going there myself. We became good friends then. I got to know him well enough to hear his problems."

After five movies, Jackie came East again to do more club work, along with Broadway revues like *Follow the Girls*. In January 1947, tastemaker Walter Winchell caught Jackie's act at Club 18 and gave it raves in his column. The accolades brought Jackie a thirty-five-hundred-dollar-a-week engagement at Billy Rose's Diamond Horseshoe. But a night-club booking, unlike driving for Gotham Bus Company, is not a job for life.

Says Durgom, "Gleason's back in New York. A friend of mine puts us together. Gleason doesn't have a manger. I'm interested in talking, he's interested in talking. We come to a talent–manager understanding.

"Those days, I was in and out of town. I had some clients in the East, and I'd brought in Jack Philbin as a partner. Philbin had also been a manager with the Glenn Miller Orchestra. In fact, I'm pretty sure he first met Gleason during *Orchestra Wives*. But the point is, I had other things to take care of, so Philbin came in to pretty much look after my interests in the East.

"Well, anyway, I really got hooked when television came around the corner and Milton Berle was such a hot item on NBC. Berle was really making television an important situation in the entertainment business. And I thought, I know Berle, I know his work, and Gleason is as sharp as Berle is, and as fast as Berle is, and I thought, I should really get Gleason on another network. If I could get him on. Well, I couldn't get him on. They weren't interested. So I figured they didn't believe in him, they didn't know enough about him. I had seen enough of him to know. I'd seen him in clubs on both coasts. There was a club on Wilshire Boulevard where Jackie played, and there was a small club on Fairfax across from CBS where Jackie played, so I'd seen him work in places other than the one where he ribbed me in Singac, and other than on *Orchestra Wives*. I thought he was ready for a big network show."

In 1949, Jackie landed, not a big network show, but a well-received part in the Broadway revue *Along Fifth Avenue.* His work earned him the prestigious George Jean Nathan Award, but again, no job for life.

Ironically, Jackie Gleason's first TV show was on the same network as Milton Berle—NBC. The show wasn't anything Uncle Miltie was likely to lose sleep over. As Chester A. Riley in *The Life of Riley,* Jackie inherited a role created on radio by William Bendix, a role Bendix was unable to assume because his RKO movie contract wouldn't let him do television. The show itself was far from the ideal Gleason vehicle, but it did put his face in the public eye. People were starting to recognize him on the street, calling, "Hi, Chester," and "Hey, Riley," and—the sweetest music to his ears—"Aren't you Jackie Gleason?"

"Now, look," remembers Bullets. "I knew what I knew. Any idiot knew that Berle had opened up the doors, the possibilities, of television. Television was coming to life. Also, Berle was a different kind of comic from Jackie Gleason, meaning that there was a certain good-sized crowd that loved Berle, and the crowd that didn't would love Gleason. Because they had two different types of acts. So I was convinced that I had to get Jackie on one of the networks, on CBS, NBC, or ABC. That didn't work, but there was still the DuMont network."

Indeed, there was. The DuMont network was small, with a limited budget. Its broadcasts didn't even cover the whole East Coast, though the other networks seemed to envy its hold on Pittsburgh. After a while, its basic strategy was to be affordable to sponsors who couldn't afford the other networks. Among the highlights of its low-budget programming were *Captain Video, Life Is Worth Living, The Plainclothesman, Rocky King,* and *Cavalcade of Stars.*

Joe Cates was with DuMont's *Cavalcade of Stars* at the time. "Probably I'm the only member of the production staff left who was there the thirteen weeks before Gleason came, during Gleason, and probably thirteen weeks after he left. It was a variety show, with sketches, and comedy, a song and dance number, and that sort of thing. Milton Douglas was the producer. I was the assistant to the producer, later promoted to the associate producer. I also wrote the *Cavalcade of Bands,* which was its sister show for about two years. We did the show at the Adelphi Theater, across the street from a famous music-business steak house, Al and Dick's Restaurant, where we rehearsed on the third floor, which was our rehearsal studio.

"We were sponsored by ethical drug products. The company was called Drugstore Television Productions. It was owned by a group. I don't remember how many, I think five or six drug chains, with Whelan Drugs the dominant one. The commercials were done by Don Russell, an announcer who wore a little druggist coat and stood behind a little counter. *Cavalcade of Stars* was a hit because of its marketing strategy. These drug chains commanded a counter display, window display, that sort of thing. Really, *that* was the star of the show. When a client bought a commercial on *Cavalcade of Stars,* he was getting all these hidden extras. His product was stocked by these various drug chains, and he was given counter-display and window-display space.''

Initially, Jack Carter hosted the show, then was coaxed away by NBC to do *Saturday Night Revue*. He was followed by Jerry Lester. When Lester left to do *Broadway Open House* (forerunner of the Tonight show), the host slot opened up again. It was offered to Peter Donald, who turned it down, but suggested that perhaps someone should consider Jackie Gleason.

In July 1950, Joe Cates remembers "going through lists with *Cavalcade of Stars* booker Benny Piermont. We were asked to go through a list, to prepare a new list. We sat one afternoon, going through *Variety* and who knows what else, checking our memories, checking everything. And somehow, on a very big list, we remembered Jackie Gleason from *Follow the Girls*. He'd also done *The Life of Riley*, which we remembered. And there was a debate. And we went through this list of names, and—I've done it all my life—names evaporate. They're not available, they don't want to do it, they're not right, someone doesn't agree, whatever, whatever. We ended up with one or two names. All of a sudden, this name at the bottom of the list, Jackie Gleason, seemed right . . .''

Gleason was in Los Angeles, playing Slapsie Maxie's, at the time L.A.'s most famous club. He'd also, as Joe Cates recalls, "just graduated from a school of hypnotism. He had graduated from some school just a week before.''

The fact that *Cavalcade of Stars* was interested, and that Bullets Durgom had been waiting for just this chance, didn't instantly hypnotize Jackie. He'd just relocated his family out west. He wasn't exactly in love with his previous experiences on television. He wasn't in any hurry to go east again. He needed certain guarantees, and got them. According to Bullets Durgom:

"I said to Jackie, 'I got you on DuMont. The money's great. A thousand a week.' And he said, 'How long?' I said, 'Well, we've got a couple of years of options, and with increases—' and I was lying, because if I'd just said there was no guarantee, he wouldn't have wanted to bother. And this way, if he had a year, at least he'd be in action. I figured when the time came, if I had a problem explaining to him, I'd get out of it somehow. But I really thought he had a great chance with this show. And it worked out that way. He came off very strong. He stayed on two years. The next year I got him more money, and never gave them an option beyond that, because I wanted to keep him open, and that's when we got him to CBS, from DuMont.''

Gleason's recollection, in a 1985 Showtime interview, was minus the subterfuge: "I was working at Slapsie Maxie's and a guy came in and caught me one night and asked if I wanted to go to New York for a week and do *Cavalcade of Stars*. I said no, I wasn't interested. He said, 'How about two weeks?' I said, 'All right, I'll go for two weeks.' I thought I was coming right back. I told Sammy Lewis, who owned Slapsie Maxie's, 'I'll be right back in a couple of weeks.' But I went to New York, and things turned out well.''

CAVALCADE

Cavalcade of Stars, *a variety show hosted by that*
rolling boulder of showmanship Jackie Gleason.
JAMES WOLCOTT, *VANITY FAIR*

It was a toss-up in the summer of 1950 whether DuMont or Jackie Gleason
had gotten the bigger break. In Gleason, DuMont had a talented new host
for the tried and true *Cavalcade of Stars.* In *Cavalcade* Gleason landed, at
worst, a job that could lead to a better job on a rival network with more
money to spend.

DuMont's *Cavalcade* had the track record. DuMont also had the sense, with
Gleason's arrival, to reposition *Cavalcade* from Saturday to Friday night, where
its main challenger for the time slot would be NBC's boxing matches and not Sid
Caesar's directly competitive *Your Show of Shows.*

As for Gleason, he had wild moves, a grab bag of funny lines, a great face,
and a natural gift for reaction. His moves com-
bined Charlie Chaplin, Buster Keaton, and another favorite, Jack Oakie, all subsumed by
what Gleason developed himself. He was a
physical comic more than a joke man,
though his way with words extended to
subtleties like an innocuous "Mmmmmmm
—boy!" that, from him, was hilarious.

"I always like Ed Wynn's distinction,"
Gleason says. "A comic *says* funny things.
A comedian *does* things funny."

Adds *Honeymooners* writer Walter
Stone, "With some comedians, if you don't
throw a pie in their face there's no life. With
Jackie, you can do subtle innuendoes. He's a
great performer. I'd say that even if I didn't work
for him."

Looking "as though
he belongs in Ebbets
Field with a container
of beer in his fist."

As early as 1950, Gleason's face was a national treasure. It could be strikingly handsome. Or it could look as the New York *Daily News* described it, "As though he belongs in Ebbets Field with a container of beer in his fist." Or, according to *Time* magazine, "like a big basset hound who had just eaten W. C. Fields . . . a mélange of smugness, mischievousness, humility, humor, guilt, pride, warmth, confidence, perplexity, and orotund, bug-eyed naivete." As to any nuances not covered above, his face could project those too. Pete Hamill has called it "a face made for expression."

Very simply, Gleason had a vocabulary of facial gestures that was enormous. On one level, they enabled him to convulse an audience. On a deeper level—one that would come increasingly to the fore as *Cavalcade* metamorphosed under Gleason—they allowed him to react, to underscore another performer's attempts to convulse the audience. When the other performer was Art Carney, as would soon be the case, the concept of "cast chemistry" would find its perfect embodiment.

Initially, Jackie's gifts were applied to the established *Cavalcade* format. "The first week," says Joe Cates, "Arnie Rosen and Coleman Jacoby, the writers, needed some time to get started, so we rented two sketches. You used to be able to do that, rent sketches from Broadway shows. We rented them from a writer-actor named Hank Ladd. We rented them for $250 apiece. Jackie was infinitely better than the material. I don't remember the other one, but I remember the checkroom sketch. Jackie kept jumping over the checkroom door, as though that was what it was there for, and he was brilliant. He was brilliantly funny.

"Jacoby and Rosen had their hands full. They had to write something like four sketches and a monologue each week, and they had three days to do it. We bought them this extra week. Then they wrote a sketch called 'The Man of Distinction,' where the role for Jackie was what ultimately became Reginald Van Gleason III. Perhaps you remember those whiskey ads going in 1950 for the Man of Distinction, who was very elegant, in a cutaway, on a throne or some sort of regal chair. So we had our man of distinction, and he had to keep posing for a photographer. Now, the photographer was fluttery, all over the place. And the whiskey was there, total temptation to drink, and get drunk, and get drunker, with the photographer showing the playboy how to imbibe for the camera, and that was the nature of the sketch.

"We needed someone to play the photographer. Art Carney was suggested to me by Arnie Rosen and Coleman Jacoby when I went to pick up the sketch. Art used to play the doorman, and Jacqueline Susann played the hatcheck girl, on Morey Amsterdam's show. I went to Irving Mansfield, the producer, as a courtesy, and asked if he'd mind my talking to Art. We were on Fridays, they were on Thursdays, so it wouldn't interfere. It was okay with Irving, so I went to Art. Art was interested, so Ben Piermont called Art's agent, Bill McCaffrey, and they made a deal.

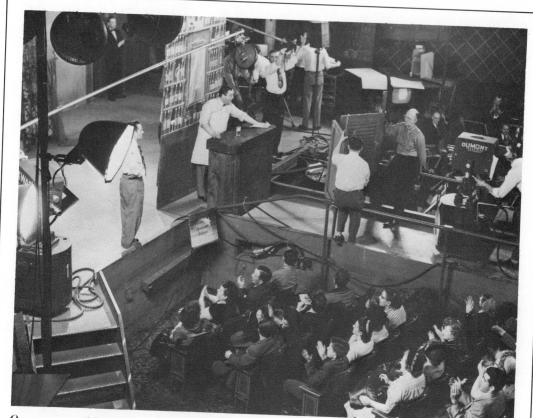

On camera with a "Joe the Bartender" sketch, on DuMont's **Cavalcade of Stars.**

"So there we were. We had this 'Man of Distinction' sketch, and we had Jackie Gleason as our star, and we had Art Carney who was going to play the other part in the sketch. Jackie had no idea what the sketch was until he came to rehearsal Wednesday. Jackie met Art Carney when I said to him, 'Jackie, this is Art Carney.' Jackie said, 'Do I know you, pal?' I said, 'Well, he's been doing that Morey Amsterdam show,' and I remember distinctly Art Carney saying, 'We may have met. I used to be with Horace Heidt and his orchestra.' And Jackie said, 'Well, maybe.' I remember that, and I remember how Art was so terrific in the 'Man of Distinction' sketch, there was just no big discussion about signing him to anything. It was just a given that he'd be on every week. 'What's Art gonna play?' Like that."

One critic later wrote of this historic introduction, "In recommending Carney, Coleman Jacoby and Arnie Rosen equalled the perfection of their hilarious, original scripts."

Already the old *Cavalcade* was becoming something new, on multiple levels. After the second show, Jackie went to Milton Douglas and said, "Look, there's something missing on this. We need some girls. You know, precision dancers. And I've got just the choreographer to do it. I know her from vaudeville." Milton Douglas said, "But I know the right person too." They were both referring to June Taylor, who came by way of *Broadway Spotlight* and the Ed Sullivan Show (where her dancers were called the Toastettes because Sullivan's program was "Toast of the Town"). June Taylor and her dancers joined *Cavalcade* by the third week.

In a matter of about as many weeks the sketches, rather than being largely generic, would be tailored to the star. Gleason believed that no one personality was rich enough to sustain an hourlong variety show week after week, doing the same shtick in three or four sketches a night. The writers concurred. A whole stable of sketch characters ensued, all played by Gleason. There was Reginald Van Gleason, the pompous, philandering playboy who mixed drinks at a conveyor-belt bar or on a model train set and bought new cars when the old ones pointed the wrong way; Joe the Bartender, neighborhood listening post and philosopher; Rudy the Repairman, who wrecked what he was repairing with righteous indignation; the Bachelor, whose housekeeping argued eloquently for never being single; the Poor Soul, a Chaplinesque pantomime; Stanley R. Sogg, fast-talking late-late-late show pitchman; and others, each of them destined to be as familiar to the man on the street as the face on a dollar bill.

"I liked Rudy the Repairman," June Taylor remembers. "Picture a thirty-five-year-old man, fairly heavyset. Now, you know the height of an ordinary table. Can you imagine putting your right foot on the top of that table and then lifting yourself up to stand on it? Jackie did that three times during a Rudy the Repairman sketch. In that one, Art Carney and Zamah Cunningham played a husband and wife who made the mistake of hiring Rudy. That was the quality physical sketch comedy

As Joe the Bartender.

As Rudy the Repairman.

evolving on *Cavalcade of Stars.* In others, whenever Jackie got his hands on a hose, as Rudy, he loved squirting everybody. Art and Zamah. The cameraman. The audience.''

"I heard something about a Reggie Van Gleason sketch," reports Jack Philbin. "I wasn't there when it happened, but I don't doubt it's true. The writing always went up to the last minute, and *last* minute means just that. Jackie was doing one Reggie sketch at DuMont, and the writers were backstage trying to get a blackout for him. When he went out there at the start of the sketch, he literally didn't know how it was going to end. Jackie did his lines and broke into his Reggie dance, and then danced offstage and asked the writers, 'Have you got it yet?' And they said, 'No,' so back he went, dancing. Then he did more lines, then danced off, then on, and back and forth until they gave him the blackout. These were the days of live TV. Backstage it was a riot, but the audience didn't have a clue what was going on. I don't think they could imagine such a thing."

Naturally, there were occasions when props wouldn't work. Gleason would hurl himself against a breakaway door. It wouldn't break away. Breakaway bottles would be shatterproof, and lethal. Fake window panes would be anything but. The crew would be taken to task, but things would continue to go wrong. Gleason

As the Poor Soul.

was forever bruising and braining himself. No wonder the show was a howl.

Joe Cates recalls another deathless moment on *Cavalcade of Stars*. "It was Thursday night. It was so late Thursday night, it was really Friday morning. We'd rehearsed. He'd read the sketches Wednesday, rehearsed Thursday. Now it was two A.M. Friday. The show was that night. I get a call. 'Pal, I'm not doing it. It's garbage. I've got a better idea. I'm gonna do the tag-team wrestling match, with Jerry Bergen for my partner. We'll fight real wrestlers. I'll come out in a sedan chair, with dancers strewing flowers in front of me. Only don't get one of those phony rings. Get me the ring from St. Nicholas Arena.'

"I said, 'Jackie, come on.' He said, 'No, you can do it. It's portable. When they're not using it, they rent it.' So I got it, and I got the wrestlers. I got them because I was on the phone waking people up all night. The ring probably arrived at noon. It took two hours to set up. Then it hit us. The ring took up the whole stage. You could die.

"Gleason arrives. Now he starts laying out the sketch, and one of the wrestlers comes out of the blue with, 'Hey, he don't beat me. I'm the champ. He can't be the winner. I'll kill him.' Jackie starts to laugh. We try to explain to the wrestler that it's only a game, and that when it's over, Jackie will call him out for a bow and tell everyone he's the real champ. He doesn't care. This isn't bad enough. We're trying to rehearse the rest of the show, which we have to do on the side of the stage, or in front of the curtain, because the whole stage is dominated by this ring. We have Eddie Fisher. We have the June Taylor Dancers, but we have no room for them to dance.

"Now Gleason says to one of the wrestlers, 'I used to do stunts, so you can throw me and I'll know how to fall.' The wrestler doesn't want to. Gleason says, 'Pal, just a little shoulder slam. I'll bounce up.' And the guy says, 'Jack, I—' and Gleason says, 'Go ahead, do it,' and the next thing we know, he throws Jackie and Jackie can't get up. He's flopping around like a dead fish. It's five-thirty. We call his doctor. Jackie can't perform. He's got to go to the hospital.

"Milton Douglas says, 'We've got to get someone.' I call Morey Amsterdam,

As the Bachelor.

who lived in Scarsdale. 'Morey, you've got five minutes to get in a suit, get in your car, and come down here. Jackie had an accident at rehearsal.' Morey says, 'What should I bring?' I don't think he ever forgot the answer. I say, 'About forty-five minutes.' And I hang up the phone. Actually, the show came off all right. That was Friday. Monday morning, Jackie's better. I go to the meeting. He says, 'Get the ring again.' And he made me get the ring, and we did the sketch.''

By today's standards it might seem primitive. But for what it was, *Cavalcade of Stars* was turning to gold, and Gleason rapidly emerged as the man with the Midas touch.

"Four weeks after I started the DuMont show,'' recalls Jackie, ''I took a date to Coney Island. We were strolling around, and I noticed people staring at me. Three, four, then ten, then we're on the boardwalk and we're the center of attention. I knew then, as I never knew before, how powerful television was. I also knew,'' he smiles half ruefully, ''I was never going to be able to walk around Coney Island with a broad again, maybe not for the rest of my life.''

Within months, events on another network were contributing to Jackie's—and by extension, to *Cavalcade's*—success. The Frank Sinatra Show on CBS was up against *Cavalcade's* old nemesis, *Your Show of Shows*. It was based in New York, though its star lived out of town. Way out of town, in Los Angeles. The weekly commute represented a gamble. Hard though it is to fathom, planes have been known to be late. When your star is as big as Frank Sinatra (who Fred Allen said was entitled to $10,000 for a burp), you take your gamble, but you also hedge your bets. Director Frank Donahue thought a regular comedian guest star would be in order, someone who might be an asset to Frank in any case, and a lifesaver if Frank didn't land on schedule. Frank's choice was his pal from club days, big-band days, Jersey days—Jackie Gleason.

Writer Harry Crane was with the Sinatra show then. ''I said to Hubbell Robinson, who was then the CBS president of programming, 'It has to be like Hope and Crosby. We need two people.' It was very difficult for Frank to function in sketches without someone to play off, and I knew Jackie was great when it came to that. I knew Jackie from the old days. We were both performers as kids around Broadway. When he played at Slapsie Maxie's, I used to give Gleason's stage call by yelling, 'They have just fired on Fort Sumter.' Anyway, we got Jackie on the show, and he was a smash. Hubbell Robinson said, 'Where did you get that fat guy?' I said, 'You can get him for a dollar and a half. He's on Whelan Drugs.'''

In truth, Gleason was well out of the dollar-and-a-half range, although, as a gesture of long friendship with Frank Sinatra, he'd offered to work for free. Free, according to AFTRA rules, was out of the question. So he wound up working for scale.

"In those shows with Frank,'' Crane continues, ''in all of them, he was hilarious. I wrote those sketches. Then Jackie asked me to go with him, to write for his *Cavalcade of Stars*. Frank's head wasn't with The Frank Sinatra Show by now, it was with pictures, with Ava Gardner, other things, and he was ready to quit. I respected Gleason. He had tremendous talent. I saw that. I said to myself, maybe I'll do it. Maybe I'll go with Gleason. And I did.''

Those six shows with Sinatra netted Jackie a new writer, Harry Crane. Moreover, they were fun for Jackie—"Frank and I hit it off like Abbott and Costello''—and they were fun for a huge new audience of fans, many out of the DuMont broadcast range, seeing this side of Gleason for the first time. A new fan worth special mention was CBS founder Bill Paley, who made a mental note that, in autumn 1952, it would make television history.

And by no means the least of the benefits derived from the Gleason-Sinatra teaming was a valuable lesson learned when Sinatra guested—in a casual walk-on—on *Cavalcade of Stars*. "It was a Happy Jack sketch,'' says June Taylor. "Happy Jack was Gleason's answer to Harold Teen or Mack Sennett. In this one, Happy Jack goes to Coney Island. It ends up with a pie-throwing melee. We didn't use actual pies at rehearsal, so we weren't prepared for what happened. In the show, we used lemon meringue pies from Lindy's. With whipped cream, the works. What happened, totally unplanned, was that everyone slid, stumbled, fell, everything, on the pies. Even Sinatra. The lesson we learned here was that Jackie told me, all things considered, it wasn't a good idea to engage in pie-throwing stunts using real whipped-cream pies.''

As Reggie Van Gleason III.

The Jackie Gleason Show *toured as a stage show in the summer of 1952.*

CREATION

The Honeymooners *set a precedent for TV's*
exploration of marital strife.
HIGH TIMES

Sometimes it happens that a creature of fiction takes on legendary status, a life of its own. Never mind that Don Quixote and Sancho Panza were dreamed up by Miguel Cervantes. Cervantes was only the first to expound and embroider on who and what they were.

That this has happened with the Kramdens and the Nortons, who were invented for TV fiction and then evolved into popular folk heroes, comes as no great surprise. That it happened from the first instant someone said, "I have an idea for a sketch," and someone else said, "Hey, here's something you can add," is equally unsurprising. That it happened to the legends behind the legend—from the day and the hour of the inception of *The Honeymooners*—is perhaps more surprising, though easy enough to acknowledge.

If you think of Kramden as Don Quixote and Norton as Sancho Panza—which is ultimately inescapable—can the image of a windmill be far behind? And if you picture the windmill, whose description do you go by? Don Quixote's? Sancho Panza's? Or do you ask the man who runs the mill? Or the carpenter who built it?

Like it or not, the birth of any legend begins with so many people encircling an enormous windmill, pressed up against it, some outside, some inside, absorbing what they see. Each version is entirely accurate from its own perspective. But no perspective is identical to another. Try to draw a composite description from the various versions. What you get might look less like a windmill than a Madison Avenue bus.

In the case of *The Honeymooners*, especially in the beginning, the windmill was a live weekly spectacle with dancing girls, pop-music singers, opera singers, musicians, speciality acts, actors and actresses, writers, technicians, stagehands, directors, producers, and every other kind of show person and star, racing against the clock. Scratch windmill. It was a treadmill. Arms and legs and torsos with people attached ran the minute mile to air time, on an insane treadmill, lucky to stop for air. Each came from a different direction, with a different direction to go in. So they have the occasional different perspective of a particular detail that whizzed past at a hundred miles per. So what? Can you remember the precise moment at which you turned on the oven for dinner last night?

Nonetheless, let history record that *The Honeymooners* was born, in the manner dictated for all great creation epics, on the first day—

One day, the writers were knocking their heads together, trying to come up with a new sketch, perhaps a new character to add to Gleason's stable. Already Jackie Gleason had come up with Reggie Van Gleason, Rudy the Repairman, Stanley R. Sogg, the Poor Soul, Joe the Bartender. Each of these creations was funny. Each drew from, and grew from, various facets of human nature to ring appealingly true. But each, by his own unique situation, was set somewhat apart from the everyday guy on the street. Gleason felt it was time that the guy on the street got his due. In his own home. In his own situation. In his own way.

Jackie Gleason had an idea for a guy like this—but not set on the street. It would take place in a sparse, hardly furnished apartment. It would involve, along with the loudmouthed guy, his long-suffering (though not the kind to suffer in silence) wife. The couple would be poor, argumentative, but very much in love. Gleason took the idea to writers Joe Bigelow and Harry Crane.

Joe Cates, associated with the production end of things, recalls the point at which "Jackie turned to Harry Crane and Joe Bigelow and said, 'Look, here's what we'll do. I'll be a bus driver in Brooklyn. I got a wife.' And someone said, 'What'll Art Carney do?' Jackie said, 'He'll be a neighbor upstairs. And you know, the wife and me can get in these arguments. Back and forth. Lower middle class. I want a sketch like that. And at the end, I'll come to the realization of what a mistake I made. We'll play soft music and I'll grab her and say, 'Gee, baby, you're the greatest.'"

Gleason had very definite ideas about the couple's relationship. It wouldn't be one of those two-dimensional husband-wife spats heard on the radio. It would reflect the give-and-take of real life. "I always wanted to do this thing. The man isn't a beast. The guy really loves this broad. They fight, sure. But they always end in a clinch."

According to the most frequently quoted account, writer Joe Bigelow said, "I've got the opening line. The guy comes home tired. He worked all day. He's beat. He walks in, mad at the whole world, and his wife says, 'Don't take your coat off. Go downstairs and get me a loaf of bread,' and the guy gives her a look that would split a grapefruit and he shakes his head sarcastically and says, 'I'm not getting anything. I worked all day. What did you do?' and they're off to the races."

By the same account, Jackie replied to Bigelow, "That's the general idea. Make it real. Make it the way people really live. If it isn't credible, nobody's going to laugh. The guy at home has got to be able to look at it and say, 'That's the way my old lady sounds.' I even know who can play the wife. Pert Kelton. Is anybody more natural than Pert for this bit? Did you guys ever see her in a part where she gets mad at a guy? Holy smoke!'"

Suggests Jackie Gleason, "The very first *Honeymooners* that we did, I had an idea for two people such as I knew in Brooklyn, who were always arguing. While

Norton's office.

As Ralph Kramden.

they stayed together, they loved each other, they still had these continual fights. And then we took it from there. I decided that Kramden should be a bus driver. But not until, I think, about the second time we did it. He came in wearing a uniform in the first one, but I don't think he mentioned bus. And Norton, as soon as I saw the way Carney was playing the character of the neighbor, I decided he should work in the sewer. But that didn't come right away. In the first one, he wasn't even a neighbor. He was a cop.''

The first *Honeymooners* had several working titles. "The Beasts" was one, which was immediately rejected because it made it sound like the guy was doing all the fighting. "The Lovers" came up, but being lovers doesn't make a couple husband and wife. "The Honeymoon Is Over" was offered, but sounded like the couple didn't even want to be husband and wife. "Love, Honor, and Obey" and "The Couple Next Door" were similarly rejected.

They were shooting titles back and forth, and Gleason said, " 'Honeymoon Is Over'? 'Love, Honor, and Obey'? Why don't we just call it *The Honeymooners*?"

With this, *The Honeymooners* was born—the episode that initiated it all, about a man and a woman and a loaf of bread.

As Joe Cates reconstructs the search for the first Alice Kramden, "We had to get a wife. Now, you understand, I'm talking about a sketch where Jackie discussed it on a Monday. Tuesday afternoon it was written. And I had to get someone at one o'clock Wednesday to rehearse with him. There were no big meetings or consultations. I called Jackie and I said, 'For your wife, I have a friend, Ralph Bell, the radio actor. He's married to Pert Kelton. She would be terrific.' Jackie remembered her from the early movies that she did in the Thirties, so he went for the idea. Now, from Monday, morning meeting, late morning, to the sketch being delivered Tuesday afternoon, to showing up Wednesday for rehearsal, that was about the size of the thought. And the set was delivered Thursday. That was what weekly television was about. That's all the preparation we had."

Pert Kelton came in to play the role of Alice, split-a-grapefruit look and all.

As Harry Crane remembers Pert Kelton, who had been in show business

Pert Kelton, the first Alice Kramden.

since age three, and did everything from Hal Roach movies to radio and Broadway comedy, "I knew her. I worked with her. I wrote a Broadway show called *All in Fun*. She was in it with Imogene Coca. So I said, 'Gee, there's a redhead, Pert Kelton, that I did a thing with.' Then I didn't hear anything about it. Then they found out about her, and interviewed her, and she had the job."

As to the set, says Joe Cates, "DuMont television network had no services. They didn't have Music Clearance, Trucking, Set Building, Rental, Props. There wasn't some department you could call to do it for you. I had to do our arrangements. I selected the drops used to back the numbers. I'd order the sets from Kay Velden, a company in New Jersey, by describing them or pointing to examples in magazines. And at the beginning, the set to us was just an excuse to back up the artists. So Jack said, 'Get a Brooklyn tenement and make it scruffy.' I don't really remember details like the candy dish on the dresser, but we had a property man, Skippy, at the theater. He had a lot of properties, like all good theatrical-property men, and he probably put it there, because I wouldn't have ordered it. Jackie liked Skippy. Skippy liked Jackie. He'd offer him things for the set, and Jackie would say, 'Yeah, put that, that's right.' My guess is that Skippy would have come up with the candy dish and asked Jackie about it, and Jackie would have said, 'Yeah, but keep it empty.' That sounds like something Jackie would have said,"

The set, whatever its specific origin, was soon a facsimile of the apartment where Jackie Gleason was raised. That Chauncey Street dwelling is described by Frieda Broodno Storm—who grew up in the same real-life building—as "a railroad flat you walked through. The bedroom had, essentially, no windows. The main room, where everyone would congregate, was the kitchen. There was an icebox, not a refrigerator. There were no curtains on the windows. The sink had a drape over the pipes. The kitchen table was the focal point of the whole place. The one big difference between the Kramden apartment and Jackie's was that in Jackie's, the bathroom was in the hall, and the tub was in the kitchen adjacent to the sink."

"One day," says Joe Cates, "someone wanted to hang a picture on the wall near the door to the bedroom. Gleason asked, 'Hey, what are you doing? We didn't have a picture in the flat. No, strike it. Take it down.' So he had a pretty accurate picture of what he wanted."

Initially, the overriding theme of *The Honeymooners* was Ralph's perennial need to top Alice. For instance, in one DuMont episode, Ralph and Alice come home having just lost big prizes on a quiz show. It appears they lost because Alice answered a question wrong. Back in their miserable kitchen, surrounded by cartons of free breakfast cereal won as a consolation prize, Ralph can't think of enough ways to tell Alice how stupid she is. Then there's a knock at the door. It's the people from the quiz show, saying that Alice was right after all, and that the only fair way to settle things is to ask Ralph a question. If he answers correctly, the Kramdens will win everything they could have won on the show. The quiz master asks Ralph what Marconi invented. Ralph, his face a puddle of baffled contortions, can't produce a better answer than, "Ma—caroni?" With this, Ralph loses the prizes and his pride but not Alice, who says she puts up with his insults because she loves him so much.

To Gingr[sic] Jones, who played dozens of different roles in the *Cavalcade* (and later CBS) days, "The way she loved him was one of the wonderful things about Pert Kelton's Alice. I can see her in that dark green sweater with the elbow out, tossing that gorgeous head of bright red hair down, and putting a ribbon around it, and throwing it back. And when she said, 'I love you, Ralph,' with all the warmth in the world after she'd just screamed her head off at him, you *knew* that she loved him."

Early on, *The Honeymooners* would open with Ralph doing a sort of modified monologue, along the lines of a-funny-thing-happened-to-me-on-the-way-to-the-studio. Only as Ralph did it, he'd walk into the apartment with a little story in character. Harry Crane wrote one for "Six Months to Live" (the forerunner of later "monochromia" episodes) that went:

"You won't believe this, Alice. What do you think happened on the bus today? Some guy comes in yelling, "I'm George Washington. I'm George Washington." He kept yelling this, and everybody was scared to death. Well, he had everybody crazy. But I got rid of him. I yelled, "Next stop, Valley Forge," and this bum gets off.

This was the germinal king of the castle. As described by Harry Crane, "He comes home, he's always beaten. That's going to be his job for life. A hard job, very little promotion. Step to the back of the bus, folks . . ." Night after night the king would come home, from one bad day after another, and release pent-up steam at his wife.

From that simple, badly beaten king would emerge a living, breathing entity named Ralph Kramden.

And from its humble beginnings on DuMont, the king's kingdom was destined to grow beyond measure, in a kitchen-sink world that never changed.

FROM CHAOS TO KRAMDEN

Ralph Kramden ... a character that we might be getting from Mr. Dickens if he were writing for TV.
JOHN O'HARA

Ralph Kramden never lacked a personality. But, like everything else associated with *The Honeymooners*, his personality became a totality greater than the sum of its parts. The later Ralph Kramden would display traits of the imperious Reggie Van Gleason, the blowhard Charlie Bratton, the philosophical Joe the Bartender, and the hapless Poor Soul. The early Ralph Kramden was more like a bellicose Chester A. Riley with a crabby wife.

Just as Ralph evolved, so did the texture of the Kramden–Norton saga. At first, *The Honeymooners* was a husband–wife squabble sketch, its roots going way back beyond *The Bickersons* to Adam and Eve, another couple who got into a mess when they argued about food.

To the husband–wife thread, and the step-to-the-back-of-the-bus thread, were added others as the *The Honeymooners* tapestry took shape. One of the most effective was the typically Kramden catch phrase, like "One of these days, pow, right in the kisser." As Steve Allen wrote, "Gleason's power made it easy for him to successfully employ such devices as the running gag or stock-reference line. To a comedian there can be few things more valuable—especially early in his career—than a line that catches the public's fancy. . . . The line is repeated in partial context until a habitual response is built up. From that point, the comedian has only to stop everything, look the audience in the eye, and plunge the needle into his helpless subjects; their response is inevitable."

The same was true of "fat jokes." It was a given that Ralph was fat. With Gleason's build, how could Ralph have been otherwise? But increasingly, the fact that Ralph was setting himself up for a fat joke, and that the audience *knew* he was walking into a fat joke, was at least as funny as the actual punch line.

What was true for catch phrases and fat jokes was about to be true of entire situations. To the initial rule for *Honeymooners* story lines—that the plots had to be extensions of things that *could* happen—was added the concept that the

Jackie with Pert. Note the early version of his bus driver's uniform.

audience should know where Ralph was headed while he himself still hadn't a clue.

These are crackerjack rules of thumb to a writer devising a husband–wife quarrel. But they work better yet when applied to another Ralph trademark, the fly-by-night scheme.

Ralph's scheming wasn't as early a development as Ralph's screaming, though it grew out of something endemic to *The Honeymooners*: Ralph's poverty. As seen by Walter Stone, a later *Honeymooners* writer on DuMont, "The poverty was behind the whole concept of his schemes, because he wanted to get out of his poverty, and you believe he wanted to give Alice all these things she wouldn't otherwise have. And because of his schemes, he never got any richer. If he saved his money, he probably could have gotten her a few things. But he was that type of character."

As the schemes developed, so did Ralph's need for a crony in his boneheaded notions. Art Carney's easygoing lunacy was the match. Jackie Gleason's manic friction was the sandpaper. When the two got together, sparks flew. More schemes for the Kramden–Norton fabric were the natural, incendiary result.

Before long, it became handy for Norton to have a wife, and for Alice to have a friend, so a Mrs. Norton was introduced. The first Mrs. Norton, who had almost nothing to do, was played by Elaine Stritch, who only stayed one show. The Mrs. Norton who stayed for years was played by Joyce Randolph, who got the part because Jackie had liked her work as a serious actress in a *Cavalcade* sketch two weeks earlier.

Says Joyce, "Jackie said to Joe Cates, 'Get me that serious actress.' I think Jackie also knew my work from the Colgate Comedy Hour. I'd done comedy with Eddie Cantor, Danny Thomas, Dean Martin and Jerry Lewis, so they must have known I did comedy. The sketch I had done with him on *Cavalcade* was something about vaudevillians who had been separated by show business. They were sweethearts, and they were reunited backstage. It was pretty maudlin. So he *must* have known I did comedy too."

With the increasing importance of Norton in Ralph's life and schemes, and the addition of Trixie as a foil for both Norton and Alice, the *Honeymooners* vignettes were expanding into more plotted stories. Longer, when the story dictated. With greater character development, ineluctably.

The writers were part of the process every step of the way. In the first year of *Cavalcade,* the writers were Coleman Jacoby and Arnie Rosen, who had been hired by the show's producer even before Gleason joined the team. They were not just comedy writers but "humorists, a label that puts them in a kind of celebrity status of their own," wrote Michael Drury in *Collier's* magazine. "Before the year was out they had quit, or threatened to quit, four or five times, and that has been the pattern of their relationship ever since, but they keep returning to Gleason and he to them in mutual if reluctant

Joyce Randolph, who before joining DuMont's The Honeymooners was billed as "the most murdered girl on television."

admiration for each other's talents.'' Jacoby and Rosen were *the* writing team when the earliest Gleason characters, like Reggie Van Gleason III, entered the picture.

In the second year, Harry Crane came aboard, as did Joe Bigelow. Bigelow had been a Bullets Durgom client before Jackie. He'd become pals with Jackie when they were both on the West Coast. He'd also been friendly with Harry Crane and had, in fact, brought Crame out west in 1940 to write for Edgar Bergen.

At one point, Coleman Jacoby, Arnie Rosen, and Joe Bigelow had all left. Harry Crane remained. ''I used to type and feed Joe Cates pages so he could get them to the cast. No time to brood over what would be good. They say there was a 'creative community' in New York then, all these people from the 'golden age of television,' but I never met anybody. I never spoke to anybody. You did your work and went home.''

It wasn't that other writers weren't hired. It was only that they didn't manage to stay. Gleason knew what he wanted. The writer who couldn't supply it was off the payroll fast.

It helped if the writer was clairvoyant, because Gleason's mind was on too many details to linger too long on any one. There was no getting him into a room to critique the fine points of a script. If you had his presence, it was only briefly. If you had his undivided attention, it was exceedingly rare.

''When you wrote, there was no such thing as checking with Gleason,'' says Crane. ''He'd get the pages at the last minute. I used to meet him every Friday morning—this was a Friday-night show, remember—and I read him the script while he was shaving. He'd read it first, and then while he was shaving, I'd read the other parts, and he knew already—he had a photographic memory—he already

The DuMont Honeymooners—Pert Kelton, Jackie Gleason, Art Carney, Joyce Randolph.

had his cues and lines. We went to the theater around noon. Then they'd all converge on him. 'Jackie, do we do this or that?' He'd say, 'Every man for himself, pal. Good luck.'

"Then came the run-through. He'd rehearse one time. Then the director would say, 'Let's try it again, for camera positions.' And Jackie would answer, 'What for? Just point the camera at the kitchen table. I'm not going to fool you and run off stage. That's it. Goodbye.' Then we'd break for dinner or whatever."

When Harry Crane met actor-turned-writer Marvin Marx, he hired him for the job of clairvoyant, a.k.a. writer. Marx thought of TV-and-radio writer Walter Stone, whom he met when they both wrote for Jack Carter, as another candidate for the post. Stone was hesitant about working for Gleason, having heard of his turnover rate. Then he reconsidered, and accepted the *Cavalcade* challenge. But Marvin Marx already was gone.

As luck would have it, Marx was rehired while Stone was still there. Gleason had signed himself into Doctors Hospital to lose weight. Not too fascinated by the prospect of watching the pounds melt away, he was more than willing to brainstorm with the new writers. "That was great," says Walter Stone. "We used to meet with him every day. It was Harry Crane, Marvin, myself, and Gleason, who wasn't going anywhere, for a change. It's not like he was in a hotel room. There was nothing else for him to do. The thing about having him there was, you never had to guess what he was going to go for. You said the line, and if he liked it, you went with it. If he said no, right away you went to something else. In the first week, we did two complete shows. He thought that was pretty good. So we stayed on."

"Crane, Marx, and Stone were an interesting combination," explains Jack Philbin. "Harry was from Brooklyn, the same part as Gleason. Marvin and Walter were from Jersey, and Gleason had all these ties with Jersey from working in places like the Club Miami in Newark. These writers were so close to Jackie that they took all his personality and almost made it their own. When you hear names of places like Fred's Landing in a script, you can't tell if it came from one of the writers, or from Gleason. They were that much in tune."

Though the mix was effective, Harry Crane moved on soon after. An offer came from Dean Martin and Jerry Lewis to write for their show. It meant going back west, which appealed to Crane, and it meant getting the same money to write five specials that he'd gotten to write an entire year of *Cavalcade*.

Exit Harry Crane, leaving behind two writers who would beat the odds and set an endurance record with the show. "Marvin and I stayed," says Walter Stone. "And it was crazy. Crazy. People couldn't believe it today, because nobody does live. You do one live show today and you take bows for a month. When you did them every week, you had no time to take bows. You got right back to work. You didn't worry about details like the name of Alice's sister last week. You didn't figure it was going to be a classic. Call her something. Just write it.

The only thing that saved us in those days, and most of what we did turned out all right, was that you had to go on. I mean, what are you going to do? You have to go out there and do *something* for an hour."

Says Joe Cates, "Very often we didn't have an ending. We didn't know where we were going, and Jackie and Art would have a muttered conference and Jackie would say, 'Do this, do this, do this, cross behind me,' and he'd nod to Sammy Spear, the conductor, and the sketch was over. Or sometimes he'd challenge Art. He'd do a funny fall and Art would do a funny move, and Jackie would do a double fall, and maybe end it there. And it wouldn't be the sketch they started with."

"Because," says Gleason, "we were always instructed by the audience what way to go. We could feel if they wanted more of something, or if we should soften something up. We always took that direction from the audience."

Such was the DuMont *Honeymooners*. An idea. A talented team to realize it. Instinct. Moxie.

Someone once called Gleason the "Scarlett O'Hara of show business—'I'll think about it tomorrow'—until show time. Then watch out!"

"Yes, but out of all the chaos and strife," Gleason used to observe, "comes the tempered steel of comedy."

CBS

Television eats up talent, but it could choke on Gleason.
And that's not just because he once hit 286 pounds.
NEW YORK DAILY NEWS, 1953

By 1952, the *Cavalcade* combination was far superior to anything else on DuMont, and indeed, to most network fare. Much of TV's content in those early '50s was mediocre, embarrasingly amateurish. "There were some people who were quote TV stars unquote who to this day I don't understand what they were doing in show business, much less being successful," comments Steve Allen. "And the answer is, nobody knew anything about television, everybody was stumbling around. So they were taking has-beens, and people's girlfriends, and putting them on the air. But out of this general lousiness emerged a true Golden Age. The best comedians floated to the top, the best singers, and a great many very gifted directors, writers, and actors."

The mature *Cavalcade*—to the extent that *Cavalcade* was ever mature—was solid Golden Age entertainment. At its peak, it was as close to the big time as DuMont ever got. The Gleason gang was a hit. *The Honeymooners* drew raves. Gleason wasn't oblivious to the fact. "In the beginning of the second year," according to Joe Cates, "Jackie came to Milton Douglas and offered to sign a contract for another three years, or maybe it was two years, because he needed the advance. I forget the amount he wanted. But we knew what a star he was. Milton went to the DuMont network. Now, at the time, we had the two big shows on DuMont, *Cavalcade of Stars* and *Cavalcade of Bands*. Next to us, I guess, was Dennis James doing wrestling. Milton went to DuMont, and DuMont said, 'We have a certain amount of development money. Let us think about it.' They came back a week later and said, 'We have a limited amount of money, and rather than sign Gleason, although he's our biggest star, we would prefer to put the money into a dramatic show with Joseph Schildkraut hosting it.' Now, I don't deny that Joseph Schildkraut was a distinguished actor, very respected. But what a choice to make. Milton Douglas never got over that, he couldn't believe it."

As things developed, a deal was struck, but with CBS, not DuMont. Hubbell Robinson at CBS was its chief architect. Bill Paley at CBS, who had seen and liked Gleason on the Sinatra show, gave the nod. Represented by Bullets Durgom, MCA's Herb Rosenthal, and other top negotiators, Gleason signed with the CBS network in 1952. Under the contract, he'd produce as well as star in the *Jackie Gleason Show*.

When Gleason left DuMont for CBS, Joe Cates remained with Milton Douglas and *Cavalcade*. "What it came down to was an offer to go with him as associate producer. I had a secret fear that if I went as associate producer, and he was around for fifteen more years, fifteen years later I'd be a forty-three-year-old associate producer, which I had no wish to be." Instead, Cates went on to executive-producer status with award-winning TV shows, Broadway plays, and movies. Gleason assembled a new production team.

There was Jack Philbin as executive producer. There was Jack Hurdle, producer. There was Stanley Poss, assistant producer. Philbin, of course, had been with Gleason since before the DuMont days. Jack Hurdle had come by way of vaudeville, radio, and theater. In vaudeville, he'd been a straight man for Ted Healy. On radio, he'd been a sought-after director in both Chicago and New York. On stage, he was associated with classic performances like George M. Cohan's in *Ah Wilderness*—the musical version of which, years later, would win Gleason a Tony award (as Sid in *Take Me Along*). "There is great similarity between Cohan and Gleason," Hurdle once remarked. "He was a great actor, a great performer, a song-and-dance man, a director. He wrote plays, dialogue, songs. Gleason does all these things."

Scenic designer Richard Rychtarik came from DuMont. Set decorator Phil Cuoco was already with CBS. Says Cuoco, "I'd been involved with Frank Sinatra's show. Frank told Jackie, when Jackie was coming over to CBS, to get hold of me. I'd gone on vacation. I was in Phoenix. I was going to be fired if I didn't leave Phoenix and go back. I went to New York, to the Park Sheraton, up to Gleason's suite. He was sitting there, flanked by Bullets Durgom and Jack Hurdle, and all the CBS brass sitting on fold-up seats. I walked in, and Gleason asked if I was the 'bum we've been waiting for?' So I wondered aloud who the fat loudmouth was. These were the first words I ever spoke to him. I've been with him ever since." Cuoco, who was with CBS from the beginning—"I provided their first prop. There was a girl sitting in front of the American flag. I provided the flag. They brought the girl"—was still with Gleason for the last *Honeymooners* special, as associate producer.

Stanley Poss came to Gleason by way of Orson Welles and the Mercury Theater. Like Hurdle, Poss drew the occasional parallel: "Welles and Gleason have in common that they know what they want and stick with it till they get it." As to how the production staff worked, said Poss, "It's like the army. Hurdle is the Eisenhower. I'm Omar Bradley. He's command. I'm operations." There was always plenty for them to do.

Gleason brought Jack Lescoulie to be the announcer of the *Jackie Gleason Show*. Lescoulie was highly regarded for his work with Dave Garroway on *Today*. Announcers Bill Nimmo and Jimmy Blaine came too, to do the commercial spots. Nimmo was already known as a game-show announcer, and as Bill the Bartender for Pabst Blue Ribbon on the *Wednesday Night Fights*. Blaine was a singer *(Stop the Music)* and game-show emcee *(Hold That Camera)*. All three were buddies of Gleason's at his favorite watering hole, Toots Shor's, where Mickey Mantle, Whitey Ford, Roger Maris, and Billy Martin were also regulars and Gleason colleagues, as were Humphrey Bogart and Bing Crosby when they were in town.

Another feature of the new show would be "Portrettes"—beautiful girls posed behind large picture frames, smiling and delivering lines about products and station identification.

The June Taylor Dancers followed Gleason to CBS. "When we made the move in 1952," recalls June, "I was told by Bullets Durgom that the budget would permit me to have four boys and four girls. That's eight dancers. I was thrilled, because on DuMont I was working with three girls and two boys and was lucky when I got a third boy, Ron Field. Ron was a dancer in Broadway musicals then. In a few years, he was a celebrated choreographer, with *Cabaret,* and

The media never tired of reporting on Gleason's characters and show.

director, with *Applause*. Anyway—they said eight dancers. But Jackie wanted sixteen. We stammered, *'Whaaat*? How do we photograph sixteen dancers?' He solved the problem by putting a camera in the balcony.

"Our opening number for our first CBS show, 'Five Minutes to Show Time,' was big and splashy and glamorous. We had the sixteen dancers, along with production people like Stanley Poss bustling across the stage to give the feeling of getting ready to go on the air. We got fantastic reviews. If we hadn't, we'd have been limited to just the eight dancers originally budgeted for.

"But the sixteen June Taylor Dancers were *in,* absolutely *in.* This meant we couldn't goof off. By the third show, I stopped living. I ate, I slept, I worked. Period.

"After a while, I went to Jackie and I said, 'Jack, you know, it may start to get a little boring with the opening number, the precision kicks, the precision dancing. We really need something new. Why don't we do a takeoff on the Busby Berkely overhead-camera bit?' He liked the idea and took it to CBS, and they said no. They stalled us for a year, then I went back to Jackie about it, and he went back to CBS, and proceeded to show them how to do an overhead-camera effect. The problem had been that you couldn't just hang that bulky camera down pointing at the floor. They put the camera on a platform, raised it up to the ceiling, with the lens pointing straight out. Then they put a mirror in front of the lens, and the mirror angled down. That's how we got the overhead effect."

Nor was it enough to amass an imposing team for the new CBS show. *jackie gleason enterprises* needed suitable headquarters. Penthouse apartments with terraces and gardens were leased and remodeled at the Park Sheraton Hotel (now New York's Omni Park Central). The twelve-room complex ran $25,000 a year. "Almost big enough to be a suburb," wrote the *New York Herald Tribune*'s Hy Gardner. "Painted heliotrope, Kelly green, and fire engine red . . . very restless-ful." Reportedly, the first time Art Carney saw it, he observed, "It looks like it was made out of peppermint wafers." A portrait over the main fireplace was of Reggie Van Gleason III, dressed as a World War I soldier. A plaque beneath the portrait read OUR FOUNDER. The June Taylor Dancers had a complete practice studio in the hotel. The producer had a suite. The writers had a suite. Gleason had two suites. He worked out of one. He lived in the other.

All this flamboyance had a purpose beyond the obvious one of making Gleason happy. It was great for the image. The man who had signed the biggest contract in TV history had to look like a potentate worth every cent.

For its part, CBS launched a major publicity push to be sure that the world would be watching for Gleason when he came on the air on Saturday nights in September. As added insurance—considering that Gleason really wasn't well known in cities outside the limited DuMont broadcast range—*The Jackie Gleason Show* was packaged as a touring one-hour stage presentation in the summer of 1952. Consisting of a *Honeymooners* sketch, a Reggie sketch, and musical numbers, it played movie palaces across the country—four and five times a day—as the live prologue portion between the feature films.

For *The Honeymooners* segment, Jackie Gleason, Pert Kelton, and Art Carney went on the road. Only Jackie and Art were able to finish the tour. Pert suffered a coronary thrombosis and, sadly, had to withdraw. She simply could not have continued. It was more than the end of the tour for her. It was the end of her tenure as Alice.

The actress brought in to finish the tour as Alice was radio and TV star Gingr Jones. "I'll never forget it. Suddenly I'm getting this call, to take over a part almost overnight. I was sitting in a pool in Connecticut, drinking a bottle of beer on a hot day. I said I wouldn't go. Jack Hurdle called a couple of times. Finally, he prevailed and I went. But I said to him, 'You must tell Mr. Gleason there is no way I can be anything like Pert. He isn't to expect it. No one can come up to the way she does that role.' He assured me that he and Jackie understood.

"I remember that I also asked about clothes. I was told I could fit into Pert's. I flew out and the secretary met me at the airport, and took me to my hotel. There was a message from Gleason that I was to get into the tub with my script and go over and over and over the lines, and then fall asleep on them. But before I fell asleep, I was to get out of the tub.

"I was to meet him at the theater the next morning. I got down there early, and of course he didn't show for hours. He arrived a little before the first performance we were to do, before the first matinee. The movie was already playing. We went behind the movie screen. He walked me around the set and drew a stage diagram for me. He said, 'Now, when I'm at the table, you say this line. Then you cross from the icebox to the ironing board.' This was the kind of rehearsal I had before I went on.

"I said, 'I can't do this, Jackie.' My training in the theater had been to have lots of rehearsals. And he said, 'Oh, just watch me. I'll put you where I want you to be.' And he did. He's the most remarkable person to work with. He put me with his eyes exactly where he wanted me to be. It's a marvelous experience for a performer, and I never made a mistake. He just moved me wherever he wanted on this great big stage. With his eyes.

"The plot was something about the Kramdens going to a dance with the Nortons. Trixie was referred to, but she wasn't actually in the show. Alice was at the ironing board, ironing something. She wore a long, blue satin, very full-skirted evening gown, and I think her hair was in curlers. In these days, *The Honeymooners* still concentrated on the domestic-argument angle, though Norton was already very, very important. It all took place on the typical *Honeymooners* set.

"It was terrific fun, doing the show and getting to know everyone. Art and I and Zamah Cunningham, who was in the Reggie sketch, had a ball together. But it wasn't entirely a picnic. I broke my toe in Boston when I got up in the middle of the night and jammed it into a piece of furniture in the dark. The toe turned black. When I woke up the next morning, it was still throbbing. Rather than tell Jackie, I called Art. He bought me a pair of ballet shoes, and cut them up so I could get them on my feet. Then, for each performance, he helped me to the theater. He'd bring a tub of ice into my dressing room so that I could thoroughly numb the toe before each performance. Then he'd help me onto the stage. Five shows a day. Jackie never knew it. Of course, I was wearing the long evening gown, which had the virtue of covering my busted toe.

"Jackie finally found out after the last show, when he brought me onstage for an extra curtain call. You always ran onstage, and ran offstage, for the curtain call, because it was a huge stage. I could barely manage running out for one call. But when he wanted to do the second, I had to limp.

"Naturally, I had to tell him what happened. Jackie showed his appreciation by having a little medal made, which read 'For distinguished service, courage, and valor beyond the call of duty during the '52 Gleason Tour.'"

Despite Pert's misfortune, and Gingr's mishap, the tour was, from a marketing standpoint, a total success. The nation was clamoring to see *The Jackie Gleason Show* on CBS in the fall. *The Honeymooners* had scored a major triumph.

Unfortunately, *The Honeymooners* was still *The Honeymooners* minus one. Pert Kelton was unable to work. Gingr Jones was "not asked, because, I eventually heard from Jack Hurdle, Jackie thought I was 'too much of a lady.'" Perhaps she just looked too good in a long blue satin evening gown.

Now the search was on for a new Alice, with dozens of actresses vying for the chance, and precious little time to make a selection. Bullets Durgom was asking everyone he could think of for suggestions. One of the people he talked to was his old friend, manager Val Irving. Val represented Audrey Meadows, who was then in Phil Silvers's *Top Banana* on Broadway.

As Audrey recalls, "I was in this hit Broadway show, so neither of them thought of me. They asked me for names, and everyone I came up with had been dismissed as inappropriate or considered or interviewed already. I was running out of names, then it came to me. I wasn't really serious, but I wasn't *not* serious, and I said, 'I thought of the perfect person.' I listed all sorts of qualifications this person had, and they said, 'Who?' and I said, 'Me.' Jackie had seen everyone else in New York and Hollywood. The only person he hadn't seen was me. I went up to see him. We chatted. He was noncommittal."

Says Bullets Durgom, "Jackie meets with people alone. He doesn't have anybody sitting there, the staff or myself or anybody. That's his decision. That's fine. That way, it's his responsibility. So they had their meeting, and she left, and about twenty minutes later, Jackie buzzes me. We had offices all over the Park Sheraton. I went over to his office, and he said, 'What's the matter with you? She's not right for Alice. She's too attractive.' I said, 'Well, okay, I thought we

Audrey Meadows—the first CBS Alice Kramden.

might take a chance and see if it would be worth trying.' He said, 'Now what are we going to do?' I said, 'I don't know. We'll have to keep thinking about it.' Then I called Val Irving and gave him the verdict.''

Says Audrey, ''This next part of the story has been told wrong a number of times, with different people taking credit for the idea. Here's what really happened. *Top Banana* was about to go on the road, and I didn't want to go on the road. I also couldn't believe an actor would say I was too attractive. I'd take that from a producer who didn't know anything about acting. But Jackie should have known I could do the part without makeup and be Alice. I told Val we should get a photographer to take pictures of the way I look first thing in the morning. I'd pose with a coffee pot and a frying pan and a ratty dress and apron, in my terrible, miserable apartment over a rug company. We'd have them developed right away, and send them to Jackie with no identification.''

Bullets Durgom has a similar recollection, except that ''I said to Val, 'Listen, it didn't work. Jackie thought she was too attractive. All dressed up, and the makeup, and the hair and all.' And Val said, 'Do me a favor. Will you go over with me? Will you explain it to her?' It was just a few blocks away, right off Fifth Avenue. She lived in a walkup flat, a dingy little place. With a kitchenette, not a kitchen. She had the window just like *The Honeymooners* set. It scared me. I said, 'My God, this is the set.' We were laughing. I said, 'Audrey, the problem is, you were too attractive.' She said, 'What am I supposed to do?'

"We sat around, and talked about it. I said, 'We've got to do this in a hurry. Get a photographer over, and Audrey can take her makeup off, pull her hair down, put on an apron, and stand over by the fridge and the window,' And they took pictures."

Or—as reported in a 1955 issue of *Cosmopolitan*—Audrey was leaving the Park Sheraton with Val Irving when she remembered a routine she did on *Bob and Ray*. It was a spoof of the Good Housekeeping Seal of Approval called "The Bad Housekeeping Seal of Disapproval." In it, Audrey was a dumpy housewife with a broken vacuum cleaner. According to *Cosmopolitan,* Audrey said, "I wish I had

a picture of myself in the costume and makeup that I used in the Bad Housekeeping bit." Then Val Irving snapped his fingers. He had an idea.

By all accounts, Audrey next found an old blouse and tore the sleeve. She pulled her hair back, without combs, and slept with it that way. At seven o'clock the next morning, photographer Bill Mark appeared, ready to go to work. Audrey's mother was there, fussing over Audrey, trying to spruce her up. Luckily, Audrey's sister Jayne Meadows was also there, in the next room with a cold. She finally had to use it as an excuse to separate Audrey and her mom.

"Now," says Bullets Durgom, "Val brought me the pictures, and I brought them to Jackie's office. I had three photos. I said, 'Jack, what do you think of this girl for *The Honeymooners*?' In the pictures, Audrey was a sorry sight. Said Jackie, '*That's* the girl! Who is it?' I said, 'Audrey Meadows.' He said, 'What? Get her!'

"So that was settled. Audrey was going to do just fine. Incidentally, there was never any worry about public resistance to her filling Pert's shoes, because CBS had a different audience. Actually, compared to CBS, DuMont had *no* audience. CBS had a much wider audience, and if only because they could afford it, they had a better grade of show. Then there was all this energy and money they were putting into kicking off the Gleason program on CBS, the tremendous publicity."

Once Audrey had the job, she told Phil Silvers. He was glad she'd been given the opportunity, and would not let her *Top Banana* commitment stand in her way. Audrey recalls that "Then I said, 'Phil, you've got to see these pictures.' Phil looked at them very seriously. I said, 'Aren't they the worst you ever saw?' He said, 'I don't know what you're talking about. When did you ever look this good?' "

The next step, or so it seemed to Audrey, was to read scripts and attend rehearsals for *The Honeymooners*. In attempting to, she learned what performers both before and after her had discovered about Gleason. He doesn't like to rehearse. After the barest run-through, without costumes or props, she asked Art Carney when the rehearsal would be. He said, "You just did it."

It got better. Sort of. Soon *TV Stage* magazine would be reporting that Audrey, feeling it was impossible for her to work without rehearsing, tried to quit in her third week. Gleason refused. So she resolved to get herself fired. "Just before the show was scheduled to go on the air, she told him she'd go on stage, but not say a word. 'If you don't have to rehearse,' Audrey said, 'then you're good enough to get by without my lines, too.' Audrey really didn't live up to her threat, but as the show went along, she did feed Jackie a number of the wrong lines. When the show was over, Audrey was stunned by Jackie's reaction. Instead of firing her, the next night he tossed a party in Audrey's honor."

Some months later, Jackie asked Audrey how she made chicken. When she told him, he invited her to his home for a chicken dinner and asked if she wouldn't mind doing the cooking. She agreed, only to discover twenty guests at Jackie's and twenty birds in the kitchen. None too happy, Audrey gave it her best shot. When dinner was over, Jackie said, "Have you ever wondered why I hired you so quickly last fall?" She said she had wondered, and Jackie replied, "Audrey, I very seldom make a mistake. I wasted no time hiring you because I knew, the minute I laid eyes on you, that you were a girl who could cook twenty chickens without getting excited."

Pulitzer Prize winner Ron Powers recently wrote of Audrey, as Alice, that she could "stand still better than anyone in TV history, providing the essential counterpoint of defeated sanity." It's a tribute to her acting skills, of course. But when you consider what Audrey went through to get the part and, over the years, to play it, it's apparent that defeated sanity was her medium. And that standing implacably still was her best defense.

WATCHING THE LOST EPISODES

The remarkable thing is that the new "lost"
Honeymooners are less Stone Age precursors to the 39
telefilms that have thrived on reruns lo these 30 years
than prime examples of a fully developed concept.
FILM COMMENT (1985)

[The lost episodes] might strike "Honeymooner"
devotees as, by and large, promising but primitive works.
THE NEW YORK TIMES (1985)

It is likely that *Honeymooners* fans, TV critics, historians of the medium, and observers of pop culture will be analyzing, dissecting, and scrutinizing the Lost Episodes, and comparing them to the Classic Thirty-nine for as many years as the lost sketches sat in Jackie Gleason's film library. And once the Lost Episodes have been seen often enough by enough people, highly opinionated factions will form—*Honeymooners* "camps," if you will—to debate, over tables full of pizza and bottles full of grape juice, the merits of the "Lost *Honeymooners*."

Some, giddy with the knowledge that there are now more than one hundred black-and-white vintage Fifties sketches and episodes in syndication, will embrace the Lost Episodes wholeheartedly and without reservation. Others will decide that a dozen, a score, half, or maybe more of the lost sketches are in the same league as the Classic Thirty-nine. And then there will be those who won't much care for the Lost *Honeymooners* at all.

Gleason has an opinion about all this. He told Tom Shales of the *Washington Post:* "You have to remember, it was because of those sketches that Buick wanted us to do the thirty-nine episodes, so they gotta be funny. As a matter of fact, they might be a little funnier because at that time we weren't having as many script problems. It was a new thing; we had ideas all the time. It was after a while that we had done so many of them that there just wasn't anything else to say."

"I have an open mind," Ralph once said to Alice. To which she answered, "Well, you better close it before your brains fall out." But even Alice wouldn't argue with Ralph if he suggested that *Honeymooners* fans watch the Lost

Episodes with an open mind. That means remembering, for instance, that in the first couple of seasons of sketches the actors were struggling—in front of several million people each week—to give their characters definition, to mold their personalities, and to develop relationships with the other characters. It also means remembering that the actors, who were so at ease with one another when they made the Classic Thirty-nine that they seemed to be reading each other's minds, were just getting to know one another in '52 and '53.

Keeping an open-mind also means expecting the characters to look and act differently on occasion, especially in the early seasons: Ralph thinner in the first few sketches, and more bellicose over the first few seasons; Alice sometimes looking like a Brooklyn bag lady, and sounding so shrill and acting so quarrelsome you wonder how Ralph refrained from belting her; Norton looking and sounding like a lobotomized version of his later self; Trixie with a different hairdo, and in the earliest sketches, looking young enough to have been recruited from a high-school drama club.

Viewing with an open mind also means not being put off by an often highly exaggerated, slapstick brand of comedy rarely found in the thirty-nine. Walls split in two. Sinks and pipes squirt people. Ovens go haywire and spill food onto the floor. Ralph rips his pants in half as he tries to put them on. He throws, slams, pounds, bangs, and punches things. Plaster falls from the ceiling onto people's

heads. Ralph dives
onto a dusty couch in
pursuit of a mouse
and comes up in
"whiteface." Nor-
ton sets up a cot that
collapses   when
Ralph lies on it.

It may require
some self-control,
too, to keep from
groaning when one
sees Ralph in the
tight, button-down
jacket that was the
early, poor man's
version of his
famed bus-driv-
er's uniform, or
Norton dressed in
unexplained variations on his patented outfit: T-shirts in different colors or
different styles.

But for those who resist scoffing at what may seem like uncharacteristic
behavior by the characters, and who don't allow the differences between the Lost
Episodes and the Classic Thirty-nine to distract them, viewing the old sketches
has its payoffs. Where in the thirty-nine, for example, is the name of the founder
of the Racoon Lodge mentioned? In the lost sketches the writers were so generous
they gave two names: Toots Mondello and Herman Hildebrand. Ralph never gets
promoted in the half-hour shows; in the Lost Episodes he gets several promotions
and a few raises. Norton hardly ever mentions his family in the thirty-nine; in the
sketches he reveals a brother, Willy, five sisters, and a father and grandfather who
worked in the sewer. And Trixie's long-rumored career as a burlesque dancer is
no longer rumor. It's fact.

There is much that the half-hours and the sketches have in common. A lack of
continuity, for one, in things such as the names and numbers of relatives; how
characters met and got their jobs; the Kramdens' street address. The puzzle pieces
that don't fit, the conflicting stories and pieces of information, and the dangling
threads in the thirty-nine are well known to *Honeymooners* buffs. But it wasn't
just in the thirty-nine that no one seemed to keep track of these details. The fact
is, no one ever did. That is why, in the Lost Episodes, Alice appears to have an
endless number of siblings; why the Kramdens' apartment seems to have existed
at two other addresses: 358 and 358½ Chauncey Street; why Norton seems to

have gotten his job in the sewer as many ways as Wonder Bread builds strong bodies; and why the Kramdens are on record as having met in at least three or four different places. Ditto for Ralph and Norton.

But there's an excuse for all this. "There was a failure to communicate with each other in our rush to get the show out," says Leonard Stern. "Though we seemed to have a commonality of understanding and purpose in terms of the characters, there was almost no chance to discuss anything in depth. We just did it. That weekly deadline."

Or, as Walter Stone put it, the writers were writing for their lives. Who cared from Frank and Bill and Pete and George.

Ad libs and goofs, stubborn props that don't work right, and plain old accidents—all things that helped create a mystique around the Classic Thirty-nine—are liberally scattered throughout the lost sketches. These were often the result of Gleason's style of working, which meant rehearsing with the cast as little as possible, and of the fact that with live television there are no retakes. (There were none in the half-hours either, even though Gleason had the luxury of refilming scenes or editing things out.)

The classic ad libs from the thirty-nine—Art Carney's "Leave it there, the cat'll get it," when Bert Weedemeyer clumsily bumps into a table in "Alice and the Blonde"; Gleason's "Maybe we oughta say something about spear fishing," when a piece of the Handy Housewife Helper (or Helpful Housewife Happy Handy, as Gleason once calls it) he's waving around flies off, in "Better Living Through TV"; his "denaturizer" line, when a piece of his spaceman costume falls off as he's modeling it for Alice in "Man from Space"—are prime ingredients in the magic of *The Honeymooners*. So are those classic moments where things happened that weren't supposed to, as when Gleason knocked down the wall of pots and pans at the end of the Handy Housewife Helper commercial, or when the house phone won't stop buzzing in "Dial J for Janitor."

The Lost *Honeymooners* have more than their share of faux pas, props that won't cooperate, and *Twilight Zone*-like happenings. In "Ralph's Sweet Tooth," Gleason keeps forgetting which side of his mouth is supposed to ache; he accidentally breaks a glass and sets up a rare ad lib for Audrey Meadows in "Boys and Girls Together"; exasperated, he wonders out loud if a boxtop he's trying to rip off its box is welded on in "Boxtop Kid"; Art Carney can't get a door open in "Stand In for Murder," and George Petrie is forced into what must have been one of his few ad libs; Frank Marth accidentally drops a huge hunk of ice on the floor in "The Adoption"; Carney slips on some wet paint and nearly takes a tumble in "My Fair Landlord," and Gleason immediately responds with a line about Norton having a good sense of balance; Audrey puts her hand through the "window pane" to pull in a telephone Trixie has lowered in "Kramden vs. Norton"; Gleason is on stage with his zipper open in "Hot Tips."

Audrew Meadows vividly remembers "Teamwork Beat the Clock," because

Alice washes a window pane that obviously isn't there in "Kramden vs. Norton."

it was one of the few shows in which she—not Gleason or Carney—was doing the ad libbing.

"There's a scene in that show where it's about two o'clock in the morning and we're still practicing to be on *Beat the Clock*. Well, we were playing the Paramount the same week we were doing that show. We were doing six shows a day, running back and forth to rehearse, do the show, go on the air. And in the scene I just got tongue-tied. It was supposed to be late at night, and we're doing this dumb stunt. Artie is the machine rolling the lemon down this chute, and Jackie and I had to catch the lemon in a cup and put it on a saucer and keep a balloon in the air at the same time. I'm supposed to say something like, 'Wait a minute. This is what we do. He rolls the lemon down the chute and we go through the whole thing properly.'

"We get on the air, and I got so tongue-twisted that it would not come out right no matter what I did. Like, 'You roll the cup down the thing. I mean the saucer . . . ' Gleason just backed off. Then I said, 'I am going to say this until I get it right.' Then I said very deliberately, 'Now you just stand there. Now, he-rolls-the-lemon-down. . . .' all very slowly, until I got all through. Jackie says, 'Big deal,' and the audience didn't notice the mistake. They screamed.

"He was so happy, afterward he said, 'Aud, you should have seen your face when you said, 'I'm going to say this until I get it right.'"

There are several expressions common to both groups of *Honeymooners*.

"Baby, you're the greatest" runs from the first to the last seasons. So do the Nortonisms "Hey there, Ralphie boy," "Sheesh, what a grouch," and "Va va va voom." But "Bang! Zoom!" used frequently in the thirty-nine appears only once in the lost sketches. Conversely, "One of these days, Alice, pow! Right in the kisser," a fixture in the Lost *Honeymooners*, is used just once in the half-hours.

Walter Stone recalls that stock lines like "Pow, right in the kisser" were both written into the script and tossed in by Gleason when he was looking for a laugh.

"Sometimes we would put it in and sometimes Gleason'd say, 'Leave it to me. I'll put it in where it fits,'" says Stone. "It would work both ways. If we saw an obvious place we'd put it in. But we wouldn't do it like 'Make sure you got one in each script.'

"If he was out there and maybe he didn't feel happy with the way things were going, he figures, you know, this is a sure laugh. It fits, because there was always some sort of conflict between the two of them. He was always thinking on his feet out there. I mean, he was never lost because he was that kind of guy."

A lot of familiar names pop up in the lost sketches, but they're not always attached to the people or places they're associated with in the thirty-nine. In the Lost *Honeymooners* there are two Freddie Mullers: the "real" Freddie, a bus driver, and another who is a bus-company executive; Herman Gruber is an old school chum of Ralph's, not the Racoon who provides pizza, knockwurst, and pig's knuckles and sauerkraut at bowling tournaments; Grogan is a bus driver, not the neighborhood cop; Fensterblau is Evelyn Fensterblau, a girl who worked at a cigar stand, not Joe Fensterblau, a guy at the bus company who's always needling Ralph; Wohlstetter is not Harvey (or Harvey Jr.), but an opportunistic entrepreneur; Freitag is a meat market, not a delicatessen, and Krauss's is a deli, not a meat market.

Then, in the Lost Episodes there are characters (both seen and unseen) and places too numerous to mention that were forgotten by the filming of the half-hours, and lines and pieces of business that similarly disappeared. "Boy, would I like to drive one right through" and "You're going up in the air," were two of Ralph's threats that didn't stick. The "lost" Alice said "Awww, shaddup!" and "From this blow I may never recover" a lot; the later Alice never did. Another oft-used but finally discarded Ralph–Alice bit: Ralph goes into a spiel about other men's wives standing behind their men, and then asks "What do I have behind me?" Alice looks at his posterior and is about to burst forth with the big answer when Ralph, realizing he's set himself up, cautions her, "Don't you dare!"

One line that pops up in numerous episodes between 1952 and 1954, but

George Petrie as Freddie Muller, assistant bus dispatcher for Gotham Transit.

never in the half-hours, is "You are a mental case," Ralph's response to a crazy idea or dumb comment by Norton. Walter Stone doesn't remember why the line was dropped, but he says it's a line a writer couldn't use today.

"We used that a lot, but don't forget we're talking a different era. Now "mental case" means something. Today you say "mental case" and people look at you, but they didn't have the same feelings then. Things weren't publicized at the time like they are today. They didn't have these drives where people say, "This is Mental Health Week." Those days, comedians didn't know yet that they were going to have certain charities they were going to plug and that mental health was going to be one of them. So nobody cared. You got a laugh, it was funny, and people didn't object to it.

"People say to me today that Ralph was a real chauvinist pig. But it was a different era and it was a different kind of comedy. You couldn't do it as broad today as we did it then, because, you know, the women's movement. Same with the "mental" thing. If a person is a mental case today it's not funny."

What fans may find most striking about watching the Lost *Honeymooners* is that two episodes of the Classic Thirty-nine—"The Loudspeaker" and " 'Twas the Night Before Christmas"—are actually remakes of "lost" sketches. ("A Matter of Life and Death" is a remake too, but of a DuMont sketch presumably lost forever. In that one, Ralph has "cerebral monochromia" and discovers he's

not dying before trying to sell his story to a magazine.)

"The Loudspeaker" is 1952's "The Guest Speaker," beefed up and slightly altered. The main difference is that in the half-hour version Ralph discovers that rather than giving an acceptance speech for being named Racoon of the Year he's supposed to introduce Norton, the real winner; in the original sketch Ralph learns he's supposed to introduce the head Racoon at a meeting, not give a speech, as he thought. (Trivia note: Norton's not even a member of the lodge in this one.)

" 'Twas the Night Before Christmas" is the "lost" sketch, "Anniversary Gift" with tinsel on it. The anniversary gift in the sketch of the same name is a hairpin box made out of two thousand matches glued together; Ralph and Trixie have bought Alice the same present, and Ralph scrambles to find a way to raise money to buy Alice another gift. A few years later, Marx and Stone dusted off that script and made it a holiday show in which a neighbor, Mrs. Stevens, gives Alice the same gift Ralph bought for her.

Seventy-plus sketches. The original cast. Filmed live. Black and white. New characters. Different sets. More shtick. Familiar faces. Recycled plots. Busloads of trivia. More contradictions. Goofs and ad libs. Crazy hare-brained schemes. The Lost *Honeymooners*. For *Honeymooners* fans who've been wondering when their ship was gonna come in, wonder no more. Here it is, the Queen Mary!

THE FIRST CBS SEASON: 1952–1953

*On one level it was like third-rate vaudeville and on
another level it was one of the greatest things ever done.*
COLEMAN JACOBY

I t wasn't until 1952, following Gleason's move from Dumont to CBS, that a
national audience had a chance to see the misadventures of the Kramdens
and the Nortons.

The earliest *Honeymooners* sketch now back in syndication was
performed on November 1, 1952 (a few episodes were done in September
and October of '52, but they have either been lost for good or aren't being
rereleased because the quality of the original kinescopes is poor). That episode,
entitled "The Cold," is noteworthy not only because it is now the oldest
Honeymooners sketch in circulation, but also for what it does and doesn't contain.
First, the skit contains what would become three signatures of the *Honeymooners*:
one of Ralph's pain bits—those dozen or so seconds where Ralph careens around
the apartment like a greased pinball, waving or holding a wounded limb; the
"walking speech," where at the end of a skit or episode Ralph admits to being a
moax and apologizes for whatever foolish thing he's done; and the line "Baby,
you're the greatest," arguably the most famous closing line in the history of
entertainment.

Three other things distinguish this episode. The most obvious is the absence
of Norton. It's the only "Lost *Honeymooners*" sketch in which he doesn't appear.
Trixie, however, does appear (it wasn't until January 1953 that all four characters
appeared in the same sketch), just long enough to become a target for Ralph's
sarcasm and nasty disposition. Though Ralph flares up at Trixie a couple of times
in the Classic Thirty-nine, those instances don't come close to the run-ins he has
with her in several of the Lost Episodes. Finally, in this episode, as in eleven
others done during this season, Ralph doesn't wear the bus driver's uniform.

When Ralph does wear his uniform, it is not the familiar one from the half-hour shows; this uniform is no more than a button-down jacket. Norton appears "out of uniform" on occasion too: in "Jellybeans" he wears a strap T-shirt under his vest, and in a couple of other sketches he wears a collarless, button-neck, long-sleeved thermal shirt. The outfitting of Mrs. Kramden is a little erratic too: in one sketch she looks almost like a bag lady; in another as if she's going to a cocktail party.

Unarguably the most jolting visual of these early lost episodes is a slim Ralph! In "Pickles" and "Jellybeans" he looks downright skinny—at least compared to the Kramden in a later lost episode where he is almost suspended from the bus company for being overweight.

Fans will be amazed to find three episodes from this season in which Ralph doesn't once yell at Alice; on other occasions they'll be tempted to put their fingers in their ears when Ralph's barking gets especially vicious, and Alice's rejoinders are so shrill that one actually roots for Ralph to belt her one. He threatens to more than once, not with a "Bang! Zoom!" as he would a few years later, but with a "Pow! Right in the kisser!" the standard threat of the lost episodes. (Gleason would use this line only once in the Classic Thirty-nine.)

A number of "Gleason actors" make their first CBS *Honeymooners* appearance in this season: Zamah Cunningham, George Petrie, Dick Bernie, and Ethel Owen. Cunningham, throughout the lost episodes, played either an Italian or an Irish neighbor; Petrie is in his familiar role as the first man off the bench; Bernie has a handful of parts, and Owen appears as both Alice's aunt and her mother.

Other firsts: a mention of the Racoon Lodge, in this instance the International Order of Friendly Sons of the Racoons ("Guest Speaker"); the first episode in which Ralph thinks he's going to be a father ("Pickles"); Ralph's first brush with a promotion ("Alice Plays Cupid"); the first—and by no means the last—explanations of how Ralph met Alice and Norton met Trixie ("Anniversary Gift"); the first appearance of a box made out of two thousand matches ("Anniversary Gift"); the first reference to Trixie's being a burlesque dancer ("Anniversary Gift"); the first time the Kramdens have an electrical appliance—a radio!—in the apartment ("Ralph's Diet"); the first episode in which the characters move outside the Kramden's apartment ("Vacation/Fred's Landing"), and the first sketch to run longer than thirty minutes ("Vacation/Fred's Landing," the last sketch of the 1952–53 season; no episode that preceded it ran longer than fourteen minutes).

TITLE: *"The Cold"*
DATE: *November 1, 1952*
LENGTH: *7:47*

Ralph has a cold, but the way he's acting you'd think he had arterial monochromia. He's turned the Kramden apartment into a hospital ward and poor Alice into Florence Nightingale. She serves Ralph juice and crackers, refills his hot-water bottle, applies a mustard plaster to his back, soaks his feet, etc. But it's Ralph's disposition, not his health, that takes a turn for the worse when Alice lets it slip out that she's taken an insurance policy out on his life. Ralph gets so worked up that he accuses Alice of actually wanting him to die. A few seconds later, though, he feels like crawling into a six-foot-deep hole when Alice tells him that she also has a policy on her own life, with Ralph as the beneficiary. Ralph does his obigatory moax routine and predicts immortality for himself and Alice.

TITLE: *"Pickles"*
DATE: *November 8, 1952*
LENGTH: *7:08*

Alice has Ralph running all over the neighborhood, shopping, on his day off. He's steamed because Alice has dragged him to three different stores just to save a few cents on groceries. And worse, after buying the groceries and paying the bills Alice has spent Ralph's entire paycheck—$42—leaving Ralph without his allowance. Ralph screams poverty—until Norton comes down in desperate need of five dollars. Ralph takes a five-dollar bill he had hidden under a bureau drawer and gives it to Norton. Before Alice can chew him into chopped meat, Ralph explains that the money was for an anniversary present he bought for Alice that was being delivered to the apartment. The delivery man shows up and Ralph is about to send him away without payment when—*voilà!*—out pops five dollars from one of Alice's hiding places. She was saving it for an anniversary-night celebration. Then Alice remembers to eat the pickles she bought at the grocery. Ralph thinks she's pregnant and begins dreaming up names for the child. Alice says she's eating the pickles because her doctor wants to see if she's allergic to them. Ralph won't be a father after all, and he expresses his disappointment by threatening Alice with a "One of these days, Alice" and a big fist, to which Alice gently and encouragingly replies, "Ralph, one of these days . . ."

TITLE: *"Jellybeans"*
DATE: *November 22, 1952*
LENGTH: *8:18*

A local furniture store is having a guess-how-many-jellybeans-are-in-the-jar contest. Ralph wants to win the hundred-dollar prize, so he buys a jar and a few thousand jellybeans and begins counting. Alice could care less: her mind is on a dress she's been coveting for weeks that's on sale one last day. Ralph has Norton call the store with his guess, which turns out to be right. But the prize isn't a hundred dollars in cash like Ralph thought—it's a hundred-dollar gift certificate, redeemable only after the purchase of a thousand dollars worth of furniture. Now that that's over, Alice wants Ralph to take her to buy the dress. She discovers her money is missing, and Ralph sheepishly admits he spent it on jellybeans.

TITLE: *"Alice Plays Cupid"*
DATE: *January 17, 1953*
LENGTH: *11:55*

Ralph is bringing home George, the traffic manager at the bus company, for supper. Alice decides to play cupid and invites Henrietta, a girl from the ladies' auxiliary, to be George's date. Ralph wants to make points with George because a bunch of drivers are about to be transferred to Staten Island and Ralph doesn't want to be one of them. He bawls out Alice about the dinner because he thinks the menu—Yankee bean soup, meat loaf and french fries, and fruit cup—is too common. Henrietta arrives first and Ralph can think of only one word to describe her: *monster*. She goes into the bathroom to freshen up and George arrives. Ralph tells him that Alice is playing matchmaker and then throws in a few nasty remarks about Henrietta. George says he appreciates Alice's gesture, then adds that he recently became engaged. Ralph takes that as a cue to rip into Henrietta some more. She returns and George—dumbfounded, and enraged at Ralph's remarks—introduces her as his fiancée. As the couple leaves, George makes an appointment with Ralph for the following morning—to discuss a Staten Island run.

TITLE: *"Suspense"*
DATE: *January 24, 1953*
LENGTH: *10:38*

Does Alice really hate Ralph? Enough to kill him? No, she's just rehearsing for a play in which she portrays a woman plotting to murder her husband. Trixie and Alice are in the Kramden bedroom, going over Alice's lines, when Ralph and Norton walk into the apartment and overhear them. Ralph naturally thinks the worst, but he just can't believe it; he thinks he's been a model husband. The Nortons leave, and Ralph begins to steam as he tells Alice he overheard her talking to Trixie. Alice is nonchalant about the whole thing because she thinks Ralph knows she was rehearsing for the play, and is just against her acting. She finally catches on that Ralph thinks she's going to kill him when she puts a vitamin in Ralph's juice and he accuses her of trying to poison him. Alice then gives a Tony Award–winning performance: She "confesses" to Ralph that yes, she was planning to kill him and that if she can't do that she'll kill herself instead. Alice gulps down the "poisoned" juice, and Ralph erupts into hysterics, thinking he's about to lose Alice forever. Gleason is superb as he makes a completely believable split-second leap from comedy to pathos, causing the audience to simultaneously laugh at his stupidity and sympathize with his despair. Alice "recovers" and Ralph regains his composure—and threatens to beat up Alice. She reminds him that when he thought she was dying he said she was his whole world. Ralph comes to his senses and gives her a kiss instead of a right hook.

TITLE: *"Lost Job"*
DATE: *January 31, 1953*
LENGTH: *8:58*

The Kramdens and the Nortons are going to the Royal Chinese Gardens for dinner—until Alice finds a pink slip in Ralph's pay envelope. Ralph is angry and melancholy. He reminisces about his twelve years as a bus driver, recalling highlights such as the time he drove his bus when his sacroiliac was out of place. How will the Kramdens live? Alice offers to hock her wedding ring and to get a job. Ralph decides the best thing to do is to send Alice to live with her mother while he leaves town in search of work. In walks Dutch, the guy who stuffs the pay envelopes at the bus company. He's ready to go bowling with Ralph, who'd rather bust a bowling ball over his head because of the pink slip. Dutch explains that he was using the slip as scrap paper and that if Ralph had turned it over he would have seen a note about going bowling. Relieved, Ralph says he can't go bowling—he has a date with his wife at the Royal Chinese Gardens.

TITLE: *"Anniversary Gift"*
DATE: *February 21, 1953*
LENGTH: *10:17*

It's the Kramdens' anniversary and they're going to celebrate it dancing at the Hotel New Yorker, the site of their first date. Alice is giving Ralph twenty-five dollars to buy a suede coat he wants and—shades of Christmas Future!—Ralph has bought Alice a box for hairpins that's made of two thousand matches glued together. They decide to exchange gifts, but before Ralph can give Alice hers, Trixie gives Alice the same box. Ralph is flabbergasted and tells Alice her present is being delivered later. While Ralph and Norton are trying to figure out where Ralph can get some money to buy another gift, a delivery man with a package for

Mrs. O'Leary arrives and asks Ralph if he can leave the box with him until she returns home. A moment later Alice comes out of the bedroom, and, thinking the package is for her, snatches it from Ralph and opens it. It's a dress, and as Alice is trying it on Mrs. O'Leary arrives, looking for her package. She demands to know why Alice is wearing her dress. Ralph wants to avoid a scene, so he pays Mrs. O'Leary for the dress—with the money Alice gave him for a suede coat.

TITLE: *"Income Tax"*
DATE: *March 7, 1953*
LENGTH: *10:37*

Ralph is trying to fill out his tax return and it's driving him nuts, mainly because he hasn't the slightest idea of what he's doing. Alice isn't helping matters either, complaining about Ralph's salary, which in this episode is $42.50 a week. Ralph finally concludes that he owes the government fifteen dollars, and that's fifteen dollars more than he says he has. Alice remembers that Ralph has stashed away fifteen dollars for a new bowling ball, but Ralph tells her that that money is off limits to everybody, including Uncle Sam. The neighborhood priest stops by, asking for donations for the poor, and Ralph is shamed into giving him the bowling ball money. He tells Alice he'll find some way to raise the fifteen dollars for the IRS, and then delivers a patriotic speech about what a great country America is and that she's welcome to any taxes she wants from the Kramdens.

TITLE: *"Alice's Aunt Ethel"*
DATE: *March 14, 1953*
LENGTH: *8:34*

Alice's Aunt Ethel arrives for Thanksgiving—toting more luggage than someone leaving for Africa, according to Ralph. Why is Ralph so upset? Because in Hotel Kramden there's only one bedroom, and Alice and Aunt Ethel are sharing the one bed, leaving Ralph to sleep on a cot in the kitchen. All that's left for Ralph to do is to scheme to get rid of Aunt Ethel. Norton, slightly out of uniform in a Wallace Beery–type long-sleeved undershirt, tries to help out Ralph with some dumb ideas, like having Ralph yell "Fire, Aunt Ethel," so she'll rush out of the apartment. Ralph has a better idea: he'll stage a phony backache and tell Aunt Ethel that the only way he'll get better is to sleep in a nice, soft bed. Ralph begins bellowing in pain, and Alice and Aunt Ethel rush out of the bedroom—where Aunt Ethel was just beginning to pack for a trip to Cousin Mildred's!—to see what's the matter. When

Ralph tells Aunt Ethel about his backache and that he's got to sleep in his bed to get rid of it, she hits him with a bombshell: she was just about to leave for Cousin Mildred's, but now she's going to stay and help nurse Ralph back to health. Oh, and by the way, Aunt Ethel's remedy for a bad back is to sleep on the kitchen floor, not on a soft bed.

TITLE: *"What's Her Name"*
DATE: *March 21, 1953*
LENGTH: *7:02*

Ralph, Alice, Norton, and Trixie have been to the movies. Round One begins when Alice tells Ralph she'd like him to be more like Ronald Colman—suave, smooth, and sophisticated. Ralph says he'd be more like Ronald Colman if Alice were more like Lana Turner. Round Two. Alice says she prefers the other actress in the movie to Lana Turner, and then can't remember her name. That puts the whammy on Ralph, because he can't sleep until they think of the actress's name. All the noise keeps Norton awake, so he comes downstairs—but can't remember the name either. As he's leaning out the Kramdens' window, trying to read the movie-theater marquee, a cop comes to the door. He tells Ralph that if the noise doesn't stop he's going to wind up in front of a judge. That's it! declares Ralph. Judge! Arline Judge is the actress's name.

TITLE: *"Lunchbox"*
DATE: *March 28, 1953*
LENGTH: *9:08*

Ralph comes home in a foul mood because he hated what he found in his lunchbox that afternoon. He complains to Alice that the food was horrible, and then gripes that there wasn't enough of it. Frankie, another driver, shows up and tells Ralph that somehow their lunchboxes got mixed up, and that Ralph ate his lunch and Frankie got the one Alice had prepared for Ralph. Frankie raves about the food, and Ralph realizes Alice packed him a gourmet feast. Ralph eats his words.

TITLE: *"Hot Tips"*
DATE: *April 11, 1953*
LENGTH: *11:10*

Ralph, Alice, and Norton are going to the racetrack. Half the people in the neighborhood know it and want

Ralph to place bets for them. Ralph takes bets from Eddie, the delivery boy; Mrs. Gallager; and Max, the butcher, and when word about the bets gets around the neighborhood, the police—thinking Ralph may be a bookie—make a beeline for his apartment. Ralph and Norton panic, and Norton tells Ralph to eat the list on which he has written down the names of the horses he was supposed to bet. When Alice tells the cop the list will actually prove Ralph's innocence, Ralph discovered that he didn't eat the list after all—it was a fifty-dollar bill he swallowed. The cop is convinced that Ralph's not a bookie and leaves him with an expensive case of indigestion.

TITLE: *"Norton Moves In"*
DATE: *April 18, 1953*
LENGTH: *12:02*

The Nortons have had their apartment painted and they can't stand the smell, so Trixie comes down to the Kramdens' at three A.M. to ask if she and Norton can spend the night there. Ralph is incensed at being awakened in the middle of the night. ("Norton works in the sewer all day and he can't stand the smell of paint!" he moans.) Ralph ends up in the kitchen sleeping with Norton on a cot that collapses as soon as Ralph lies down on it. No sooner does Ralph close his eyes when Norton wants a cigarette, and then a match. Norton lights up and then accidentally drops the match in the bedding. This burns Ralph up—literally. He so brutally insults Norton that he and Trixie leave. Alice then reminds Ralph of all the favors Norton has done for him, and he relents. Re-enter Norton—who had been standing right outside the door.

TITLE: *"Ralph's Diet"*
DATE: *April 25, 1953*
LENGTH: *11:30*

Mrs. Rafferty is throwing a surprise party for her husband, and she wants to hide the cake and a turkey in the Kramden apartment. She'd like the Kramdens to attend the party, but Alice says no—Ralph's on a diet and the food at the party would be too great a temptation. The diet is driving Ralph crazy: for breakfast he had a poached egg and half a grapefruit, and for lunch a hardboiled egg, two stalks of celery, and an apple. Alice has a raw vegetable salad ready for his dinner, and that sends Ralph over the edge. He's seen more food dragged into holes by ants than he's eaten all day, he says. He tries to get his mind off of food by listening to the radio (!), but when a commercial comes on for fried chicken Ralph turns off the radio—by putting his fist through it. When Alice leaves the apartment, Ralph discovers Mrs. Rafferty's cake and turkey, which Alice has hidden in the bureau drawer. He does a Dr. Jekyll–Mr. Hyde transformation into a two-fisted eating machine, turkey leg in one hand, a hunk of cake in the other.

Alice offers to replace the cake and turkey, and Ralph gets to finish his feast after he promises Alice he'll begin a new diet the next day.

TITLE: *"Dinner Guest"*
DATE: *May 2, 1953*
LENGTH: *9:45*

Freddie Muller (not the same Freddie from the Classic Thirty-nine) and his wife are dinner guests of the Kramdens. Promotions are coming up at the bus company and Ralph is trying to make a pitch for himself, yet every time he's about to sell himself to Freddie something happens to interfere. Freddie suggests they all go to a drive-in movie, but Ralph vetoes the idea. Alice turns on the radio (!) and everyone dances the mambo. Norton comes down and kills Ralph's evening by reminding Alice that Trixie was expecting her to go to a club meeting that night. That sends the Mullers home, and as soon as they're out the door, Ralph rips into Alice for distracting Freddie all night. Freddie comes back for his wife's purse— and commends Ralph for being the only bus driver not to pester him about a promotion. Ralph's going to get a promotion after all—thanks to Alice.

TITLE: *"Manager of the Baseball Team"*
DATE: *May 9, 1953*
LENGTH: *9:50*

Alice is worried because Ralph is long overdue from work. When he finally comes home he has flowers for Alice, cigars for Norton, and champagne for everybody. Ralph's celebrating what he thinks is a promotion to manager of the bus company. Ralph is giddy with the idea of making more money and he promises Alice that the first thing he'll do when he gets his raise is to have the bunion removed from her foot. Soon Ralph is dreaming about becoming president of the company, and boy, would he change things. On each bus he'd add stewardesses, outlets for electric razors, and long straps for short people, and he'd have each driver start his run a minute later for people who always just miss the bus. When Ralph goes out to Krauss's to buy cold cuts and beer, a telegram comes—announcing Ralph's appointment as manager of the company *baseball* team. When Ralph hears the news he feels as bad for Alice as he does for himself, but her consoling words make him feel like he's just won the World Series.

TITLE: *"The Prowler"*
DATE: *June 6, 1953*
LENGTH: *11:03*

A prowler's been spotted at 328 Chauncey St. Alice is petrified and she wants Ralph to sit up with her. It's four A.M. and he wants to sleep. Alice convinces

Ralph to barricade the door with the bureau, but no sooner has he done this than Norton comes banging at the door, scaring the wits out of the Kramdens. Alice is worried about Trixie being alone in her apartment, but Norton tells her that Trixie is armed—with a frying pan. (Ralph: "A frying pan? That's no weapon." Norton: "It is when she cooks.") Trixie comes down to retrieve Norton, and a minute later the prowler climbs in the Kramdens' window and bops Ralph on the head with a blackjack. Alice screams and the police barge in and nab the prowler. Ralph, who never knew what hit him, wakes up from his stupor and reassures Alice that as long as he's around she has nothing to worry about.

TITLE: *"Guest Speaker"*
DATE: *June 13, 1953*
LENGTH: *13:31*

Ralph gets a message that he's supposed to speak at a meeting of the International Order of Friendly Sons of the Racoons, and he's in a tizzy because Alice sent his uniform pants to the cleaners. Worse, he can't get Alice or Norton to laugh at his joke about the Racoons working like beavers, and Alice and Trixie keep interrupting him while he's trying to memorize the speech he wrote. Just when Ralph gives up trying to recite the speech, George Williams, head of the lodge, arrives with Ralph's remarks for that night. Ralph thinks he's a bigger big shot than he thought he was, until he discovers that all he's supposed to do is introduce Brother Williams at the meeting. Alice reminds him he's still the Number One Racoon in their house. (This skit was embellished a couple of years later and became "The Loudspeaker," an episode of the Classic Thirty-nine. (Above: *Petrie and Gleason exchange a friendly Racoon ooo-woo.*)

TITLE: *"Vacation at Fred's Landing"*
DATE: *June 20, 1953*
LENGTH:

This episode is an earlier version of "Vacation/Fred's Landing," which was broadcast June 19, 1954. This version of the vacation escapades of the Kramdens and the Nortons will not be syndicated but will be available from MPI on videocassette. The 1954 episode is in syndication.

TITLE: *"Glow Worm Cleaning"*
DATE: *June 27, 1953*
LENGTH: *9:53*

Alice is going to be a Glow Worm Girl. That is, she's been picked to appear in a magazine ad for Glow Worm sink cleanser. Ralph is immediately against it because he figures one ad for Glow Worm will start Alice on a career as a model. Ralph changes his tune from "Tell Her No" to "Count Me In" as soon as he thinks he's going to be in the ad too. But an executive from Glow Worm's ad agency tells Ralph he's not the right type for the ad and Ralph begins to glow— like hot lava inside a volcano. He's about to throw the ad exec, his cameraman, and a male model who's to play Alice's husband in the ad out of the apartment, when the exec promises Ralph he can appear in another ad. Ralph cools off, but only until he hears he's going to portray someone "fat, flabby, and forty." That's when he shoves the ad people out the door, to Alice's chagrin. Ralph realizes he's been a jealous fool and is about to leave the apartment when Alice stops him in his tracks by forgiving him. The episode ended with an affectionate "One of these days, pow! Right in the kisser."

THE TRANSITION SEASON: 1953–1954

*As I recall, "Letter to the Boss" was the show that
turned it around because it was so well received that
we started to do more long shows.*
LEONARD STERN

Except for the decision in 1955 to spin off *The Honeymooners* from a sketch on the *Jackie Gleason Show* to its own half-hour series, the most significant programming move regarding *The Honeymooners* took place during the 1953–54 season. Less than two months into the season *The Honeymooners* was permanently expanded from a short ten-to-fifteen minute sketch into a thirty-minute-plus centerpiece of each Gleason show.

The season began with a hint that maybe America would see more of the Kramdens and the Nortons than it had the year before. The opening sketch, "Lucky Number," ran just over seventeen minutes, which, except for "Vacation/Fred's Landing" from the previous season, was the longest *Honeymooners* ever done. A few weeks later another thirty-minute-plus sketch, "Hot Dog Stand," aired, but it was followed by more nine- and ten-minute quickies.

Then *it* happened: *The Honeymooners* went into long-form, half-hour and longer episodes that allowed more time for character development and gave the writers the flexibility to create new situations for the characters and the freedom to take them out of the Kramdens' apartment and put them into places such as the bus depot, the sewer, the boss's office, the pool room, the bowling alley, restaurants, on the sets of popular TV shows, and onto the front stoop at 328/358

Chauncey Street. (The following week's episode and one other later in the season ran less than thirty minutes, but every other sketch done during this and the 1954–55 season ran for at least a half hour.)

The pivotal episode was "Letter to the Boss," a thirty-two-and-a-half-minute sketch that is certain to become an immediate favorite among *Honeymooners* buffs. Here is a microcosm of the life and times of Ralph Kramden. In it are found the elements that would characterize him for all time: his attack/ceasefire relationships with Alice and Norton; how his feelings of self-worth are tied to his job; how the Fickle Finger of Fate always seems to motion to him to advance to Go, and then pokes him in the eye just as he's about to make his move; his unpredictable, childlike personality; his sentimental side; his scheming mind.

The length of the sketches was not the only thing that put the '53–'54 season into sharp contrast with the preceding one. This second season of CBS–era *Honeymooners*—with its frequent set changes, its more sophisticated plots, its use of more actors on stage—was as different from what viewers saw the season before as a Broadway show would look like next to a summer-stock production.

In this one season, the Kramdens and the Nortons were found at the Gotham Bus Company; the bowling alley; on the streets of Brooklyn; in jail; in a hotel lobby and a ballroom; on the set of a popular TV show; in a hospital; in a cottage in the country; at the poolroom; in an apartment in the Bronx!; at a rescue mission; in the park; at the racetrack; and back at Fred's Landing.

Gleason's repertory company was enlarged too. Back were Zamah Cunningham, George Petrie, Dick Bernie, and Ethel Owen, and used for the first time since the move to CBS were Frank Marth, Sammy Birch, Eddie Hanley, Cliff Hall, Les Damon, Gingr Jones, Victor Rendino, Nick Stantley, John Seymour, Humphrey Davis, Sid Raymond, and Jack Albertson. Well-known guest stars were also used in *The Honeymooners* for the first time: Tommy and Jimmy Dorsey appeared with their big band in a New Year's episode, and Elisha Cook, Jr., best known for his role as the small-time thug in *The Maltese Falcon,* did a bit as a bookie in "Santa and the Bookies."

This season also marked Ralph and Norton's first appearances in costumes. In the season's shortest episode, "Halloween Party," Alice dresses up Ralph as a Zulu chieftain, and Norton appears in drag—as silent-film star Clara Bow. For the Christmas show, Ralph wears a Santa Claus outfit and Norton dresses up as an elf. "Hot Dog Stand" is a sort of preview of Ralph and Norton as Chef of the Future/Chef of the Past in "Better Living Through TV." The costumes got such big laughs that putting Ralph and Norton in crazy outfits at least a couple of times a season became obligatory.

Honeymooners trivia buffs will find this season fascinating—for the new information it contains—and frustrating for the contradictions it sets up. For instance, the Kramdens once owned a refrigerator!—but Ralph sold it. And Norton once owned an Essex. Norton fought in the Golden Gloves tournament.

Phil Cuoco (named after the CBS prop man) introduced Ralph and Alice (he must have done it at the WPA, in school, or at a hot-dog wagon, because these are all places at which the Kramdens are said to have met) and was Ralph's best man. Garrity (a.k.a McGarrity) Ralph's nemesis in the building, lived on the sixth floor. Ralph had seven brothers and sisters. His father's name was Ed; Alice's was Mike. Ralph and Norton met at a snooker parlor or at a pool hall, depending upon which episode you watch (from this season). And their first partnerships in crazy, hare-brained, get-rich-quick schemes were in KramNor's Miracle Hair Restorer and a roadside hot-dog stand in New Jersey.

As significant as any other development of the 1953–54 season was the emergence of Norton as the near equal to Ralph in on-screen time. When the sketches were bumped up from eight- or ten-minute bits to half-hour episodes, Norton's role—previously three- or four-minute bits that would provide comic relief to Ralph and Alice's squabbling—was expanded in kind. Gleason has always been generous in attributing to Art Carney much of the reason for the success of *The Honeymooners*, and it is more than likely that had Norton's role not been expanded as the episodes got longer, *The Honeymooners* would not have remained popular enough with audiences to be lifted from the Gleason show and made into a series.

Gleason remembers the decision to beef up the Norton part as simply the outgrowth of both his own and the audience's affection for the character. "Because he was very, very funny and the audience liked him, I wanted them to see as much of him as possible."

"Gleason knew that I wasn't out to upstage him or steal his thunder," says Carney, "and he let me do and say anything I wanted to because he trusted me. That's the way it was and the way it always has been."

TITLE: *"Lucky Number"*
DATE: *September 26, 1953*
LENGTH: *17:02*

Norton has tickets to the ballgame, so he and Ralph play hooky from work. At the game, Ralph wins a thousand dollars by having the winning ticket in a pumpernickel-bread contest. Ralph wants to spend the money immediately—on a new pan to put under the icebox, a car, a rubber plant for the fire escape, and to have a bunion removed from Alice's foot—but Alice wants to save it. Mr. O'Keefe from the bread company arrives to take Ralph's photo for the newspaper. Alice realizes that if Ralph's picture appears in the paper, his boss will see it and know Ralph was lying when he called in sick. Ralph's ready to take his chances, because the bread company won't give him the money unless they can use his picture for publicity. He wants the thousand bucks—until a doctor from the bus company arrives to give Ralph a physical. Ralph suddenly gets sick—mostly from having to give up the money.

TITLE: *"Hot Dog Stand"*
DATE: *October 10, 1953*
LENGTH: *34:49*

Ralph and Norton want to buy a hot-dog stand in New Jersey, but they need six hundred dollars first. The Kramdens have $158 in their bank account, but it's a joint account and Alice won't let Ralph use the money. Ralph is bitter over this because Alice has caused him to miss other opportunities—his brother Willy's used-tire and rug-shampooing businesses—because she wanted to save their money for their retirement years. It's the same story with Norton and Trixie, so the boys are forced to go first to friends and relatives for the money, and finally to a bank. Mr. Foster, the banker, refuses to lend Ralph and Norton the money, until Norton mentions that they were planning to work their regular jobs nights and run the hot-dog stand during the day. Foster is impressed with their dedication and approves the loan. Alice and Trixie help the boys get the stand ready for the grand opening, while Ralph and Norton practice a code that's supposed to help provide quick and efficient service. (H-D-O-R-W-M, for instance, is a hot dog on a roll with mustard.) Things look rosy when a customer tells Ralph and Norton that a building is going up right down the road from the stand. But their kraut goes sour a moment later when they learn that the building is going to be a Howard Johnson's restaurant.

TITLE: *"Two Tickets to the Fight"*
DATE: *October 24, 1953*
LENGTH: *10:41*

Uncle George from Pittsburgh is in town and Alice has invited him to dinner. Ralph has other plans: He and Norton have front-row seats at the fights. Alice is especially fond of Uncle George because he's been generous with the Kramdens. Among other things, he once bought them a refrigerator that Ralph later sold. Ralph could care less. He says, "I'm not missing the best fight of the year!" Alice answers, "You try and walk out that door and you'll be in the best fight of the year!" Uncle George arrives before Ralph can get out of the house, so Ralph tries to get rid of him by faking a backache. Norton walks in on the middle of Ralph's act and is taken in by it too. Not wanting to go to the fight alone, he offers Ralph's ticket to Uncle George.

TITLE: *"Halloween Party"*
DATE: *October 31, 1953*
LENGTH: *9:12*

It's Halloween and the Kramdens and the Nortons are going to a bus-company party. They're all in costume: Trixie's a sailor, Alice is an angel, Norton's dressed as Clara Bow, and Ralph's outfitted as a Zulu chief. Ralph hates his costume, though (a top hat, a sweat shirt, and a grass skirt pulled up to his chest), so he decides to rip up his tuxedo and go as an "elegant bum." Freddie Muller and his wife come to pick up the Nortons and the Kramdens and they're dressed to the teeth. Freddie explains that though the party's on Halloween, it's not a costume party—it's a formal dinner-dance to celebrate the boss's birthday. Since Ralph's tux is now in rags, he misses a chance to hobnob with the muckety-mucks, but Norton doesn't consider the evening a total loss: he figures since everyone's in costume, they might as well go out trick-or-treating. (*This episode was done again in 1954 but that version has not been rereleased.*)

TITLE: *"Champagne and Caviar"*
DATE: *November 7, 1953*
LENGTH: *10:45*

Mr. Marshall is dropping in on the Kramdens, and Ralph, who desperately wants a promotion and a raise, is going to extremes to impress him—he buys champagne, caviar, and expensive cigars. Norton comes down and embarrasses Ralph in front of Marshall. Ralph finally gets rid of him by giving him money to take Trixie to the movies. Then Ralph gets poked in the eye by the Fickle Finger of Fate. The board of directors for the bus company has been pressuring Marshall to give his drivers a raise, but now that he sees how well Ralph lives on the $62 a week he already pays him, he wants to use Ralph and his gracious life style as proof that he already pays his drivers enough. Ralph is crestfallen, but he dines that evening on caviar and champagne.

TITLE: *"Letter to the Boss"*
DATE: *November 14, 1953*
LENGTH: *32:29*

Ralph comes home in a rage; after driving a bus for the Gotham Bus Company for nine years, he's been told to turn in his uniform. He is incensed, frustrated, and humiliated, and the loss of income has him bordering on panic—he actually suggests to Alice that they move in with her parents until he gets another job. Norton comes down to pick up Ralph to go bowling and, as only he can, he makes Ralph feel worse while trying to cheer him up. Ralph feels cheated and betrayed—both by life and by J. J. Marshall, president of the bus company—so he decides to write Marshall a letter to tell him how he feels after being fired after nine years of loyal service. Norton writes what Ralph dictates. His opening line: "You dirty bum," delivered with such conviction by Ralph that it sounds as if he invented the insult for the occasion. After calling Marshall a miserable low-life and telling him to turn in his membership card to the human race, he tells Norton to sign the letter, "Respectfully yours, etc., etc." Ralph's too depressed to go bowling, so he gives Norton the letter and asks him to mail it on the way to the alley. Moments later Ralph finds out he hasn't been fired: he was told to turn in his uniform because he was getting a promotion. Ralph races out of the house to catch Norton before he mails the letter. Norton, meanwhile, asks a custodian at the bowling alley to mail the letter. Ralph arrives at the alley, but by the time he finds out what happened to the letter, it's too late—the custodian's disappeared and presumably dropped the letter in a mailbox outside the alley. Federal offense or not, Ralph is determined to retrieve the letter from the mailbox—until a postman catches him and Norton trying to turn it over and shake out its contents. Ralph's only chance now is to intercept the letter before Mr. Marshall has a chance to read it. Marshall walks into his office just as Ralph is sorting through the mail and Ralph greets him with a friendly *homina-homina*. The first letter Marshall opens is Ralph's, and he begins reading it out loud to acquaint Ralph with the crank mail executives occasionally receive. Marshall is getting a kick out of the letter until he gets to the end. He doesn't mind the nasty remarks but he becomes infuriated when he thinks the author didn't have the courage to sign his name. Norton had written down exactly what Ralph said: "Respectfully yours, etc., etc." Ralph is so shocked by the turn of events that he has a spastic fainting attack (it looks like a precursor of break dancing) and collapses on Marshall's floor. Ralph recovers and races home to tell Alice the good news—because of Norton's stupidity he didn't lose his promotion. The Kramdens are preparing to celebrate with a Chinese dinner when Norton comes in with his good news: he went down to the bus company and told Mr. Marshall that Ralph was sorry for calling him a dirty bum. When Ralph hears this he has fainting spell number two, a "cartwheel faint" that plops him squarely on his backside.

TITLE: *"Finger Man"*
DATE: *November 28, 1953*
LENGTH: *11:42*

Ralph spots Bullets Durgom, a wanted killer, on his bus and helps the police capture him. Ralph races home with the news, just a step ahead of the reporters who descend upon Chauncey Street for photos of the hero and a firsthand account of how he helped apprehend one of the country's meanest thugs. A police chief comes by to congratulate Ralph, and while he's there one of his men races in with the news that Bullets has escaped. Ralph is terrified, because Bullets has threatened to get him. The cops figure Bullets will head straight to Chauncey Street to carry out his threat, so they set a trap for him: two cops will wait in the Kramden's bedroom, ready to spring out when Ralph says "Bullets, it's you," when the killer enters the apartment. Bullets appears and Ralph is tongue-tied. Just as Bullets is about to shoot, Norton walks in, and upon seeing him blurts out "Bullets, it's you." The cops fly out of the bedroom, nab Bullets, and commend Ralph for being so brave.

TITLE: *"Santa and the Bookies"*
DATE: *December 12, 1953*
LENGTH: *34:05*

Alice is knitting baby clothes to make some extra money for Christmas. When Norton comes down and asks Ralph if he can hide Trixie's Christmas present in the Kramdens' apartment, Ralph says yes and sticks the present in the bureau drawer—where Alice has hidden the baby clothes. A moment later, when Norton tells Ralph that Trixie has made a doctor's appointment for Alice, Ralph is sure that Alice is pregnant. He decides he has to make some more money in a hurry so that his future son can go to college, so he answers a newspaper ad for a Santa Claus job. What Ralph doesn't know is that the guys who placed the ad are bookmakers and that they plan to use the Santa to collect bets. Ralph is hired and so is Norton—as an elf. Ralph and Norton set up shop on the sidewalk, and bettors walk by and drop in their money and slips of paper with the names of the horses they want to bet. When a cop drops some money into the pot and Norton asks him where his slip is, Santa and his helper wind up in the slammer. Ralph is frantic. He explains to the cops that he was playing Santa Claus because he wanted to earn some extra money because his wife is pregnant, and that he thought he was collecting money for charity. Alice shows up at the jail, and when Ralph asks her to corroborate his story, he finds out he's not going to be a father after all. The cops think Ralph's a liar and want to throw the book at him. The boys finally convince the cops to bring them back to where they were collecting the money, and to set up a stakeout to catch the real bookies when they show up to pick up the loot and betting slips from Ralph. The cops nab the real bad guys and for a few seconds it looks as if Ralph may have a merry Christmas after all. But only for a few seconds. While Alice, Norton, and Ralph—still dressed in his Santa costume—are waiting for a bus to take them home, a woman hands Ralph some change and another cop pinches him for soliciting money without a license.

TITLE: *"Honeymooners Christmas Party"*
DATE: *December 19, 1953*
LENGTH: *37:23*

This episode is invaluable among Lost and Classic Thirty-nine *Honeymooners* because no other trots out a representative sampling of the Gleason repertory of characters that had so much to do with Jackie Gleason's success. The plot depends on the premise that the characters live, work, or bar-hop in the Kramden neighborhood, but who's to say they don't? And besides, it's Christmas Eve. Alice is decorating the tree and setting out holiday refreshments. Ralph comes home with potato salad, but Alice says it's the wrong potato salad. It came from DeVito's, which would have been the right place to go for lasagne, but the right potato salad would have come from Krauss's. Ralph can't believe that Alice is

Rehearsing for "Honeymooners Christmas Party," 1953.

actually asking him to go out for different potato salad, and he's right. She's not asking him. She's telling him. He leaves. Trixie enters, and describes to Alice what Ed gave her for Christmas—a juice squeezer that looks like Napoleon and squirts juice out of its ear (foreshadowing the later-model Napoleon-shaped juice squeezer of the Classic Thirty-nine's "'Twas the Night Before Christmas"). Fenwick Babbitt (played by Jackie Gleason) comes by, to deliver ice and beer. After hauling the beer barrel all over the apartment and standing around with the block of ice, he discovers he's in the wrong apartment, and leaves. Ed enters, escorting Frances Langford, the next in the series of guests (and *Jackie Gleason Show* guest stars and characters) to appear in the program. Frances used to know Trixie in vaudeville. She sings "Great Day" and "I Love Paris" for Alice, Ed, and Trixie, and dances with Ed. Then Joe the Bartender (played by Gleason) stops in. He says a poor soul down at the bar was the victim of a nasty practical joke by Fatso Fogarty, who told him he had "won" a diamond and then handed him a cheap rhinestone. What made the hoax particularly pathetic was that the poor soul, totally taken in, cherished his prize. Alice, moved by the tale, tells Joe to send the poor soul up, and she'll give him a real present. Joe leaves, taking Frances Langford with him. Now the Poor Soul (played by Gleason in pantomime) arrives. Alice offers him refreshments and a gift, probably the first gift anyone ever gave him. He touchingly returns the favor by giving her his "diamond," then leaves. The next visitor is Rudy the Repairman (Why is his face familiar? Answer: he is played by Gleason). Rudy is accompanied by his regular assistant, Whitey, whose chief trait is that he speaks unintelligibly. Rudy makes a pass at Alice and Trixie, destroys the television set, and departs. Alice tells Trixie that it doesn't really matter, since she just had the set on trial. (Not that she has any cause for alarm. Live entertainment is mere moments away.) Ed brings in little Eddie Hodges, who stands as high as the kitchen chair and sings "Walking My Baby Back Home" not much more intelligibly than Whitey spoke. Eddie goes, and—what do you think?—Reggie Van Gleason III (hmmm, that face...) shows up with a band ("now appearing at the Swan Room of Toots Shor's") and the June Taylor Dancers. Reggie has been throwing a party at Joe the Bartender's. Now he's come to bring joy upstairs. The band plays. The dancers dance. Reggie does his inimitable Reggie dance. Then he and his entourage file out. Alice realizes it's been a while since she saw Ralph. Ralph (played by...) reappears,

Frank Marth, Jackie Gleason, Audrey Meadows in "Honeymooners Christmas Party," *1953.*

with a cop. Seems Ralph was knocking on the window of Kraus's, and was arrested for attempted break-in. Alice straightens things out. The cop leaves. Alice and Ralph exchange presents. He gets rabbit-lined gloves. She gets a juice squeezer shaped like Napoleon ("and it's practical, too . . . ").

TITLE: *"New Year's Eve Party"*
DATE: *December 26, 1953*
LENGTH: *36:33*

It's the day before New Year's Eve, and Alice and Trixie want Ralph and Norton to take them out to celebrate the arrival of 1954. Ralph, who says he hates going out on New Year's Eve, anticipates that Alice is going to ask him to take her out, so he decides to pick a fight with her so she'll be too mad at him to want to go anywhere. First he screams about dinner; but Alice doesn't retaliate because one of her New Year's resolutions is not to argue with Ralph. Ralph gropes for other things to get her riled, and when they fail he blurts out that he's not taking her out for New Year's Eve. Then they fight. In walk Tommy and Jimmy Dorsey, who've come to retrieve a briefcase full of sheet music Alice found earlier that day in a telephone booth. They invite the Kramdens and the Nortons to be their guests New Year's Eve at the Statler Hotel, where the Dorsey Brothers band is playing. Suddenly Ralph is in a festive mood. Moments later Freddie Muller arrives with bad news: Ralph has to work New Year's Eve. The next day Ralph goes to see Mr. Marshall to ask for the night off. While he's there Marshall has a fit over six other drivers all trying to do the same thing. When Marshall says the only way a driver is going to get the night off is to be sick—really sick—Ralph begins to bellow "in pain" and Marshall tells him to go home. Ralph leaves and Marshall calls his secretary to confirm his reservations for that night—at the Statler. In the Statler lobby Ralph meets Marshall, who fires him for lying. Marshall's wife reminds him that he also lied—to her mother so they wouldn't have to spend New Year's Eve with her. Marshall forgives Ralph and rehires him, and the Kramdens, Nortons, and Marshalls usher in the New Year swinging to the music of the Dorseys.

TITLE: *"This Is Your Life"*
DATE: *January 16, 1954*
LENGTH: *39:48*

Ralph has been chosen to appear on the *This Is Your Life* TV program, and Alice must meet secretly with Mr. Wilson, the show's producer, to discuss the arrangements. Ralph finds out about the meetings and thinks Alice is fooling around with another man. He thinks the best way to uncover Alice's lover's identity is to play detective at the pool room. He already knows that the mystery man likes Italian food and is going to California; when he finds out who the guy is, he'll invite him to the house, find a way to leave him and Alice alone together, and then barge back into the apartment to catch them red-handed. Phil Cuoco, the best man at Ralph and Alice's wedding, becomes the prime suspect when Ralph overhears him telling a friend that he's going to California, and when he tells Ralph that he's eaten at an Italian restaurant two days in a row. Ralph invites him to the apartment and then leaves him alone with Alice so he can spy on them from the fire escape. Phil leans over Alice as they are looking at old photographs and Ralph thinks they're cuddling. Phil leaves the apartment and Mr. Wilson shows up as Ralph is racing up to the roof and back down the stairs to the apartment. Ralph barges in and without looking at who he's hitting, belts Wilson—killing his spot on *This Is Your Life*.

TITLE: *"Cottage for Sale"*
DATE: *January 23, 1954*
LENGTH: *39:25*

Ralph and Norton have a secret that Norton can't wait to blab to the wives—he and Ralph are going to buy a cottage in the country. They want to spend nearly a thousand dollars for it, and Alice and Trixie are immediately against the idea. Ralph convinces Alice to go look at a model cottage, and she and Trixie fall in love with it—not knowing that they're looking at a model that costs more than twice as much as the one Ralph and Norton want to buy. Alice changes her mind and decides she'd love to own a summer cottage. The boys send the wives away so they can bargain with the salesman, a shady character who'd give a used-car salesman a good name by comparison. He tells Ralph and Norton he'll give them a "modified" version of the two-thousand-dollar cottage for $989, the price of the model they wanted originally. When the Kramdens and the Nortons arrive at Paradise Acres to spend their first night in their dream cottage, they discover they've been sold a nightmare instead. The wives are infuriated, and soon everyone is yelling at everyone else. Trixie blames Ralph for dragging Norton into another fiasco, but Alice jumps to Ralph's defense. The Kramdens storm out, and when they get home Ralph takes out a house-for-sale ad in the paper. A Mr. Wohlstetter answers the ad, and pays a thousand dollars for the cottage. Ralph and Norton think they've pulled a fast one—until they learn that a highway is going through Paradise Acres and that Wohlstetter is going to sell the cottage property to the developers for four thousand dollars.

TITLE: *"Lawsuit"*
DATE: *March 27, 1954*
LENGTH: *15:00*

Ralph broke his leg in a bus accident and now he wants to break the bank at the bus company by suing it for ten thousand dollars. According to Ralph, the accident occurred because of company negligence: the windshield wipers on his bus didn't work and he smashed his bus into a tree because he couldn't see in the rain. Ralph doesn't care that suing the company may cost him his job because he has other plans anyway—when he gets the money from the lawsuit he's going to buy a grocery store in Jersey City. A claims adjuster from the bus company comes and offers Ralph back pay for the time he missed while recuperating and complete payment of his medical bills, but Ralph refuses the offer. Instead, he has Norton call a lawyer, who tells Norton that Ralph has a can't-lose case. The lawyer comes to the Kramden apartment, and while he's asking Ralph questions he learns for the first time that Ralph was the driver of the bus, not a passenger. He tells Ralph about a city ordinance that requires a bus driver to be sure that all the safety equipment on his bus is working properly before taking the bus out of the depot. Ralph has no case after all, and, after kicking the adjuster out of the apartment, maybe no job either.

TITLE: *"The Next Champ"*
DATE: *April 10, 1954*
LENGTH: *37:17*

Ralph and Norton are at the poolroom, when in walks Dynamite Moran, a small-time boxer who's come to New York to make it big. He's had two fights and two quick knockouts, and when Ralph sees him punch a cigarette machine he decides he wants to manage the kid. Alice feels like KO-ing Ralph when she hears this scheme, but she's placated when Ralph says it won't cost him any money to manage Moran. Then he drops the bombshell: Moran is moving in with them. Ralph and Norton go to see Jack Philbin, a fight promoter and member of the Racoon Lodge (and in real life the executive producer of the *Jackie Gleason Show* and *The Honeymooners*), to try to arrange a match. When Armstrong, another fight manager, tells Philbin he's heard Moran can punch, Philbin schedules a fight for Moran. Armstrong offers to buy Moran's contract from Ralph for five hundred dollars, but Ralph refuses. Armstrong drops by the Kramdens' one morning to watch Moran train, and while he's there a neighbor comes in to complain about the noise. Moran grabs him menacingly and the neighbor pops him on the chin, knocking Moran cold. Glass jaw, says Armstrong. Ralph's career as a fight manager ends in a TKO.

TITLE: *"Stand In for Murder"*
DATE: *April 17, 1954*
LENGTH: *40:37*

A mob boss, who is a dead ringer for Ralph, is holed up in his apartment because a rival gang leader, Barney Hackett, wants to bump him off. Nick, one of his henchmen, takes a ride on Ralph's bus and gets the idea of somehow setting up

Ralph to get knocked off in place of his boss. He offers Ralph a ''job'' as a top executive with an insurance company, as the pretext of getting Ralph to the boss's apartment so he can be set up. When Ralph tells Alice he's been offered a job as boss of the ''eastern district'' of an insurance company (whose name he doesn't even know), with a salary of six hundred dollars a week, a Park Avenue apartment, and a chauffeured limousine, she is—what else—skeptical. The next day Ralph reports to work on Park Avenue, while the mob boss moves to another hideout. Nick makes a deal with Hackett to bump off Ralph (Hackett, of course, isn't wise to the switch), but the assassination attempt fails, thanks to Norton's interference. Next, Nick sends Ralph to Hackett's headquarters, to ''sell him insurance.'' When Ralph walks in, Hackett thinks it's his archenemy looking for a showdown. Ralph doesn't suspect a thing, and just as he's invited to step into the back room, a cop walks in and insists that Ralph move his car. When Ralph shows up at the apartment again, Nick decides they'll have to bump off Ralph themselves, and then dump his body in front of Hackett's joint. He mistakes his boss for Ralph, knocks him cold, and deposits him in the bedroom. Alice comes by to visit Ralph on his new job, and right behind her is the boss's girlfriend, who thinks Ralph is her boyfriend. As she's cuddling up to Ralph, Alice re-enters the room and sparks fly. Ralph goes into the bedroom and sees the mob boss out cold on the bed. He puts two and two together and realizes what's been going on. Alice calls the cops and Ralph's career as an insurance executive comes to a sudden end. (*Only the studio audience saw the ending of this episode. As Leonard Stern recalls, the show had not ended by nine o'clock and without explanation CBS just cut away from the sketch before it finished. ''There was so much laughter we ran out of time before the solution,'' he says. ''The television audience was left up in the air. Each of the major dailies, certainly the tabloids, did stories on it, speculating how it would end. It made page two, page one, in each of the New York newspapers. The following week Gleason, who never did superb mono-logues, tried to explain this convoluted story on the air so the audience would have satisfaction. In so doing, he took up so much time that we ran over again.''*)

TITLE: *"Move Uptown"*
DATE: *April 24, 1954*
LENGTH: *36:40*

The Kramdens leave Brooklyn for the Bronx?!? Yes, if Ralph has his way. His friend George and his wife are moving to Albany, and Ralph and Alice have a chance to rent their apartment, a spacious, nicely decorated place that looks like the Taj Mahal next to the Kramdens' flat. For only fifteen dollars a month more than they're paying at Chauncey Street, the Kramdens can experience comfort and luxury; but first they have to sublet their apartment. When a couple of prospective tenants wash out, Ralph decides to move out in the middle of the night. That doesn't work—Norton falls down the stairs carrying a load of pots and pans and Ralph's brother Charlie doesn't show up with the car—so Ralph tries to get kicked out of the apartment by making a racket and painting the apartment in crazy colors. The landlord of the building in the Bronx drops in to interview the Kramdens, and Ralph, who's never met the Chauncey Street landlord, thinks he's the landlord of his building. Ralph does his best to prove he's a troublemaker, and his landlord-to-be rips up the lease for the new apartment before Ralph realizes who he is.

TITLE: *"The Man in the Blue Suit"*
DATE: *May 1, 1954*
LENGTH: *32:55*

Ralph wins $73.85 playing poker and hides the money in the pocket of an old suit so Alice won't find it. The next day, a man from the Help the Needy Society comes to the apartment looking for old clothes and newspapers. Alice gives him Ralph's old suit. When Ralph hears this he and Norton race down to the mission to retrieve the suit. They decide that if Ralph goes in and asks for the suit because his money is in the pocket, the society may check with Alice to verify the story. Instead, Norton makes up Ralph to look like a bum in need of new clothes. Ralph gets on the clothes line, but when he gets to the counter the man tells him he can't get clothes without a ticket. Then Ralph learns he can't get a ticket until he fills out some forms and is investigated by the society. He gives the clerk a nutty sob story, gets a ticket, and grabs the suit he thinks is his. It's not. He sees another guy about his size wearing a similar jacket and tries to pick a fight with him, hoping the guy will take off the jacket, giving Norton a chance to search the pockets. Instead, he and Norton get kicked out for being troublemakers. A moment later, in walks the guy who collected Ralph's suit from Alice. He looks it over and decides he'll keep it for himself. He finds the money in the pocket and heads back to Chauncey Street to return it to Alice. Ralph gets home and discovers Alice has the money. He rants and raves that it's his money—and Alice graciously returns it to him. Ralph feels like two cents.

TITLE: *"Hair-Raising Tale"*
DATE: *May 8, 1954*
LENGTH: *37:13*

Two con men pull a scam on Ralph as he sits in the park eating his lunch. One poses as the inventor of a miracle hair restorer and the other as an unscrupulous businessman trying to buy the formula. The second man "gets rough" with the smaller one and Ralph intervenes and chases off the larger man. The "inventor," Prof. Steinhardt, tells Ralph about his hair restorer and lets Ralph talk him into selling him exclusive rights to sell the formula in New York. Ralph races home for the money, but Alice won't give it to him because of his dismal track record with guaranteed get-rich-quick schemes. Norton hears the whole fight and comes downstairs for a ringside seat. Ralph figures he can get three hundred dollars against his life-insurance policy, and invites Norton to become his partner for a two-hundred-dollar investment. Norton says no—he's still smarting from the beating he took on the shoe polish that glows in the dark. He finally gives in—before he came down Trixie bet him a quarter he would—and KramNor's Miracle Restorer is born. Steinhardt arrives with the formula and the ingredients and Ralph and Norton begin mixing a batch. Mr. Mitchell, traffic manager at the bus company, drops by to tell Ralph he has to take another driver's shift. Ralph tells Mitchell—who's half bald—about KramNor's, but Mitchell is skeptical. Ralph offers him a free treatment that not only doesn't grow hair but kills most of what Mitchell had. Ralph and Norton go to the park to try to pull the scam on another sucker. The guy they pick isn't interested in the formula because he's got an invention of his own he's trying to market—an electric zipper. Ralph forgets all about unloading KramNor's and wonders how much money he can make selling zippers.

TITLE: *"Boxtop Kid"*
DATE: *May 22, 1954*
LENGTH: *40:10*

Alice's sister, Helen, and her husband, Frank, have won a cruise to Europe, and Ralph and Alice go to see them off at the dock. Ralph is jealous and he acts it. The next day he buys every product that's running a contest—$23.50 worth of dog food, cereal, cake mix, detergent, etc.—so he can win something too. Ralph eventually wins two contests: his prizes are a dog from the Happy Hound dog-food people and a trip to Europe from Slim-o Bread. (Ralph's winning slogan: "Slim-O Bread adds to the taste and takes away from the waist.") When Ralph reads the telegram that notifies him about winning the trip, he discovers that the company wants to use before-and-after photos of him; Ralph said on his entry blank that he used to be a fatty but that his weight dropped down to 170 pounds after he began eating Slim-O. Ralph cons Norton into posing as him, and stuffs him with a pillow and takes his picture, which is to pass as the "before" Ralph. The ruse works—until Mrs. Manicotti comes in and refers to Ralph as Mr. Kramden. When the Slim-O man questions her, she tells him that Ralph is Kramden. Ralph is also fat, so he doesn't get to go to Europe.

TITLE: *"Two Men on a Horse"*
DATE: *May 29, 1954*
LENGTH: *37:58*

Ralph's been elected treasurer of the Racoon Lodge—he won by promising to spend the Lodge's budget surplus on beer and hot dogs. On the way home from the lodge he loses the two hundred dollars he's supposed to deposit in the Racoons's bank account. The next day he meets Norton at Jerry's Lunch Room to figure out where he can get another two hundred dollars. He tries to make some of it back by playing pinball against a guy in the lunch room. Ralph rolls up a score that Norton says will put him in the Pinball Hall of Fame, but his opponent tops it with his first ball. As Ralph and Norton are leaving, Jerry gets a telephone call—a hot tip on Cigar Box, a horse running that afternoon at the track. Jerry closes the lunch room to go to the track, and Ralph figures the horse must be a sure thing. He and Norton go to the track, hoping to win two hundred dollars. When the odds on Cigar Box start dropping, Ralph goes around dissuading people from betting on the horse. He and Norton split up, and Norton tells one man who's going to bet Cigar Box that he's the horse's owner, and that the horse can't win. Norton tells him to bet Happy Feet instead. Ralph bumps into the same man, who tells Ralph Cigar Box won't win because his owner just told him the horse is in the race only for a workout. Ralph bets Happy Feet instead, and then finds out Cigar Box's "owner" is Norton. Ralph rips up his ticket in despair. The race begins and Cigar Box leads the pack by a mile. Suddenly Happy Feet charges in front and wins the race, sending Ralph and Norton scrambling to the floor for the ripped-up ticket.

TITLE: *"Good Buy Aunt Ethel"*
DATE: *June 5, 1954*
LENGTH: *41.24*

This is an expanded version of the March 1953 skit "Alice's Aunt Ethel." In this episode, Ralph comes home from work in a fabulous mood—which lasts only until Alice tells him Aunt

Ethel is coming for a visit. The middle sequence of this episode—in which Ralph is trying to sleep on a cot in the kitchen while Alice makes coffee for Aunt Ethel—is "Alice's Aunt Ethel" all over again. When Ralph's scheme to get rid of Aunt Ethel by faking a bad back fails, he concludes that the only way to get rid of her for good is to marry her off to somebody. Freddie Zimmerman, the butcher from Freitag's Meat Market, is chosen as the pigeon and invited over for dinner. Ralph goes all out to ensure that the evening is a success. He sends Aunt Ethel to the beauty parlor and buys her a corsage; he borrows the Nortons' love seat and his pal George's record player and records; he sprays the apartment with perfume, and buys four pounds of chopped meat from Freddie to make sure he's in a good mood. Aunt Ethel and Freddie discover they have something in common: she used to stuff sausages for a living when she lived in Ohio, and Freddie gets his meat from the same meat packer. Three weeks later they're married and Ralph thinks he's finally rid of Aunt Ethel. Not so fast: Freddie lives at the YMCA, and he and Ethel can't move in there, so they barge in on the Kramdens—just until they can find their own place. Ralph goes to live at the Y. (Above: *Ethel Owen as Ethel.*)

TITLE: *"Vacation/Fred's Landing"*
DATE: *June 19, 1954*
LENGTH: *30:52*

The Kramdens and the Nortons are going on vacation together. The girls think they're going to Atlantic City, but the boys decide they want to go fishing at Fred's Landing. They get their way—and wind up having to push their borrowed car halfway to Fred's. After two days at Fred's, Alice and Trixie are worn out—cooking, cleaning, toting water, collecting firewood. They decide to annoy the boys enough to get them to want to leave. They don't know that Ralph and Norton are miserable too. Ralph decides he'll dress up in a bear suit to scare the girls into begging him and Norton to go home, so the boys can leave and save face at the same time. Ralph returns with the suit, to find Norton face to face with a real bear. Ralph admits he made a mistake wanting to go to Fred's and it's off to Atlantic City. *(The 1953 version of this sketch has not been put back into syndication.)*

As Laurel and Hardy in "Songs and Witty Sayings."

COUNTDOWN TO THE THIRTY-NINE 1954–1955

How does it happen that a rowdy, thirty-nine-year-old comedian who often has not known where his next meal was coming from is today the biggest single commodity in the competitive and tricky market place that is television?
COLLIER'S (1955)

This was the season that convinced people that *The Honeymooners* could stand alone as a weekly series. The Gleason show finished the season second in the Nielsen ratings, behind *I Love Lucy,* and with this the Great One earned himself a new title: "Mr. Saturday Night." Buick, which had been a sponsor of Milton Berle on NBC, desperately wanted a piece of that Gleason magic, and sent Mike Kirk of the Kudner advertising agency to get it. When Kirk approached Gleason and his executive producer, Jack Philbin, on Buick's behalf, the idea for a half-hour *Honeymooners* series was born.

Some of the funniest and most unexpected moments in the more than a hundred existing black and white *Honeymooners* shows and sketches are found in the episodes filmed in '54 and '55. Scenes such as Norton helping Ralph rehearse for an appearance in a candy commercial, in "Ralph's Sweet Tooth"; Ralph, Alice, Norton, and Trixie in the pool room in "Kramden vs. Norton"; Norton's milk 'n' cookies break at the opening of "A Little Man Who Wasn't There"; the stickup in "The Great Jewel Robbery"; Alice's attempt to restore romance to the Kramdens' marriage, in "Boys and Girls Together"; and Norton's swami routine and his and Ralph's Laurel and Hardy impersonations in "Songs and Witty Sayings."

This season also featured what may become the most talked-about Lost *Honeymooners* Episode: "The Adoption." After flirting with the idea of children for the Kramdens in earlier episodes ("Pickles" and "Santa and the Bookies"— episodes where Ralph jumps to the conclusion that Alice is pregnant), the writers actually gave them a child in this episode, a girl they adopt and name Ralphina.

In this funny, bittersweet sketch, a couple that hardly ever mentions children suddenly wants one desperately. Their desperation extends to borrowing furniture and furnishings from the Nortons, and fixing up their apartment to make it look like a suitable place in which to raise a child. They lie, but they can't escape what they are: as they are going through the motions of trying to impress the woman from the adoption agency, an iceman comes with a delivery for the Kramdens' icebox—which has mysteriously been replaced by a refrigerator. In typically Kramdenesque fashion, the more Ralph tries to sustain the deception the more transparent his scheme becomes.

The Kramdens get their child anyway—ironically, on this occasion Ralph's scheme works to his advantage, because the woman from the agency figures that anyone who wants a child badly enough to decorate his apartment with someone else's furniture should have a child—but not before Ralph puts Alice through an emotional wringer. He had his heart set on a boy, and when the doctor tells him and Alice that the baby they've been gazing upon with loving affection is a girl, Ralph insists that the doctor replace her with a boy. A pall falls over everyone in the room and they all exit, leaving Ralph one on one with the infant girl. He changes his mind and the Kramdens keep the girl, setting up the inevitable tragic ending.

One could not imagine, for instance, Lucy Ricardo suffering a miscarriage and its "playing" to a TV audience. But the loss of a child in *The Honeymooners*—in this case, the natural mother asks for the child back and the Kramdens reluctantly give her up, though the baby is legally theirs—and the emotional agony it precipitates "plays" because the audience has been conditioned to accept it: in each *Honeymooners* sketch pathos is always crouched just at the edge of the humor. Not even Gleason's continual flub during the scene— referring to the baby as "he"—can dull the kick-in-the-gut impact of the moment. Crunching together humor and pathos is a device that always worked with *The Honeymooners*, for two reasons: Gleason's uncanny ability to swing from one mood to another without missing a beat, and the fact that the audience never questioned Ralph's behavior, no matter how erratic it was.

"I always say that one of the reasons *The Honeymooners* was a hit," contends Gleason, "besides it being funny and all the other stuff, was that it was actually a play, and there was no reason we shouldn't do drama as well as comedy if we were doing plays."

Steve Allen once wrote about Gleason: "Even in a sketch, what he lacks in sheer comic ability he more than makes up for in warmth and naturalness. It is this ability to seem like a real flesh-and-blood human being that makes it possible for Jackie to make a quick switch from humor to pathos."

The longest of the Lost Episodes—"Weighty Problem" at 48:09—ran this season. That episode was also one of the season's two (the other was "People's Choice") to be expanded from earlier sketches ("Ralph's Diet" and "Finger Man," respectively). "Ralph's Sweet Tooth," "Game Called on Account of Marriage," "The People's Choice," "Brother-in-Law," "Kramden vs. Norton," and "Songs and Witty Sayings" put Ralph and Norton back into crazy costumes, or into zany variations of their usual outfits. In "Peacemaker" it's Norton and Trixie quarreling instead of Alice and Ralph. And "Kramden vs. Norton" is a treasure trove of previously unknown facts about the characters.

The 1954–55 season was an eventful one for Ralph. He appeared on television twice more; he helped capture a killer and ran for elected office; he became an uncle; he bought a hotel; he wrote a hit song; he got two promotions and raises at the bus company; he attended his first Racoon convention; he visited a psychiatrist; he befriended a neighborhood kid; he redecorated his apartment; and he entered a local talent contest.

Norton is finally seen at the sewer—both surfacing and submerging. His mind still works like a Rube Goldberg toy run amok, but he doesn't sound as dumb as he did in earlier sketches. He's revealed to be an expert mambo dancer, and the meaning of the "L" in Edward L. Norton is a mystery no more: it stands for Lilywhite (Lilywhite was Norton's mother's maiden name. Norton was his father's, he tells Ralph). Not to be outdone, Trixie reveals her real name too: Thelma.

Alice's family continued to grow: added were siblings Sally, Helen, Grace, Agnes, Mary, Ginny, and Frank. Freddie and Charlie had been introduced the previous season.

Jack Benny has a cameo role as the Kramdens' miserly landlord, and another Jack, Jack Norton, does one of his famous drunken walk-ons (he would have appeared in the half-hour show "Unconventional Behavior," had he not gotten sick on show day). Ned Glass, famed for his bit as Teddy Oberman, a crude lout Ralph befriends during his feud with Norton in "Pal O' Mine" from the Classic Thirty-nine, shows up too, as Herman Gruber, an old school chum of Ralph's. And add two more names to the list of Gleason Actors: Anne Seymour and John Gibson.

TITLE: *"Ralph's Sweet Tooth"*
DATE: *September 25, 1954*
LENGTH: *35:39*

It's one of the greatest days—again—in Ralph's life: He's going to be on television. No, not as a quiz-show contestant, but in a commercial, for Choosy Chew candy. Ralph's going to be paid a hundred dollars to be interviewed by the Choosy Chew Roving Reporter on the *Choosy Chew Symphony Hour,* where he will tell the whole world how much he loves the candy. Ralph has lines he has to memorize, and he enlists Norton—dressed in Bermuda shorts and a pair of yellow shoes he won at a mambo contest—to help him. The rehearsal scene is priceless, but the rehearsal isn't worth two cents, and when it's over Ralph knows less about what he has to say than when he began. Later, Ralph has a real problem: he gets a toothache. (Gleason has a problem too: he keeps forgetting on which side of his mouth he's supposed to have the bad tooth.) It's the middle of the night, the night before he's supposed to do the commercial, and Ralph spends most of it screaming at Alice and Norton because none of their home remedies—salt water that Ralph's supposed to slosh

George Petrie and Jackie Gleason in "Ralph's Sweet Tooth."

around on the tooth but drinks instead, self-hypnosis, a string tied to a doorknob, and others—don't work. Alice finally suggests a last resort that terrifies Ralph—a visit to Dr. Durgom (named after Bullets Durgom, Gleason's manager at the time), the family dentist. Ralph goes, but instead of allowing Durgom to pull the aching tooth he grabs a bottle of liquid painkiller and scrams when Durgom steps out of the office to answer a telephone call. What he doesn't know is that unless the medicine is kept refrigerated, it is useless. A few hours later Ralph bumbles and stumbles his way through a rehearsal for the commercial. Just before air time, he applies the painkiller to the bad tooth, thinking it will deaden the pain when he bites into the Choosy Chew bar during the commercial. Instead, candy + toothache = excruciating pain, which sends Ralph rampaging around the set and through the Choosy Chew orchestra. (Above: *Les Damon as the dentist; Gingr Jones—Mrs. Les Damon—as the nurse;* far right: *George Petrie, center.*)

TITLE: *"Game Called on Account of Marriage"*
DATE: *October 2, 1954*
LENGTH: *33:50*

Ralph doesn't want to go to Alice's sister Sally's wedding because he has tickets to the World Series. He wouldn't miss the game if the Gabor sisters were marrying the Ritz Brothers, he says. He and Alice battle for nine innings, without resolution. Ralph meets Norton for lunch and they hatch a surefire scheme: trick Stanley, the groom-to-be, into eloping right away. That night Ralph and Norton show up at Sally's house with a ladder. Stanley's afraid of heights, so Ralph has to climb the ladder to get Sally's luggage. When she comes down, she and Stanley have a fight and call off the elopement. Ralph climbs back up the ladder and begins tossing Sally's bags back through the window. Stanley and Sally return and announce they're going to elope after all. Off they go. As Ralph is taking down the ladder a cop appears and demands an explanation. Ralph tells him the whole story, and then the cop gives him the bad news: earlier in the day the New York Giants clinched the Series by winning four straight games.

TITLE: *"The People's Choice"*
DATE: *October 23, 1954*
LENGTH: *40:01*

This episode is an expanded version of "Finger Man," and its first dozen minutes is the earlier skit done again. The new material picks up when Messrs. Morgan and Weaver, from a corrupt local political party, visit Ralph and ask him to run for assemblyman on their ticket. Ralph is so impressed with himself that the pair actually has him believing he might be President some day. Alice suspects that Morgan and Weaver want Ralph to be their stooge, but Ralph interprets her skepticism as a lack of faith in him. The Kramdens and the Nortons take to the streets to campaign, and Ralph quickly learns that capturing killers doesn't qualify one to serve in the State Assembly. Morgan and Weaver call Ralph an idiot for exposing himself to the public, and it begins to dawn on Ralph that maybe Alice is right. At a rally the next night, instead of giving the speech Morgan and Weaver prepared for him, Ralph tells his "supporters" that he's not qualified to run for office and that they should vote for his opponent.

TITLE: *"Battle of the Sexes"*
DATE: *November 13, 1954*
LENGTH: *35:28*

Ralph and Norton are at the pool hall, in a scene

that was later adapted for "The Bensonhurst Bomber," one of the thirty-nine half-hour shows. Trixie telephones Norton and tells him to get home—her mother has come for a visit. This is Ralph's cue to give Norton a "King of the Castle" speech, and to tutor him on what to tell Trixie when he returns home—after he and Ralph have finished playing pool. Norton is so inspired that he says Ralph's words should be recorded and played at every wedding instead of "Here Comes the Bride." Later, Trixie comes down to the Kramdens' apartment in tears—Norton's been playing king and she doesn't want to spend the night with him. Alice wakes up Ralph, and when he gives her his "king" speech, she gets suspicious. When Norton comes down and begins bullying Trixie again, it confirms to Alice that Norton has become Ralph's understudy. Alice and Trixie walk out together, leaving Ralph and Norton as roommates in the Kramdens' apartment. A week later the apartment looks like Yucca Flats after the blast and Norton is complaining about Ralph's cooking. (He tells Ralph that he's become so weak from the bad food that he had to wear an inner tube in the sewer to keep from drowning.) Ralph's too proud to apologize to Alice, so he and Norton scheme to get the wives to make the first move. They fake having a party in the apartment, but while Ralph is yelling jovial remarks out the window so Alice and Trixie can hear him upstairs, Alice walks in and the party crash-lands. After three more schemes fail—the sympathy routine, the threat to cut off Alice's household money, and the "I'm leaving forever" warning—the boys break down and apologize. The girls open their arms to welcome them back but Ralph and Norton sweep right past them and dive at the table full of food Trixie has prepared for her own and Alice's dinner.

TITLE: *"Teamwork Beat the Clock"*
DATE: *November 20, 1954*
LENGTH: *32:08*

Ralph and Alice are contestants on *Beat the Clock*. They succeed on their first stunt, where Alice has to propel a cup with a can of whipped cream into a net Ralph is holding in his teeth, and are in the middle of their second, where they have to catch lemons in a cup and stack the cups while keeping a balloon from hitting the ground, when time runs out and they're asked to return the next week. Of course they will—a 21-inch color TV is at stake. Ralph and Alice practice their stunt at home, with Norton's help. Jerry, Alice's brother-in-law, arrives with the news that Alice's sister Helen is expecting their child any day. He has to leave town on business and he wants to know if the Kramdens will look after Helen while he's gone. As the Fickle Finger of Fate would have it, Helen goes into labor Saturday night, just before the Kramdens are supposed to be at the TV studio. Helen has twins, and Alice decides to stay with her. Norton accompanies Ralph to the studio, and the show's host, Bud Collyer, invites him to take Alice's place in the stunt when Ralph explains why Alice isn't there. They win the TV set, and a bonus—a pair of baby buggies. *(This episode, the first sketch written by Leonard Stern and Syd Zelinka as a team, was also the first "physical" show, where a lot of the comedy depended on the action.)*

TITLE: *"Brother-in-Law"*
DATE: *November 27, 1954*
LENGTH: *34:47*

Alice's brother Frank is coming for dinner. Ralph has hated Frank ever since he cheated him out of a promotion when they both worked for the WPA. According to Ralph, Frank's "a moocher, a swindler, and a bum!" Frank antagonizes Ralph during dinner, and then tries to put the finger on him and Alice for five hundred dollars to buy a hotel in New Jersey that's located right where a new highway is supposed to be built. The Kramdens don't give him the money—Alice agrees with Ralph this time—but Ralph decides to steal Frank's idea and buy the hotel with the Nortons. Ralph becomes manager by winning a coin toss. Norton is the bellhop, Alice the cook, and Trixie the chambermaid. Norton says the hotel looks like "the set for a Bela Lugosi picture," but miraculously they get it cleaned up. Their first guest is a surveyor with the highway-construction crew—who tells Ralph and Norton that the highway isn't going to pass right in front of the hotel as they thought, but over it. It's an elevated highway.

TITLE: *"Songwriters"*
DATE: *December 11, 1954*
LENGTH: *35:54*

Ralph's gonna get rich—by writing hit songs. He gets the idea when he learns that the Racoon Lodge has contracted to pay a professional songwriter one hundred dollars to write a lodge theme song—and that the hundred dollars is peanuts compared with what the songwriter makes writing pop songs. Ralph's first step to stardom is to recruit Norton to play the piano and write the music to Ralph's lyrics. Ralph keeps Norton up all night trying to write songs, while waging running battles with Alice and McGarrity (a.k.a. Garrity). After failing at writing love songs, lullabies, and holiday songs, they hit on a novelty song and take it to a publisher. Ralph is

"My Love Song to You," written for "Songwriters," became popular in its own right—both as sheet music and as a Bob Manning recording for Capitol Records.

crushed when the publisher says he loves the melody but hates the words, and that he wants to bring in a professional songwriter to write lyrics to Norton's music. In a rare gesture of unselfishness Ralph steps aside for Norton's sake. But Norton values his friendship with Ralph more than a musical career, and, unbeknownst to Ralph, takes their song to another publisher, who loves it so much he has it recorded. Ralph has the thrill of a lifetime when he hears his and Norton's song on the radio.

TITLE: *"Kramden vs. Norton"*
DATE: *January 5, 1955*
LENGTH: *33:55*

It's Norton's birthday, the Kramdens are treating for a night out, and Ralph's looking to get off cheaply. He doesn't want the Nortons to think he's cheap, though, so he tells Alice to suggest that they go to the movies (instead of to the Kit Kat Club, where Norton took Ralph on his birthday). It's been a banner day for Norton—he's gotten a new vest from Trixie, a hand-carved mahogany surf board from the boys in the sewer, and a monogrammed scarf from the Kramdens—and going to the movies is the icing on Norton's cake when he has the winning ticket in a drawing for a television set. Ralph claims the set is his because he paid for the tickets, and a feud erupts. Ralph dismantles the set so no one can watch it, and he and Norton stop speaking to each other; they write notes instead. Things get so bad that the boys are reduced to playing pool with their wives. A bitter confrontation at the pool hall spills over into night court, where, during Trixie and Alice's testimony, we learn that Trixie's real name is Thelma and that the Kramdens and the Nortons met when Ed invited the Kramdens out to dinner the day they moved in at 328 Chauncey Street. As Alice relates to the judge the history of Ralph and Norton's friendship, the boys break down in tears and each forsakes his claim to the TV in exchange for the other's friendship.

TITLE: *"A Promotion"*
DATE: *January 22, 1955*
LENGTH: *38:57*

The heat's off at Chauncey Street and the apartment's an icebox, but Ralph doesn't even notice—he's just been promoted to first assistant cashier to the assistant cashier. What a life, he muses—he can dress up every day like it's Sunday, and take his lunch to work in a briefcase. Day One on the new job Ralph is working late trying to find a three-dollar discrepancy in the day's accounting. Norton comes to visit and Ralph accidentally closes and locks the safe before he puts away the day's receipts. He takes the money home in a paper bag, with the intention of returning it to the safe early the next morning when the safe's time lock shuts off. At home, with Norton's help, the bag gets mixed up with some grocery bags and Alice discovers the money. Instead of thinking Ralph's a dope, as he thought she would, she is sympathetic. That night, at the bus company, the safe is blown open by crooks. The next morning, when Ralph arrives at work with the money, he finds a room full of bus-company executives and cops, who are convinced Ralph's the thief. As Ralph and his "accomplice," Norton, are being taken to jail, a call comes in—the real crooks have been apprehended. Ralph's relieved, but Norton's upset at Mr. Marshall for thinking Ralph would rob the company. He tells Marshall how dedicated Ralph is and enumerates Ralph's ideas for saving the company money. Marshall decides Ralph's too valuable to the company to be sitting at a desk, so he tells Ralph he's going back to driving a bus—and into training as assistant bus dispatcher. (Above right: *Humphrey Davis, right.*)

TITLE: *"The Hypnotist"*
DATE: *January 29, 1955*
LENGTH: *38:23*

The International Order of Loyal Racoons are planning a trip to Chicago for their annual convention, and

to help get themselves in the mood for the festive occasion they've invited the Great Fatchamara—"the world's greatest hypnotist," and a Racoon from Bayonne—to the lodge to entertain them. He hypnotizes Ralph and Norton and tells Ralph he is Norton, and Norton, Ralph. He tells them they're at a bowling alley, and each acts as if he's the other: "Ralph" is angry because "Norton" wants to bowl first; "Norton" rolls a strike and finishes off his turn with a Nortonesque flourish of the arms. Before Fatchamara brings them out of their trances, he gives them a posthypnotic suggestion: whenever they're seated and hear the name Chicago, they'll think they're sitting on a bed of red-hot coals. The convention ought to be a riot—Ralph's bringing a toy gun, a trick glass, chattering teeth, an electric prod, and paper bags to drop out the hotel window—but he may not get there because he hasn't saved any money. He tries the flattery routine to coax some money out of Alice, but she's having none of it—she's saving the money for furniture. Then Ralph has one of his all-time-great brainstorms: we'll get the Great Fatchamara to hypno-tize Alice so she'll tell Ralph where she's hidden the money. The next day Alice is in the candy store, making a telephone call, and in walk Ralph and Norton to call Fatchamara. They don't know it's Alice in the telephone booth, and while they're waiting for her to hang up they discuss Ralph's scheme. Alice overhears the whole thing. When Fatcha-mara shows up at the Kram-dens, Alice is ready for him and fakes being hypnotized. She shows Ralph where she's hidden the money, but he decides to play it smart and take it just before he's ready to leave for Chicago so Alice won't know it's

Rehearsing for "The Hypnotist." Stanley Poss is the one holding the stopwatch.

missing until too late. On the train to the convention, the Racoons are filling the car with belly laughs as Ralph relates the whole story. When the waiter brings the check for the Racoons' drinks, big-shot Ralph offers to pay. He opens the money box, but instead of finding the cash he finds a note—from Alice. Then, to add insult to injury, when the waiter tells Ralph he must pay up before the train reaches "Chicago," Ralph gets "burned" again. (Page 112: *Cliff Hall, left, Eddie Hanley, right.* Page 113, center: *George Petrie*; right: *George Petrie*.)

TITLE: *"Cupid"*
DATE: *February 5, 1955*
LENGTH: *39:21*

Ralph and Norton run into Herman Gruber, a boyhood friend of Ralph's from P.S. 73. Herman isn't married yet, so Ralph decides to find him a girl. He calls Evelyn Fensterblau and asks her what she's doing the following night, and she hangs up on him. He has better luck with Charlotte Stadtelman from the bus company, who agrees to date Herman. The next day at the beauty parlor Trixie hears the latest gossip—Ralph called Evelyn and asked her for a date! Trixie tells Alice, and when Alice confronts Ralph with the story he explains to Alice that he was calling Evelyn for Herman Gruber. Alice doesn't believe him, so Ralph decides to go to Charlotte's apartment to bring her and Herman home with him to explain things to Alice. While Ralph is there, Charlotte's jealous ex-boyfriend shows up and Ralph has to bluff his way out of a broken head. Back at Chauncey Street, Alice is donating some clothes to charity and transporting them in a suitcase. When Norton sees her carrying the suitcase he thinks she's walking out on Ralph. When Ralph returns from Charlotte's, Norton tells him Alice has left. Charlotte shows up to explain everything to Alice, whom Norton spots coming up the block. Ralph and Norton think Alice will never understand Charlotte's being in the apartment, so they try to sneak her onto the fire escape. Alice catches them and thinks it's proof that Ralph is seeing another woman. But in walks Gruber to confirm Ralph's story and save the Kramdens' marriage. (Above left: *Ned Glass, center.*)

TITLE: *"A Little Man Who Wasn't There"*
DATE: *February 12, 1955*
LENGTH: *38:07*

Some passengers on Ralph's bus who have been offended by him have complained to the bus company, so Ralph's boss orders him to see the company psychiatrist. Ralph thinks that the boss thinks he's crazy, and that this is the end of his career as a bus driver. Ralph takes Norton with him to the psychiatrist's office and within minutes they're fighting. The doctor enters the room and finds Norton standing on a desk and Ralph threatening to beat him up. The doctor sends Norton out of the room and gives Ralph his diagnosis: Norton aggravates him, so he should avoid seeing him or risk a nervous breakdown. Ralph can't tell Norton face to face that their friendship's over, so he writes him a letter. Norton accidentally sees the letter and thinks it's a suicide note. He decides to stick to Ralph like glue, to prevent him from killing himself. After two days of Norton's tailing him, Ralph thinks he's going nuts. One second he looks, and Norton's there; a second later he's gone. Ralph thinks he's imagining seeing Norton, so Alice sends for the doctor. As the doctor is prescribing a strong nerve tonic for Ralph, Norton enters and explains that he's been following Ralph to make sure he won't kill himself. The doctor reverses himself and tells Ralph it's okay to see Norton again.

TITLE: *"Hero"*
DATE: *February 19, 1955*
LENGTH: *39:45*

Tommy, a new kid in the building, idolizes Ralph. Ralph thinks he's a pest—until Tommy tells him he saw him playing stickball, and that he wants to grow up to be a great athlete like Ralph is. The way to Ralph's heart is not only through his stomach but through his ego, and Ralph warms up to the kid in a flash. Soon Ralph is telling Tommy he fought for the Golden Gloves championship (The Wild Bull of Bensonhurst, they called him), that he almost pitched for the Brooklyn Dodgers, that he could lift four hundred pounds when he was seventeen, that he had a glorious football career (Snakehips Kramden was his name), and that he was an Eagle Scout. Tommy writes a school composition about Ralph, and Tommy's teacher asks Ralph to come to school to talk about it. She reads the composition to Ralph and asks him to tell Tommy to stop inventing such wild stories. In the composition Tommy says he's going to invite Ralph to a father-and-son Boy Scout competition, so Ralph rushes home to learn some of the events—tying knots, blowing a bugle, leaf identification, and tracking and stalking. Ralph fails dismally at each thing he tries, so the next night he fakes having a sprained arm so he won't have to compete and be embarrassed. Tommy arrives in his Boy Scout uniform, and Ralph tells him he can't participate because of his arm. Then Ralph's conscience takes over and he confesses that he's a fake. Tommy says he doesn't care, because they're pals and because Ralph was going to the Scout meeting because he wanted to, and not out of obligation like many of the boys' fathers were. By telling the truth, Ralph's an even bigger man in the end.

TITLE: *"The Great Jewel Robbery"*
DATE: *February 25, 1955*
LENGTH: *37:30*

Ralph is collecting money from all the bus drivers for a wedding present for the boss's daughter. He hopes the gift will mean a raise for the drivers—and maybe a promotion for himself. It's Alice's birthday, and her mother pays a visit. As soon as Ralph comes home, a battle royal between him and Mrs. Gibson begins. A delivery boy from Steinhardt's jewelry store arrives with a package that contains a watch Ralph bought for the boss's daughter. Alice thinks it's her birthday gift and is ecstatic. She praises Ralph up and down to her mother, and Ralph, who forgot it was Alice's birthday, is too ashamed to tell the truth. Now Ralph has to figure out how to get the watch back without letting Alice know it isn't hers. He and Norton come up with scheme: Norton will get one of his pals to pose as a burglar, hold up the Kramdens, and take the watch. While Ralph and Norton are devising their plan, a real crook overhears them and decides to show up at the Kramdens' before Norton's friend gets there. When he shows up, Ralph thinks he's Norton's friend and practically hands him the watch. While the crook's examining the goods, Alice plunks him with a frying pan and knocks him cold. She rushes out to call the cops, but Ralph revives him and sends him on his way, with some extra loot to boot. A moment later Norton's buddy arrives and Ralph realizes what he's done. The cops catch the crook and recover the watch, forcing Ralph to tell Alice that the watch isn't hers. Alice is heartbroken, but she returns the watch. Now Ralph must decide between giving the watch to the boss's daughter as planned, or giving the watch back to Alice and being in debt to the guys at the depot. It's no contest—Alice gets the watch.

TITLE: *"Peacemaker"*
DATE: *March 5, 1955*
LENGTH: *33:15*

Ralph is trying to sleep because he has to get up early for work. Norton, trying to do a good deed, accidentally sets off Ralph's alarm clock. Ralph stumbles out of the bedroom half dressed and half asleep and heads out the door for work—six hours early. When he gets out to the street he realizes what has happened, and Norton becomes persona non grata in the Kramden household. Ralph gets back to sleep and Norton goes home—only to get into a no-holds-barred brawl with Trixie. Ralph wakes up again, and no sooner does Alice get him back in bed when in walks Trixie, sobbing because Norton has packed his things and left her. Ralph gets up again and goes out to find Norton. He catches up with him at the ice-cream parlor, where Norton is drowning his sorrows in malteds. Ralph pleads with Norton to go home, but Norton refuses. He claims he doesn't love Trixie any more—until Ralph reminds him about some of the "gourmet" meals Trixie cooks for him. Norton goes home, and Round Two begins. Norton winds up on a cot in the Kramdens' apartment, but Ralph still can't get to sleep. He drags Norton upstairs to apologize, but Trixie won't accept the apology. Round Three. Ralph sends Norton out of the apartment so he can give Trixie a speech about how much Norton really loves her. Then it comes out that Norton and Trixie were fighting over Ralph—Norton was criticizing him and Trixie was defending him. Ralph wants to kill Norton, but he's too tired. Just as he's getting ready to go to bed— again—the alarm clock goes off. It's 5 A.M.—time to go to work.

TITLE: *"The Adoption"*
DATE: *March 26, 1955*
LENGTH: *37:05*

The Kramdens want to adopt a baby. "We wanted this more than anything in the world," says Ralph. The adoption agency tells Alice her application is being considered, but that a staff worker must come to the apartment to look it over before final approval is granted. A pall falls over the Kramdens because they think once the worker sees their crummy apartment they'll be denied a child. They borrow furniture—a TV set, drapes, refrigerator, stove, new table and chairs, couch, etc.—to make the apartment look presentable. Ralph and Alice are as nervous as two kids on their first date as they wait for Miss Lawrence from the agency to arrive. As she is interviewing the Kramdens, Ralph almost blows everything when he notes with amazement that a light goes on in the refrigerator when the door is opened. But no amount of *homina-hominas* can keep the charade going when Frank, the iceman, comes in with the Kramdens' daily delivery for the icebox. Ralph and Alice finally admit they redecorated the apartment with borrowed goods to make an impression. We're not cheating to get a child, Ralph says desperately, we're fighting to get one. Miss Lawrence says the agency is not as concerned with furnishings as it is with finding couples who really want children, and that she's never met a couple who want a child more than the Kramdens. Approved! The Nortons accompany the Kramdens to the hospital to pick up the baby. When the child is wheeled out Ralph's joy turns to anger when the doctor says the baby is a girl. Ralph insists that he get a boy, and the doctor goes off to try to arrange it. Alice, near tears, leaves the room, leaving Ralph alone with the baby. In a scene he would play again—with a puppy—in the Classic Thirty-nine episode "A Dog's Life," Ralph apologizes to the baby for not wanting to bring her home. As the infant weaves her magic on Ralph, his arguments for not wanting a girl become less convincing. By the time the doctor returns with the news that the Kramdens can get a boy, Ralph turns on him like a lion defending his cub—Ralph wants the girl. "Ralphina" is a Kramden. A week later, the doctor visits with somber news: the child's natural mother wants the baby back. Ralph, enraged at the doctor for bringing the news and at the mother for trying to reclaim the child, pounces on the doctor and manhandles him. The doctor hastily explains that the Kramdens are Ralphina's legal parents now and that he and the adoption agency will support them in a custody fight; he came only because the mother was so insistent. He leaves, and Ralph, emotionally unprepared for this turn of events, reacts the only way he knows how: he hollers, in pain. Alice, as bad as she feels, empathizes with the mother. Ralph tries to suppress similar feelings, but eventually his conscience overrules his heart: they must give up the child. He goes upstairs to the Nortons' to call the doctor, leaving Alice alone, sobbing. *(Audrey Meadows remembers "The Adoption" as being "so powerful" that one viewer actually forgot she was watching a television show, and called Audrey with advice on how to keep Ralphina. "I got a call, from the mother of a guy I used to date," Audrey says. "Her husband had been ambassador to England, and she was a highly educated, well-to-do woman. She also worked for an adoption society. She called me and said, 'Audrey, you don't have to give back that baby. You don't! That mother has no right to have the baby.' I was so stunned. I said, 'Mrs. Douglas, it's not our baby. That was a script.' She started to laugh. She said, 'Oh, my God, of course it's a script. But I hope they'll straighten it out. The mother has no right to that baby.' Isn't that wild?")*

TITLE: *"Stars over Flatbush"*
DATE: *April 2, 1955*
LENGTH: *37:05*

Norton has discovered astrology, and Ralph thinks he's nuts, especially when Norton tells him the stars say he shouldn't ask his boss, Mr. Malone, for the raise he planned to request that day. Norton also sees in the stars that Ralph will have an accident that day and will be rendered speechless. When a window falls on Ralph's hand and the pain is so great that he can't utter a sound, Ralph becomes hooked on the stars too. He doesn't ask for the raise, and Alice is furious when she learns the reason why. Ralph tells her the stars say he should ask for the raise Friday night at 11:30 P.M. Alice tries to explain to Ralph that he can't possibly be anywhere near his boss Friday night at that hour. As if appointed by destiny, in walks Freddie Muller with an invitation for the Kramdens to an engagement party he's giving for Mr. Malone, Friday night—from nine P.M. to midnight. Next, Norton sees in Ralph's horoscope that he's going to have an encounter with a glamorous Aquarius. They figure that the party is the only place Ralph is likely to meet such a woman, so they decide to show up at Freddie's just before 11:30. At the party Ralph is edgy, and he nearly faints when an attractive blonde asks him for a match. He nearly has a heart attack a few minutes later when Mr. Malone's fiancée, a cute blonde Aquarius, asks him to dance with her. At exactly 11:30 Ralph asks Mr. Malone for the raise. Malone turns him down, and then dresses him down for trying to take advantage of a social situation. The next day Ralph installs extra locks on the apartment door—to keep Norton out. Up pops Mr. Malone, to apologize to Ralph for yelling at him, and to give him the raise. It seems that the stars were right after all—until Norton comes down with the news that he's been reading last year's book.

TITLE: *"One Big Happy Family"*
DATE: *April 9, 1955*
LENGTH: *37:38*

Ralph and Norton are going nuts trying to do their taxes. They compare income and expenses, and when Ralph realizes that he and Norton between them are paying $90 a month in rent, he proposes that they pool their money and share an apartment. The Kramdens and the Nortons move to 23 Mockingbird Lane in Flushing, Queens, and the benefits of the move are immediately obvious: at Chauncey Street the view from Ralph's window was the back of a Chinese restaurant; from the new apartment he can see the front of a Chinese restaurant. The euphoria of new surroundings wears off quickly, though, when Norton spends all morning in the bathtub while Ralph's waiting to bathe before going to work. When Ralph finally gets into the bathroom he takes a tumble on the soap Norton dropped on the floor and then can't get any hot water. Ralph tries to salvage his morning with a few waffles but Norton gets to them first, causing more friction. Things are no better that night; everything Norton does—eating, tapping on the table, cleaning his eyeglasses—drives Ralph crazy. Ralph tries to relax by reading the paper and listening to the radio, but Norton sends him into a frenzy by blasting the television. Soon Ralph and Norton, Trixie and Ralph, and Alice and Trixie are squabbling. The superintendent of the building comes down and kicks the blabbermouths from Bensonhurst out of the apartment house. Alice scolds Ralph for ruining the one good idea he ever had, and the episode ends with Ralph and Norton quarreling over who was to blame for the whole mess.

TITLE: *"A Weighty Problem"*
DATE: *April 16, 1955*
LENGTH: *48:09*

A bus-company inspector gets on Ralph's bus and tells him he's getting too fat to drive a bus. Ralph goes home and checks a bus company height and weight chart, and discovers that for his height—six feet tall—he's four pounds under the maximum weight for a man his height. Later that night, with a clear mind, he goes to the monthly Racoon Lodge banquet and eats up a storm. After the feast, one of the Racoons bets Ralph that he's not six feet tall, and it turns out he's right—Ralph's only 5 feet 11 inches! A five-foot-eleven bus driver is supposed to weight 238 pounds, and Ralph weighed 246—before the banquet. Ralph immediately goes on a diet, and being deprived of food turns him into a monster. Two days before his bus-company physical he's about to go over the edge: even a crossword puzzle in which one of the answers is Supreme Court Justice Frankfurter drives him nuts. The next day, Mrs. Manicotti is having a surprise party for her husband, and she wants to hide the food for the party—a ham, a turkey, and the birthday cake—in the Kramdens' apartment. Alice thinks Ralph is going to spend the night working out at the gym, so she takes the food. Ralph comes home instead, and when he sees the food he thinks he's hallucinating. When he realizes it's real, a battle begins between his willpower and his appetite. Ralph wages a good fight, until he sees the cake. He snaps, and grabs a hunk of cake with his hand. Alice returns, and prevents Ralph from eating himself out of a job.

TITLE: *"Principle of the Thing"*
DATE: *April 30, 1955*
LENGTH: *34:09*

The Kramdens' apartment is going to pot—the pipes leak, the walls are cracking, the sink won't work, doorknobs are falling off. Ralph is fed up, so he seeks out Shaughnessy, the neighborhood lawyer, who advises him to withhold his rent until the landlord makes repairs. Ralph decides to take the rent money and repair and redecorate the apartment himself. He buys a new bathtub, and wallpaper that is too gaudy even for Norton (Alice describes it as "early Halloween"). Ralph papers the apartment, but soon thereafter a painter comes in and undoes the damage. Finally comes the confrontation with the landlord (who is played by Jack Benny). Ralph rails at him for being a cheapskate and a tightwad, and tells him that a clause in his lease allows him to withhold rent money and use it for repairs. The landlord tells Ralph that another clause in the lease allows the landlord to cancel the lease entirely, and that Ralph is now an ex-tenant. The landlord says he'll renew the lease if Ralph agrees to pay an additional fifteen dollars per month—a figure that reflects the increased value of the apartment now that Ralph has fixed it up.

TITLE: *"Songs and Witty Sayings"*
DATE: *May 14, 1955*
LENGTH: *38:39*

Ralph and Norton have entered the annual amateur night at the Halsey Theater, where the grand prize is two hundred dollars. Their act consists of a mind-reading bit, jokes and a Laurel and Hardy impersonation, and a song-and-dance routine.

When Ralph comes home from work, he discovers he and Norton are going to have some stiff competition: Alice and Trixie are doing a hula song and dance. Ralph is against Alice's performing, but Norton is more understanding; Trixie had been in burlesque, he tells Ralph, and has the tradition of the theater to uphold. Alice knows Ralph is afraid she and Trixie may win, and she appeals to his pride. Ralph not only accepts her challenge but bets her ten dollars he and Norton will win and promises to eat her grass skirt if she and Trixie win. Ralph and Norton are up past midnight rehearsing, and Alice and Garrity, Ralph's upstairs nemesis, are anything but a captive audience. The "restaurant sketch" they rehearse, in which Norton does a Stan Laurel impersonation as a customer who wants a piece of custard pie, and Ralph plays the waiter à la Oliver Hardy, is a priceless tribute by Carney and Gleason to the two great funny men. At the Halsey, the first contestant is Freitag Delicatessen's delivery boy, who plays a bicycle pump. Alice and Trixie wow 'em. Norton can't even guess the first object in the mind-reading routine, Ralph bombs as a standup comic, and the song and dance is a dismal flop. Final score: Alice and Trixie, $210; Ralph, a grass skirt for dinner. ("I remember a scene from this show where I was supposed to stand on my head and sing a coloratura song," Audrey recalls. "And I'm rehearsing it in the kitchen and I'm on my head on a chair and Artie's holding my legs. I'm waiting for the music and nothing is happening. Ray Bloch, the orchestra leader, has his stick in his hand and his arms folded. Jackie says, 'Come on, Ray. Where's the music?' Ray says, 'I didn't get any music.' Jackie says, 'What do you mean, you didn't get any music? It says in the script she's going to sing.' And Ray says, 'You mean she's really going to sing that standing on her head? I thought she'd have a recording.' Nobody on the show knew I used to be a coloratura soprano, except Jackie.")

TITLE: *"Boys and Girls Together"*
DATE: *May 23, 1955*
LENGTH: *36:30*

The Kramdens have new next-door neighbors—the Fallons, from Bayonne. Ralph welcomes the new guy by inviting him to join him and Norton for pool, bowling, and lodge meetings, but Fallon is busy all the nights Ralph and Norton go out together—he spends all those nights with his wife. Alice, who earlier had been stood up for a movie date with Ralph because he had to bowl with the Hurricanes, feels like a discarded dishrag next to Mrs. Fallon. Later, Trixie tells Alice that she read in a magazine that the reason men spend so much time apart from their wives is because the wives let themselves go and allow their marriages to become dull and predictable. The girls make a pact to bring romance back to Chauncey Street. When Ralph comes home the next night and finds the apartment lit by candle-light, his first reaction is to accuse Alice of forgetting to pay the electric bill.

Alice is prepared though: fancy clothes, hugs and kisses, a bushel of compliments, a roast-beef dinner, and romantic music. Ralph reminds her that they're not Eddie Fisher and Debbie Reynolds, and it's all downhill from there. Soon each is pouring out fourteen years of frustration. Then Alice lays down the law: Ralph will be allowed out alone one night a week; any other night he goes out he has to take her with him. After four nights out with Alice, Ralph is invoking the Constitution and his right to life, liberty, and the pursuit of happiness. Alice and Trixie have said they want to spend time with their husbands but not spoil their fun, so Ralph figures the way for him and Norton to win back their freedom is to keep the girls out so late that they ask to go home, thus "spoiling" their husbands' night out and disqualifying themselves from participating in the boys' activities. Hours later—after pool, rowing boats, visiting Roseland and Coney Island, and bowling—the girls are invigorated and the boys are walking zombies. They stop in a restaurant and Ralph and Norton can't even stay awake. Half asleep, they wind up dancing together, and then fall asleep standing up. The girls give up trying to keep them awake, and ask to go home. Ralph and Norton drag themselves home, victorious.

THE CLASSIC THIRTY-NINE 1955–1956

It is the **Honeymooners** *sketch, plus the comedian's amazing talents, which have resulted in Gleason's private television uranium mine. This mine consists of a contract which will earn Jackie fifty dollars a second.*
TV STAGE MAGAZINE (1955)

S uddenly this term—"The Classic Thirty-nine"—presents a problem. It presents a problem because it implies what was never intended when the term arose. It implies that episodes outside these thirty-nine were somehow subclassic. But it only meant to suggest, back in those dark dark days before the Lost Episodes resurfaced, that these thirty-nine episodes were the classics that had been in circulation for thirty years.

However, although introduced as a designation rather than a value judgment, the term has become a self-fulfilling prophecy. Today the thirty-nine enjoy not only the status of classics, but also the history of scholarly scrutiny reserved for classics. Why is the simple greeting "Hello, Bill" from "A Man's Pride" a certifiable gem today? It is because fans have had thirty years, and about one hundred viewings, to associate the line with its context, and to experience at once its multiple layers of meaning.

So far, viewers haven't had this opporuntity with the Lost Episodes. Until they do, the thirty-nine will still be light years ahead in the scholarly-scrutiny department. A simple statement in the thirty-nine *will* telegraph more to viewers than the same phrase in a Lost Episode. Of this, there is not only ample evidence, but "proof you cannot dispute."

Ironically, these perceptions are precisely the opposite of any brought to bear on the thirty-nine when they first ran, in the 1955–56 season. Back then, the thirty-nine were the episodes that had to prove themselves, because *they* represented the departure from the familiar.

What happened to bring about this departure in 1955 was that Buick came up with the biggest contract ever negotiated for a performer in showbiz history to lure Gleason to their camp. It called for seventy-eight half-hour *Honeymooners* during the 1955–56 and 1956–57 seasons, with an option for the 1957–58 season. This $6 million contract, with add-ons, had a total value of $11 million. It made Gleason, according to *Life* magazine, "by financial standards, at least, history's greatest comedian."

Another 1955 event facilitated the format change. DuMont had developed a new process of photography called Electronicam. It was vastly superior to kinescopes. This enabled Jackie Gleason and CBS to consider spinning off *The Honeymooners* as a half-hour situation comedy that could be rerun, without losing its original function as part of a one-hour variety program. The other half of the hour, called *Stage Show*—a major add-on of the Buick deal—would also be delivered by jackie gleason enterprises. All production costs for both offerings would be shouldered by jackie gleason enterprises, and jackie gleason enterprises would be wholly responsible for the results.

Art Carney wins the Emmy for Best Supporting Actor in a Regular Series, 1955.

Audrey Meadows wins Best Supporting Actress in a Regular Series at the 1955 Emmy Awards ceremony.

The timing for this particular coup seemed perfect. Gleason's TV audience in 1955 was reckoned at 49 million, with much of his fame attributable to *The Honeymooners* and the rest to his flair for showmanship. In 1952, *TV Guide* bestowed the Best Comedian Citation on Gleason. In 1954, he received both the Fame and Peabody Awards for his show. In the same year, Gleason and Carney won the Sylvania Award as Outstanding Comedy Team. On March 7, 1955, Art Carney received an Emmy Award for "Best Supporting Actor in a Regular Series" for his work with Gleason, and Audrey Meadows got the "Best Supporting Actress in a Regular Series" Emmy for hers. Concurrently, Jackie was guest starring on dramatic shows, being courted for leading movie roles (including one to be produced by Jack Benny and George Burns), and conducting LPs of romantic mood music that were number one on the charts. Additionally, by 1955, jackie gleason enterprises owned a recording company, two music-publishing firms, and an oil-drilling venture.

Stage Show starred the Dorsey Brothers, Tommy and Jimmy, each an orchestra leader in his own right, and each the proud holder of at least one golden record. Tommy's first million seller was "Marie," in 1946; Jimmy's first was "Amapola," in 1946, followed by "Green Eyes" and "Maria Elena," also in 1946. Joining forces with Tommy and Jimmy were the June Taylor Dancers. Which is to say the *Stage Show's* credentials were in order. The TV debut of Elvis Presley on *Stage Show,* on January 28, 1956, served to enhance its credentials.

Needless to say, Jackie Gleason poured his own creative gusto into the undertaking, of which Joe Cates remembers the pilot:

"Jackie had broken his leg and couldn't get around. His regular staff was tied up doing his show, more tied up than usual, and by this time I had directed and produced a big hit, *Stop the Music,* so Jackie wanted me to produce the pilot for *Stage Show.* We had Tommy and Jimmy Dorsey, and we had what is now the Ed Sullivan Theater. The guest stars I remember were Harry Belafonte, Rosemary Clooney. I remember a lot of wonderful acts. But the biggest memory of all this is that, because it was a pilot, we couldn't afford to put in the machinery we wanted. Jack wanted to imitate the Paramount Theater stage shows, where the band had machinery to push it forward. So I must have hired twenty stagehands to push the band forward and pull it back on cue.

"The other memory, related to this, is Jackie coming in on the day of the show. He stopped rehearsal and came in on his wheelchair. He had stipulated that a microphone, like at the Paramount Theater, would come out of the floor to the correct height of each singer. We didn't have one, and for just a pilot, for a single shot, we couldn't dig a hole in the concrete and install machinery for one. We couldn't. But Jackie stopped production, and summoned the head of variety programming at CBS to the theater, and insisted on this microphone.

"We never got to rehearse the show, because that was three in the afternoon, and we spent the next three hours digging just a hole in the concrete. For the show, I lay flat on the floor, and manually fed up the microphone. Because I couldn't control it well, it wobbled. It wobbled so much that whatever artist was singing had to grab it to steady it."

When the season started, *Stage Show* held the eight P.M. to eight-thirty Saturday slot, with *The Honeymooners* following from eight-thirty to nine. Using *Stage Show* for the lead-in exposed the entire hour to competition from Perry Como's very strong hourlong variety show on NBC. At one point, NBC felt sufficiently threatened to consider starting Como at 7:30, to ensure its edge over Gleason. But the move was never effected, nor evidently, necessary.

Worse, the concept of a half-hour *Honeymooners* inexplicably set some critics gnashing their teeth in dread. Some, anticipating disappointment, were certain that the first ever of the Classic Thirty-nine—the deservedly classic "TV or Not TV"—fell flat. Others, of higher intelligence, praised it to the skies, among them *TV Guide,* which found it fast-paced and rollicking. John O'Hara wisely opined, "For the millions who have been awaiting my remarks on the Como–Gleason simultaneous broadcast situation, here is my attitude: I can hear Como any old time, but when I miss a Gleason show I've missed it forever. And that's bad." He was, of course, referring to the whole Gleason hour—since these *Honeymooners* were filmed for rerun, and would be back again.

Yet for all its supporters, the combination of the half-hour *Honeymooners* and the half-hour *Stage Show* was in trouble. The positions of the two segments were swapped, but not soon enough to save them. Beyond this, Gleason felt after one season of half-hour *Honeymooners* was done that fresh material was getting scarce, and that doing *The Honeymooners* every week, half an hour every week, was depleting it. "We were running out of ideas," he explains. "I liked *The Honeymooners*. I liked doing them. And I didn't want to denigrate them by forcing scenes that didn't mean anything." So he canceled the Buick deal, and went back to his earlier format.

A year later, he sold the one season of thirty-nine *Honeymooners* to CBS for $1.5 million. Soon after, they went into syndication. They went on to pull higher ratings in syndication than they did in the 1955–56 season. Since then—from "Hello, Bill" to "Hello, ball," to "Can, ha ha"—they've been a fixture of the American way of life.

THE CLASSIC THIRTY-NINE

TITLE: *"TV or Not TV"*
DATE: *October 1, 1955*

Ralph and Ed share the purchase of a TV set.

TITLE: *"Funny Money"*
DATE: *October 8, 1955*

Ralph finds counterfeit money on the bus.

TITLE: *"The Golfer"*
DATE: *October 15, 1955*

Ralph tries to learn golf in order to impress his boss.

TITLE: *"A Woman's Work Is Never Done"*
DATE: *October 22, 1955*

The Kramdens hire Thelma the maid.

TITLE: *"A Matter of Life and Death"*
DATE: *October 29, 1955*

Ralph thinks he's dying of arterial monochromia and sells the story to the *American Weekly*.

TITLE: *"The Sleepwalker"*
DATE: *November 5, 1955*

When Norton sleepwalks, Ralph loses sleep looking after him.

From "Pal O' Mine."

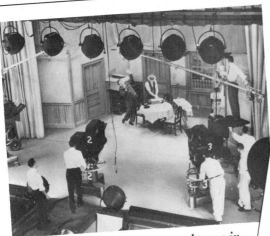

Ralph runs afoul of a vacuum cleaner in "The Deciding Vote."

Racoons reveal "The Deciding Vote."

TITLE: *"Better Living Through TV"*
DATE: *November 12, 1955*

Ralph and Ed go on TV to sell Handy Housewife Helpers.

TITLE: *"Pal O'Mine"*
DATE: *November 19, 1955*

Ralph and Ed fight over a ring, but make up after Ed survives a sewer explosion.

TITLE: *"Brother Ralph"*
DATE: *November 26, 1955*

In order to hold a job for single women only, Alice tells her boss that Ralph is her brother.

TITLE: *"Hello, Mom"*
DATE: *December 3, 1955*

Ralph sleeps at the Nortons' to avoid being at home for his mother-in-law's visit.

TITLE: *"The Deciding Vote"*
DATE: *December 10, 1955*

Ralph buys a vacuum, fights with Ed, and loses a Racoon election.

TITLE: *"Something Fishy"*
DATE: *December 17, 1955*

Ralph and Norton don't want their wives along on a Racoon fishing trip.

TITLE: *"'Twas the Night Before Christmas"*
DATE: *December 24, 1955*

Ralph hocks his bowling ball to get Alice a Christmas present.

TITLE: *"The Man from Space"*
DATE: *December 31, 1955*

Ralph enters a Racoon costume contest as the Man from Space.

TITLE: *"A Matter of Record"*
DATE: *January 7, 1956*

Ralph cuts a record to sweet-talk Alice after insulting her mother.

TITLE: *"Oh My Aching Back"*
DATE: *January 14, 1956*

Ralph wrecks his back at a Racoon bowling tournament.

TITLE: *"The Baby-sitter"*
DATE: *January 21, 1956*

Alice is babysitting, but Ralph thinks she's two-timing him.

TITLE: *"The $99,000 Answer"*
DATE: *January 28, 1956*

Ralph's category on a TV game show is popular songs.

TITLE: *"Ralph Kramden, Inc."*
DATE: *February 4, 1956*

Ed buys a share in Ralph, then Ralph is named in a will.

TITLE: *"Young at Heart"*
DATE: *February 11, 1956*

The guys hucklebuck, rollerskate, and go out with their wives.

TITLE: *"A Dog's Life"*
DATE: *February 18, 1956*

Ralph feeds his boss dog food, thinking it's an appetizer.

TITLE: *"Here Comes the Bride"*
DATE: *February 25, 1956*

Ralph's advice to lodge brother Saxon has Saxon's new bride—Alice's sister Agnes—in tears.

TITLE: *"Mama Loves Mambo"*
DATE: *March 3, 1956*

Carlos Sanchez wears out his welcome teaching good manners and the mambo.

TITLE: *"Please Leave the Premises"*
DATE: *March 10, 1956*

The Kramdens and Nortons barricade their apartments to fight a rent increase.

TITLE: *"Pardon My Glove"*
DATE: *March 17, 1956*

Alice wins free interior decorating and Ralph thinks she's carrying on with another man.

TITLE: *"Young Man with a Horn"*
DATE: *March 24, 1956*

Ralph tries to hit the high note on the civil service exam, or at least on his cornet with the sock in it.

TITLE: *"Head of the House"*
DATE: *March 31, 1956*

Ralph tells a newspaper that he's head of the house, then has to prove it to Joe Fensterblau.

TITLE: *"The Worry Wart"*
DATE: *April 7, 1956*

The IRS invites Ralph to clear up an item on his tax return.

TITLE: *"Trapped"*
DATE: *April 14, 1956*

Thugs follow Ralph home after he witnesses a holdup.

TITLE: *"The Loudspeaker"*
DATE: *April 21, 1956*

Ralph masters a speech and the hiccups for the Racoons' annual award dinner.

TITLE: *"On Stage"*
DATE: *April 28, 1956*

Stardom goes to Ralph's head when he appears in a Racoon play.

TITLE: *"Opportunity Knocks But"*
DATE: *May 5, 1956*

Ed gets a job and Ralph gets mad when the two play pool with Ralph's boss.

TITLE: *"Unconventional Behavior"*
DATE: *May 12, 1956*

Ed handcuffs himself to Ralph en route to the Racoon convention.

TITLE: *"The Safety Award"*
DATE: *May 19, 1956*

Ralph has a fender-bender on his way to receiving a Safe Bus Driver award.

TITLE: *"Mind Your Own Business"*
DATE: *May 26, 1956*

Ed sells i-rons after Ralph's advice costs him his job in the sewer.

From "Trapped." George Petrie, left; *Frank Marth*, right.

TITLE: *"Alice and the Blonde"*
DATE: *June 2, 1956*

The Kramdens and Nortons visit the Weedemeyers and Ralph and Ed go ga-ga over Rita.

TITLE: *"The Bensonhurst Bomber"*
DATE: *September 8, 1956*

After a pool-room quarrel, Ralph has to face the mighty Harvey at Kelsey's Gym.

TITLE: *"Dial J for Janitor"*
DATE: *September 15, 1956*

Ralph moonlights as the janitor of his building.

TITLE: *"A Man's Pride"*
DATE: *September 22, 1956*

Ralph claims to run things at the Gotham Bus Company to save face with Alice's old beau, Bill Davis.

THE WHAT-IF SEASON: 1956–1957

*The closing message of nearly every episode was a
simple but unshakable truth, beloved of dramatists in
every modern society since the day when the middle
class replaced the nobility as the mainstream
audience: Be it ever so humble, there is no place
like home.*
CHANNELS (1985)

Gleason shocked his fans, his sponsor, and his network when at the end of the 1955–56 TV season he canceled his multimillion-dollar contract with Buick, which called for three seasons of half-hour *Honeymooners*. Though three new half-hour shows were aired in September '56, a few months after the 1955–56 season officially ended, *The Honeymooners*, as a series, was, as Ralph would say, over, done, completed, through, finished. Gleason said he didn't want his writers to scrape the bottom of the barrel for new plot ideas, and that was that.

Gleason returned to doing an hour-long variety show, but *The Honeymooners* wouldn't die. Though Gleason admits, "At that time we'd run dry," the variety show included both long and short *Honeymooners* sketches. Gleason's explanation for the resurrection of the Kramdens and the Nortons is simply, "There were other items, other situations in society, [to] do sketches about."

So the ten sketches from this season that are now in syndication (minus the original musical "Trip to Europe" *Honeymooners* which are not part of the Lost Episodes package and a 1957 version of "Manager of the Baseball Team" not scheduled for syndication) are a glimpse of what might have been—had the half-hour *Honeymooners* run another thirty-nine weeks.

These post–Classic Thirty-nine sketches are funny, often hilarious. Just like their immediate predecessors. But strangely enough, in at least one obvious way they are more like the sketches that preceded the half-hour shows: back in use are some of Ralph's stock phrases and some Ralph–Alice shtick used in the variety-show *Honeymooners* that were abandoned for the half-hours. And mysteriously missing—except once—is Ralph's most famous signature: "Bang! Zoom!" It's almost as if the Classic Thirty-nine had never happened.

The plots here seem varied enough to make one begin to wonder if maybe Gleason hadn't been too hasty in deciding to cancel the half-hour show. Ralph fakes being an alcoholic because he wants to fail a physical he thinks is for an insurance policy; Ralph and Norton campaign for a local politician; Ralph is on the night shift and can't sleep during the day; Ralph and Norton think they've won a car in a raffle; Ralph finds a love letter in the apartment and thinks Norton wrote it to Alice; Ralph and Norton want to buy a candy store; Ralph buys a house; Ralph gets in a jam when he brags that he knows Jackie Gleason. Recurring themes, yes. Ralph is jealous; Ralph wants to make money; Ralph jumps to conclusions; Ralph schemes. But the variations on these themes are fresh enough to make these last (available) episodes from the Fifties just as precious as anything that preceded them.

TITLE: *"Double Anniversary Party"*
DATE: *October 13, 1956*
LENGTH: *13:06*

Alice is planning a surprise anniversary party for Ralph, which is going to be held at the Nortons'. Ralph, meanwhile, is secretly planning to take Alice to the Kit Kat Club the same night. He tells Alice he wants to take her to the movies—*The Bowery Boys in Baghdad* is what he chooses—but she, to Ralph's surprise, refuses the invitation and suggests they spend the evening with Norton and Trixie. When gentle persuasion fails, Ralph turns to bullying, but Alice, of course, won't change her mind. Finally Ralph is forced to tell Alice he really wants to take her to a night club. When Alice hears this, she tells Ralph about the surprise party at the Nortons'. They agree to go to the party that night, and to the Kit Kat Club the next.

TITLE: *"Check up"*
DATE: *October 20, 1956*
LENGTH: *9:50*

Ralph is being promoted to assistant starter and a doctor from the bus company stops by to give him a physical. Ralph isn't home so the doctor offers to come back later. Alice and Trixie are going shopping, so they ask Norton to wait in the apartment for Ralph to come home. When Ralph hears a doctor wants to examine him, he thinks Alice has increased his life insurance—and he wants no part of it.

He decides to fake being a drunk so he'll fail the examination and forfeit the policy. The doctor returns, and is appalled at Ralph's "condition." When Alice comes home and explains to Ralph who the doctor was he has only one thing to say: "I got a biiiig mouth!!!"

TITLE: *"Forgot to Register"*
DATE: *October 27, 1956*
LENGTH: *13:41*

It's Penrose versus Harper in a local election, and Ralph and Norton are campaigning for Penrose. They're expecting a landslide, and why not? All the influential groups in Bensonhurst—the guys at the bowling alley and the pool hall, the crowd down at the pizzeria, and the regulars at the Fascination Bar and Grill—are backing Penrose. Norton is so involved in the campaign that he dresses up as Uncle Sam and marches in a parade for Penrose. Ralph is aghast when he learns that Norton isn't voting because, he says, dressing up and going down to the polls is "too much trouble." Ralph gives Norton an inspiring speech about how the Pilgrims sailed to America and suffered deprivation and hardship so that centuries later Norton could have the right to vote, to which Norton replies, "If they'da known about me they could have saved themselves the trip." Ralph receives another shock moments later, when Alice tells him she's voting for Harper. They compare notes on each candidate's accomplishments. One reason Ralph likes Penrose is because he's promised to have the garbage picked up more frequently. The more Ralph talks the more likely it seems that no one but the boys at the pool room and the bowling alley would be dumb enough to vote for Penrose. But if Penrose is to get elected it'll have to be without Ralph's vote: he forgot to register.

TITLE: *"Expectant Father"*
DATE: *November 3, 1956*
LENGTH: *15:57*

Alice is working part time as a receptionist at an obstetrician's office, to earn some money for Christmas. One afternoon Ralph sees Alice and Trixie going into the doctor's office, and he thinks it's because Alice is pregnant. Ralph is sure he's going to have a son, and he wants to name him Ralph, just as he was named after his father. As Norton is listening to Ralph's plans for Ralph Jr., it dawns on him that maybe it was Trixie who was visiting the obstetrician and that he, not Ralph, is going to be a father. He has dreams too: to get little Norton a job in the sewer—after he graduates college. (Norton says he always wanted a son to wade in his footsteps.) When Alice and Trixie come in carrying a heavy laundry basket, each gets the royal treatment. Ralph and Norton try to get one of the girls to admit she's going to be the mother; the girls think they're nuts. Ralph finally breaks down and tells Alice he saw her going into the doctor's office. Alice thinks Ralph knows she has a job. She thinks he approves, and says she may do it every year. The prospect of being a new father every year momentarily stuns Ralph, but he's so giddy he even agrees to that. Alice then adds that if she does it every year she may have to join a union. The truth finally comes out when Ralph says he didn't know you had to join a union to have babies. Here, once again, is the Ralph Kramden of "Pickles" and "The Adoption," who confesses—both in words and by the tortured expression on his face—that his life is incomplete without children. He recovers from his grief long enough to say that maybe he'd rather have a daughter than a son, just so she could grow up to be like her mother.

TITLE: *"Good Night Sweet Prince"*
DATE: *November 10, 1956*
LENGTH: *15:27*

Ralph has been transferred to the night shift by Freddie Muller, and he's finding it impossible to sleep during the day. Alice tries to calm him down, and just as he's about to doze off Norton barges in. Now it's his turn to help Ralph sleep. Norton's idea is to stuff Ralph's ears with cotton so he can't hear any noise, and to blindfold him so he can't see daylight. Norton is leading Ralph into the bedroom but lets go of him for an instant, just long enough for Ralph to tumble head first into the bedroom. Exit Norton. Ralph cautions Alice about making noise, and returns to the bedroom. Freddie walks in and tells Alice he's putting Ralph back on the day shift. Alice calls Ralph to tell him the good news, but he races out of the bedroom and begins screaming at her for disturbing him. Ralph doesn't see Freddie standing by the door, and he goes into another tirade, blaming Freddie for his misery. Freddie's insulted, and promises to keep Ralph on the night shift forever.

TITLE: *"Two-Family Car"*
DATE: *November 17, 1956*
LENGTH: *17:27*

Ralph gets a telegram saying he's won a prize in a raffle. He assumes it's the grand prize—a new car. As he is dreaming about all the places he and Alice will go in the car, he tells Alice he couldn't have bought the winning ticket had he not been able to talk Norton into chipping in twenty-five cents—half the price of the ticket. Alice says that that makes Norton half owner of the car, and Ralph becomes delirious with anger. The wheels begin to turn, and he tries to cheat Norton out of his half of the car by offering to pay him back the quarter. Norton immediately realizes that he and Ralph must have won the car. Ralph tells Alice he wants to take her to her mother's that weekend, so he can see the expression on her face when he drives up in a new car, and Norton steps in to demand his rights: he wants to use the car on the weekend to drive to the Aberdeen Proving Grounds to see a demonstration of dum-dum bullets. The boys bicker until the man from the raffle arrives with Ralph's prize. While Norton, Ralph, and Alice look out the window for the new car, the man brings in the real prize—a turkey.

TITLE: *"Love Letter"*
DATE: *November 24, 1956*
LENGTH: *36:48*

Alice borrows a cookbook from Trixie and in it finds a love letter Norton once wrote to her. Ralph finds it too—and thinks Alice is seeing another man. Ralph and Norton—who detects something familiar about the handwriting—go to a handwriting analyst for some clues to the identity of the author of the letter. The analyst says the author is the romantic type, but that he is also disorderly, not very bright, careless, lacking in concentration, slovenly, rude, and messy. She tells Ralph she can't give him a more detailed analysis on the spot, but that she'll analyze the letter some more and mail him her conclusions. Ralph doesn't want her to send the information to his house, so Norton offers to have the letter sent to him. He writes down his address, and when the analyst reads it she is shocked to discover that the handwriting is identical to that in the love letter. She tells this in private to Ralph, who flips. The next day, Alice asks Norton to go with her to pick out a bowling ball for Ralph's birthday present. Ralph walks in while they're talking and thinks he's caught them "in the act." When Alice rushes out of the house without explanation a few minutes later, Ralph figures it's just more evidence that something's going on behind his back. While Alice and Norton are out, Ralph goes to see Trixie. He tells her what's troubling him and she tries to convince him he's wrong. As Ralph is quoting from the letter to Trixie—"I love you. I love you. I love you. I love you"—in walk Alice and Norton. Norton thinks Ralph is telling Trixie he loves her, and he challenges Ralph to a fight. Ralph belts Norton and sends him reeling onto the couch. Alice presents Ralph with the new bowling ball to prove that he's been wrong. Norton recovers, Ralph apologizes, Alice forgives.

TITLE: *"Finders Keepers"*
DATE: *December 8, 1956*
LENGTH: *37:08*

Mr. Bartfeld is selling the neighborhood candy store to the Chock Full O' Orange people. When Ralph hears this he figures the CFOO people must know something about a boom in the neighborhood, and he wants to buy the store. He and Norton form a partnership and agree to invest three hundred dollars each to buy the candy store. When Ralph gets home he discovers that Alice has just lent three hundred dollars out of their savings to her brother-in-law Harry for a car-washing machine. Ralph flips, and mourns the passing of "the candy-store dream." Norton can't get his half of the money either, so he and Ralph put their heads together to come up with a scheme. Norton turns on the radio and they hear a commercial for a find-the-missing-money contest. The prize: a thousand-dollar bill. After studying the clues, they decide the money is hidden in an automat across the street from Grand Central Station. They go there and search everything—sugar bowls, people's sandwiches, and the tiny compartments in which the food is kept. They don't find the money, but they get arrested for starting a disturbance in the automat. When Ralph gets home, he learns from Mr. Bartfeld that the Chock Full O' Orange people wanted to buy his store not because they thought it could make a lot of money, but because they want to use it as a warehouse. Ralph is relieved he didn't buy the store, but he's upset at having lost a day's pay looking for the thousand dollars and having had to pay Joe Cassidy fifteen dollars to drive his bus. Suddenly, in comes Alice with the afternoon paper and big news: Joe Cassidy found the hidden money that morning, on the visor of the bus he was driving. Ralph's bus.

TITLE: *"Catch a Star"*
DATE: *December 15, 1956*
LENGTH: *36:41*

The Racoons are holding a dance, but nobody wants to come. One of the lodge brothers suggests that they try to get a celebrity to attend the dance. Norton remembers that Ralph once told him he was friends with Jackie Gleason, so everyone at the lodge insists that Ralph bring Gleason to the dance—not only to help sell tickets but to prove he wasn't lying about knowing him. Ralph is perturbed, but Alice convinces him that the only way out is to confess to the Racoons that he doesn't know Gleason. Just as he's on his way out the door, in walks Norton—with the news that a thousand tickets have been sold to the dance. Ralph figures that maybe he can get Gleason to the dance if he tells him it's a benefit. He and Norton go to the hotel where Gleason rehearses for his show, in the hope of meeting him there. When Norton leaves the lobby to wash up for lunch, Ralph meets Art Carney, who's headed for a rehearsal. Ralph goes ga-ga. Carney leaves and Norton returns. Ralph tells Norton about meeting Carney, and then they debate over who's funnier, Gleason or Carney. Ralph bribes a delivery boy who's taking a package up to Gleason to let him take the package, and while he's going up in the elevator to see Gleason, the Great One walks into the lobby, where Norton spots him. Norton is so overwhelmed he doesn't even ask Gleason about attending the Racoons' dance. Ralph is sunk. Alice drags him to the dance, but he wants to leave immediately, because he's afraid to face the Racoons. When Ralph goes to check Alice and Trixie's coats, in walks Gleason. Alice has convinced him to come—with a homemade anchovy pizza and a note explaining Ralph's plight. Gleason goes into the dance, and Ralph returns to hear him warming up the crowd. Ralph is suddenly the number-one contender for Racoon of the Year. (Above: *Art Carney as Art Carney and Jackie Gleason as Jackie Gleason in "Catch a Star."*)

TITLE: *"My Fair Landlord"*
DATE: *January 19, 1957*
LENGTH: *36:01*

Ralph is fed up with things breaking down in the apartment, so he decides to buy a house. Naturally, he drafts the Nortons as tenants. The new house, in Queens, is also a dump but only Alice and Trixie will admit it. Ralph draws up a ninety-nine year lease for Norton, after which they have their first landlord–tenant fight—over what colors to paint Norton's apartment. It ends with Ralph throwing cans full of paint on Norton's wall, and Norton trying to get evicted by making a racket in the middle of the night. Ralph realizes Norton's intent, and joins in the noisemaking. He insists that Norton stay for ninety-nine years—after all, his rent is paying off the mortgage. He changes his mind when he gets toasted from head to toe by one of Norton's noisemakers—a giant firecracker.

TITLE: *"Manager of the Baseball Team"*
DATE: *June 1, 1957*
LENGTH: *10:36*

This is a longer, later version of the skit in which Ralph thinks he's been promoted but has instead been named manager of the bus company baseball team. The 1953 version of this skit was the one selected for syndication.

THE WRITTEN WORD

The Honeymooners *is probably the best consecutively written series of sketches ever done on television.*
JOAN RIVERS

The years in which the Lost Episodes were written were the CBS years before (and a few, after) the 1955–'56 season when the half-hour *Honeymooners* were done. They were the years when *The Honeymooners* was knitted right into a whole *Jackie Gleason Show,* when the show was an hour of dancers, singers, and other sketches galore. They were the years when Gleason, dubbed "Mr. Saturday Night," was pulling an audience share in the stratospheric mid-70s.

They were tough years for the writers, at a time in TV history when viewers never stopped to think that programs actually had to be written.

Popular comedians had huge—and hugely talented—writing staffs then, though writers rarely got public recognition. "Writers on those shows," says Leonard Stern, comedy writer for Kramden, then *Bilko,* and who later went on to produce *Get Smart,* "you were known as the boys, the fellas, the kids, so you were properly nondescript.

"I'm sure Jackie would have been delighted to have more writers, so as to be less dependent on us. Yet he was respectful of what we did. He was that most trusting of performers. He set the stage and the standards, and in that respect was demanding, *but* you had total freedom within his parameters. Since he was demanding of quality, the staff was thin and there were few of us, and it was a great learning experience as well. He really gave us a vote of confidence by never looking at the script. Not that he had many options, because we didn't finish till the end of the week or the night before the show...

"Jackie would every once in a while bring in a shipment of writers from the West Coast. It was reported in one magazine that he flew in some bunch of

Writers, left to right: *Marvin Marx, Howard Harris, Walter Stone.*

writers for four weeks at a total cost of $22,000. They invariably went upstairs and allegedly worked with him, and were going to do *Honeymooners,* or new, insightful comedy characters, and ultimately they would leave. I have a remembrance of many—my friends—who were brought in and held in bondage for a while to produce a backlog of scripts, because it was such an effort to work up a whole show from scratch every week. But I don't remember this ever producing a backlog of scripts. We'd see these people come in and disappear into some vortex upstairs. They'd surface in time to say goodbye.

"So the primary writers through the period were Marvin Marx, Walter Stone, Syd Zelinka, and I. Initially, Howard Harris was with us, until Howard left. We worked in concert, all of us working on all segments plus the monologue, and, finally, we were exhausted. At one point, we split into teams. We figured this way would give each of us two weeks to write an episode, because it was becoming increasingly apparent that we were under too much pressure and the work was suffering. Also, we never anticipated in the beginning that *The Honeymooners* would eventually be on every week. When we first started writing them, we would alternate a *Honeymooners* with three variety shows. Then, as *The Honeymooners* got more popular, we would do them every other show. Then we started to do three weeks out of four. We had to split into teams to preserve our sanity, and to keep up the quality of the work. Walter and Marvin formed one team. Syd and I were the other. Andy Russell joined the show and worked as a swing man, and then Herb Finn joined, and we split into teams of three."

Both Stern and Zelinka knew Gleason from his pre-TV days. Andy (A. J.)

Russell had come to Gleason by way of serious programs like *Studio One* and *Philco Television Playhouse*. Early on, he'd written *Studio One*'s "The Laughmaker," a television drama starring Gleason and Carney. Herb Finn was that rare exception, a writer who came to Gleason from Hollywood (though he'd previously lived in New York) and stayed. His credits included *Amos 'n' Andy, Duffy's Tavern*, and, years later, *The Flintstones*.

Arnie Rosen and Coleman Jacoby were back in the fold, specializing in non-*Honeymooners* sketches. They worked in Jacoby's apartment on the upper floor of an old mansion. The building was serviced by an ancient, coffin-like elevator. One West Coast writer, after a few turns in the elevator—once in pitch darkness—reviewed his situation and returned, with notable dispatch, to L.A.

The writers had a tremendous number of concerns to juggle. First, there were several sketches to write each week in the days of the Lost Episodes. Second, there was the fact that each writer had to produce on a rigid weekly basis. Third, there was the need for new stories for each of the sketches every time. New plots, yet fully consistent with the characters they were written for with dialogue that conveyed character along with the humor. And, of course, when you write comedy sketches, you have to churn out jokes.

In short, the actual writing process was akin to playing ice hockey while using your head as the puck. "The thing I recall," says Leonard Stern, "is that I always

Art Carney prepares to play Reggie's father in Reggie Van Gleason sketch.

The Van Gleasons—Mater (Zamah Cunningham), Pater (Art Carney), and Reggie (Jackie Gleason).

optimistically thought we'd finish at a reasonable hour, and I'd be able to go to the theater. Then I was constantly canceling tickets, because we never finished. We'd be there twelve to fourteen hours each day, Monday through Friday. No social life. No escape. It was probably more painful than I remember. Once poor Marvin fainted from fatigue. Fortunately, it was such a well-received show that at least there was some compensation for the masochism.''

"Basically," says Jack Philbin, "*The Honeymooners* was the easiest to write because it was the most honest. Reggie Van Gleason is such a caricature of a character that it's very hard to write, and very hard to write bits that are funny because they have to be physical, visual bits. To get those things to pay off, and to have a beginning, middle, and end of a bit inside of a beginning, a middle, and an end of a sketch, is very difficult. So, as a result, the toughest ones to write were Reggies. Gleason probably came up with more premises for Reggie than anybody, because Gleason *was* Reggie, really.''

According to Leonard Stern, "As far as I'm concerned, the thing we could never write was *Joe the Bartender*. It was drawn from specific people, regular customers of Jimmy Proce's Park View Tavern from Gleason's old Brooklyn neighborhood. With the exception, I think, of Gaylord Farquard. The characters were beautifully pegged. I've forgotten the name of the accident-prone one, but one day I was in the Plaza Hotel and a man came up and said, 'Aren't you one of the writers on the Gleason show?' I said yes. He identified himself as the accident-prone one. And he had a Band-aid on his head. But these were all characters known extremely well to Jackie. He knew them personally, so no matter what kind of joke we wrote, Jackie said, 'He'd never say that.'

"So *Joe the Bartender* wasn't easy. And the monologue was trouble. The day of the show, Saturday, was the most intense day. We did not stay at the theater that day. We would all be in a room trying to write those monologue jokes. It's almost impossible to write a self-contained joke. By the end of the day, whoever had a joke was welcome. The writers invariably were fading, so the busboy from the restaurant with the most current joke had access to Jackie's dressing room. One day, Howard Harris had his fill. He rose and announced, 'I quit. I quit this humiliation festival.' And he did.

"Strangely enough, we had very little to do with the behind-the-scenes and technical operation, because the script took so much time to write that we seldom visited the set until the day of the show. We didn't get down to the theater, I think, until just in time to deliver the monologue. Finally, we hired a couple of guys just to write the monologue. But still, you'd have to pitch in on everything."

The working procedure involved one person typing and everyone thinking. Whoever sat at the typewriter was the editor, because he was in the position to type what he wanted to go into the script and not to type what he didn't want. When the whole group wrote together, Marvin Marx usually typed. Says Herb Finn, "When we were working, Gleason wouldn't disturb us. In fact, he wanted to know that we were working. He liked that."

Sometimes an idea would come from a staff member—as when Jack Hurdle came up with a Santa story, or when *Honeymooners* players George and Patti Petrie's adoption of a child inspired the adoption episode.

The basic story idea would be conveyed to Jack Philbin. If there was a conflict with a story another team was writing, he'd suggest taking another tack. He'd also relay the story to Jackie at the appropriate moment. "But," says Leonard Stern, "you couldn't wait for Philbin to get back to you. With or without clearance, you went ahead and started writing. Because you didn't *have* any time to wait. So clearance was, really, automatic."

Walter Stone referred to the procedure as "A form of living dangerously."

Says Stern, "Jackie objected to one script on the basis of the fact that a network vice president's twelve-year-old daughter, a fan, didn't like it, and he had called Jackie to tell him. We replied that we had an eleven-year-old niece who loved it, and a nine-year-old nephew who was totally committed to it."

While the story ideas weren't painstakingly cleared with Gleason, all major departures were. A notion like Gleason and Carney playing double roles wasn't thought of as precedent-breaking, says Stern, "because everything we did was out of desperation. Did it work? Did it meet our standards? Was Jackie comfortable in it?" Yet even with those criteria, some changes required a huddle. When *Honeymooners* sketches were evolving into what became the first long sketches on television variety shows, discussions took place. When a totally physical concept in a new setting was contemplated, discussions took place too. Of course, not always soon enough . . .

Leonard Stern remembers one incident, over "Teamwork Beat the Clock." "It was the first one Syd and I did as a team of two. It was the first totally physical *Honeymooners* written. In those days, a television script was divided down the page. On the right-hand side was dialogue. On the left was the action. We used to have a minimum of action, because there wasn't much you could do in that one Kramden room. But this was a different setup. So, when Gleason got the script—I think it was on a Friday night—he called and said, 'It doesn't work. I want everybody to stay for a meeting. We may have to pull out an old script.'

"Syd had already left. I couldn't reach him. I had a date whom I was on my way to meet. We were going to see the Broadway musical *Kismet,* and my date was flying in from California. I was going to meet her at *Kismet.* I couldn't get word to her beforehand. I told Gleason, because he wanted to have the meeting at eight o'clock and I said it was impossible. We had to agree to hold the meeting at midnight, at which time we would discuss whether we would do the "Beat the Clock" script. That night is deeply etched in my mind. I met my date, and she had jet lag. Ten minutes into *Kismet,* she said she didn't feel well, and she left. She insisted that I stay to enjoy the show. It may be a great tribute to *Kismet* that I did in fact find myself enjoying it.

"When it was over, I got Syd, and we went over to the meeting. The staff had

Writer Leonard Stern's doodles and notations
on the script for "Principle of the Thing."

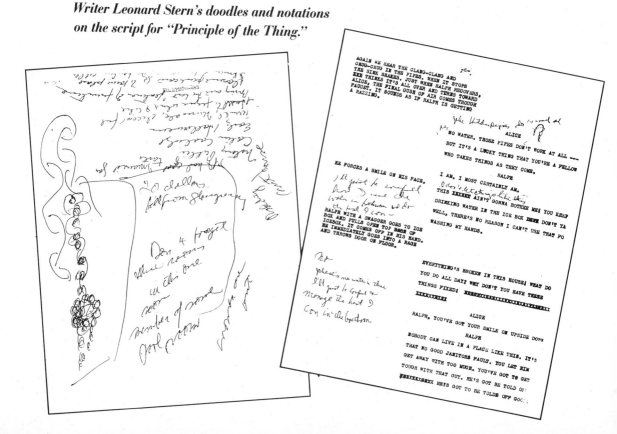

been held there for us to arrive, held there since eight o'clock. They had been drinking. It was a great collection of drunks. Jackie came back, and we discussed the script. He said it made no sense. We realized what had happened. He hadn't read the left side of the page. The minute he did, all the dialogue, which related to being on *Beat the Clock* and working with the props, was clear. He suddenly understood it and said, 'Okay, go ahead.'"

The writing of any script was carefully honed. The placing of a word, the difference between "You can't go in there" and "Don't go in there," would be weighed and pondered. As television critic Kay Gardella has observed, "Writing, acting and the sense of earthy reality has made *The Honeymooners* an all-time classic. The lines seem simple enough, but don't be fooled. They're polished gems." Writers would mull, and pace, and scan the *Racing Form,* and hook paper clips into chains, and stare out the window, until a punch line sounded just right. "It doesn't mean they were going to do it that way," adds Walter Stone, "but we were very careful about wording."

What would not necessarily be written into a script were the catch phrases. "Bang! Zoom!" and "One of these days, one of these days, pow..." were often ad libs by Gleason when the mood seemed to demand them.

What was unimportant, not only on the Gleason show but on all television sitcoms of the period, was consistency over such matters as house addresses and relatives' names. Particularly on a live program, it was inconceivable that the viewers would remember such trivia from one week to the next. "We were consistent with significant details," reflects Gleason. "A telephone never showed up unless Alice talked Ralph into getting one; then they'd get rid of it right away. Besides, having a telephone makes it too easy for writers. I realize that every week in those episodes, Alice seemed to have different relatives. But that's because we had several teams writing, and one team didn't know what the other team was doing. Nobody would think of saying, during a rehearsal, 'Wait a minute, last week her brother's name was—,' because, in those days, you didn't have much time to think. I was doing four sketches in a show, and I had a lot of other things to think about besides *The Honeymooners*. And I didn't like to rehearse, so there wasn't much time during rehearsals to go off on tangents. But, as a matter of fact, I think *The Honeymooners* had a continuity that was superior to almost every other show. We had a few things that didn't belong, or that might have been used one week and not the next, but they were really extremely minor."

After a while, the writers achieved greater consistency. They also had fun writing their own friends' and families' names into scripts. The name Nolan was a Walter Stone insertion of his wife's family name. Grogan was the name of one of her relatives. The names of Gleason's friends would show up on places like the Racoon arrears board. Shor, for instance, was Toots Shor, Falstaffian saloon-keeper to the stars. Likewise, he was the Toots in Racoon founder Toots

From "The Hypnotist."

Mondello's name. Philbin was Jack Philbin. Jack Philbin also enjoyed the distinction of being immortalized in several scripts as the Blue Philbin Hotel. "We never got into that sort of luxury on DuMont," explains Stone. "It came later."

Some names seemed natural and just stuck. "We always used the name Hurricanes for Kramden's bowling team," says Stone. "Now, years later, Gleason wound up in Miami doing *The Honeymooners,* and in Miami, it's not only that you have hurricanes all the time, but the University of Miami football team is the Hurricanes. When we first came up with the Hurricanes, there was no special connection. I think we used it because we wanted to do a big wind joke about Ralph."

The Racoons "just happened," too. "We had to have an organization they belonged to," says Gleason. "All people in Brooklyn belonged to something, the Knights of Templar or the Knights of Columbus. So we felt there was something they should belong to, and somebody came up with the idea about the Racoons." As for the uniform, it *wasn't* inspired by Walt Disney's *Davy Crockett* phenomenon, a television development that came after Kramden's lodge. Coonskin caps were known before Disney, and known to look silly when worn in fun. Several years before Disney's *Crockett,* in 1950, Frank Sinatra wore one onstage when he played the Copacabana, snapping a whip, blowing a duck call, and doing takeoffs of "Mule Train" and "The Cry of the Wild Goose." Says Walter Stone, "Forgetting Davy Crockett, look at those hats. They're hokey. That hat is hokey. And it lends itself to the Racoon salute, to waving it and going ooo-wooo."

Some plot and character devices were derived from Gleason's experiences. He had definite memories of Newark's Club Miami. Though the club had a four A.M. closing time, the bouncers were still in action at seven and eight in the morning. "The cops wouldn't go in there," he once told Jim Bacon. "They were afraid to. So fights were settled *pow,* right in the kisser. And I think that's where I first used the phrase." (According to legend of an earlier vintage—Jim Bishop's biography of Gleason, *The Golden Ham*—Jackie as a kid took on a pool player named Killer. He spotted Killer 45 points out of 50 and won anyhow. Killer responded with a warlike gesture and a "one of these days, Jackie, one of these days. Pow, right in the kisser!")

In one Lost Episode, Ralph tries to raise money by hustling a stranger at pinball. Gleason does wild moves at the pinball machine, followed by Carney doing wild moves at the pinball machine. The moves were inspired by a pinball routine done years earlier in Gleason's night-club act. The routine appears to have been the first time Art Carney saw Jackie Gleason as a performer, at the Roxy in the '40s, "doing the pinball thing."

As a child, Gleason was acutely aware of sounds. In bed, just before he fell asleep, he'd hear the sidewalk sounds, the apartment sounds, the Chauncey Street sounds. In the Marx Brothers movie *The Big Store*, these were summed up and serenaded in the "Tenement Symphony." *The Honeymooners* had its own paean to the pavement. "The garbage can goes clang. The radiator goes bang . . ." was the way the sounds were conveyed in "The Songwriters" episode. Stern and Zelinka wrote the sketch but, says Stern, "I think Jackie contracted separately for the song. I don't think Syd and I wrote it. That's the very difficult assignment of creating a good bad song. It was interesting because it did capture his frame of reference, which was limited to the world Ralph would know."

From Gleason's school days came another recognizably Kramden characteristic. "In school, I was irritating. I know what I did but I'm puzzled as to why I did it. I would sit back until Miss Pappen or Miss Caulfield or Miss Miller would make a point to the class, then I would get on my feet and argue with the teacher. I would say that, by coincidence, I had just been reading up on the subject and the authorities did not agree with whatever the poor woman had said. They'd always try to shut me up, then I would tell them they were losing their tempers because they were wrong."

Throughout his life, Gleason has always been fascinated by occultism, seances, hypnotism, and the like. He was an accomplished hypnotist. He was familiar with the extrasensory experiments of Professor J. B. Rhine of Duke University and the psychic powers of Edgar Cayce. He wrote the beginnings of a novel, *Brother Miracle,* that dealt with psychic phenomena in a monastery. As a rule, these themes were sidestepped in '50s comedies—a sitcom about the occult was deemed dangerously close to ridiculing the religious views of some of the audience—yet hypnotism figured in one Lost Episode, and astrology in another.

The smallest details from Jackie's past might appear in *The Honeymooners*. In a Gleason *Life of Riley* episode, Riley's son, Junior, and Junior's friend go in for chemistry. Junior's friend refers to NaCl (sodium chloride) as N-A-C-L. The boy's father calls it *nackle*. In the *Honeymooners* episode "Hair Raising Tale," when Kramden and Norton attempt to whip up a batch of hair restorer, they wade through a list of chemical symbols and formulas. When they try to pronounce them, Na_2Cl_3NPH comes out as *nackle-nipfh*, and H_2O (water) as *ho,* because: "You see, in chemistry, you never pronounce the numbers."

The Brooklynism *moax* found a permanent place in Ralph's vocabulary. Gleason and Crane had used it in their old neighborhoods, where it would have been uttered, not spelled. "When we wrote it in scripts," says Herb Finn, "it was *m-o-a-x*. It could very well have been *m-o-k-e-s,* properly, and maybe the person who wrote it first didn't know how to spell. I haven't used that word since I left the show. I haven't met anybody I would call a moax."

Another reference to Gleason's personal history occurs when the Kramdens and Nortons go to the movies. We see the poster outside the theater. It reveals that the movie inside is *The Desert Hawk,* starring Richard Greene, Yvonne De Carlo, and Jackie Gleason. The joke that Kramden was going to see a Gleason movie wasn't lost on the audience. To those in the know, the joke was still funnier. *The Desert Hawk* was made in 1950, when Jackie was still relatively unknown before he hit his stride with *Cavalcade of Stars.* He'd never have had third billing, having been awkwardly miscast in a small part, as a blue-eyed Arabian camel driver. (Jackie's best line in *Desert Hawk* wasn't even in the script. When he fell off a horse during filming and the director lit into him, Gleason said "What's the matter? You never see a great stunt man before?")

As on *Cavalcade,* a great deal of *The Honeymooners* was based on what Gleason did best—move funny, show embarrassment, register pain, project his eyes well out of his face, react to people, and be fat. "His consummate skill," says Leonard Stern, "was his ability to interact. When we were friends on the West Coast, before he was doing his TV variety show, he was working in Las Vegas. I went to see him. He was on

From "Kramden vs. Norton." Note the movie they go to see—and who gets third billing in the cast!

Gleason with writers Harry Crane (center, seated), Walter Stone (standing), and Marvin Marx (right, seated).

the bill with Chas Chase. Chas was an act who ate his cigarette, his shirt collar, his shirt front, his cuffs, and everything was edible and went in his mouth. And Jackie worked with him. It was the most successful I'd seen him in a club, because he just stood there and reacted. Together they were devastating. That was the first time I got a glimpse of Gleason's genius, that ability to look and listen.

"So when we were writing *The Honeymooners,* sometimes we'd say to him, 'Jackie, we don't have many lines for you tonight. They fell to Audrey and Art.' He'd say, 'Do I have something to react to?' If we said yes, he'd say, 'Okay, I can take care of myself.' And he would. He was such a great listener. He could punctuate other people's speeches with his responses. Instinctively. We wouldn't have to write a word."

Ralph's weight was still a given, because Gleason's weight was still a given. When, on a diet, Ralph tells Alice, "I've lost a pound. I can quit now," she snaps, "When you lose a pound, it's the same as Bayonne losing a mosquito." Ironically, once the characters were established in viewers' minds, it wouldn't have mattered whether Gleason weighed 220 or 280. Even when Gleason had *lost* weight, the writers would do fat jokes—and they'd work. People were so used to seeing Ralph heavy, it didn't register when he was not.

Ralph's weight, though a comic element, had psychological overtones that advanced both character and plot. When he was young, Gleason was never absolutely certain of getting enough to eat. Therefore eating gave him a sense of security. When he was a television star, in a monstrously insecure profession, eating continued to give him a sense of security. Just as consuming food was associated with security, lavish consumption of anything became his security blanket. "When you first begin to make money and become a success," Gleason once told a reporter, "you say to yourself, 'I'd better get all these things I wanted,' because how fruitless it would be if you *could* afford these things and *didn't* get them. So you accumulate everything. And then finally you realize that the materialistic things aren't of great value. The big thing is getting them. Once you've *got* them, they lose their greatness."

A driving force—perhaps *the* driving force—behind Ralph Kramden is the desire to improve his life by getting more money so he can acquire *things.* The things he can't have are endowed, in his estimation, with greatness. Things, he is certain, will give him security. Moreover, things will make Alice's life the dream he has always wanted it to be. He isn't frantic to win *Beat the Clock* so he can hoard money in a bank. Nor is that why he counts jellybeans and collects box tops. He thinks the prizes will improve the quality of his and Alice's lives. When Norton wins a television set with a ticket Ralph bought, Ralph risks his friendship with Norton because the possibility of possessing this *thing* makes him lose sight, momentarily, of what he is giving up to possess it. Ralph isn't a selfish man. He is just obsessed. Not coincidentally, Ralph is fat. Eating—consumption— approaches the security he believes will be his when he owns *things.*

Over the years, the characters acquired new traits and intensified old ones. To Leonard Stern, one aspect of character that slowly gathered steam, then became virtually symbolic of the characters, was their costumes. "It was like Chaplin's little tramp. They took even something like a hat, which has almost disappeared from our lives, and they made it contemporary. People weren't wearing hats in those days. The bus driver's hat and Norton's hat became signatures, comic signatures. If you hold up an extra-large bus driver's uniform today, people equate it with Ralph Kramden. If you hold up a hat, vest, and T-shirt, people see Norton."

Beginning with the first Norton appearance in *The Honeymooners,* the Norton–Kramden friendship developed on stage and in the scripts. Much of its growth stemmed from the nature of the stories—the need for Ralph to have a friend, a fellow schemer, a fellow Racoon. Says Herb Finn, "Kramden, of course, was stupid. Stupid is too harsh a word. Norton would say stupid things, and Ralph would recognize they were stupid. But if Carney said, 'I know a guy who wants to sell glow-in-the-dark shoelaces,' Ralph would say, 'There's money in that. We should do it.' "

The writers created an upstairs neighbor, but Art Carney created Norton.

A contributing factor to the Kramden–Norton chemistry was certainly what Art Carney brought to the role. The writers had created an upstairs neighbor. But it was Carney who created Norton. Or, as Jackie told *Newsweek* in 1959, "Just like a guy might be presented with a diamond and cut it into magnificent stones, Art did the same with the character, Ed Norton."

In some personal traits, Carney was not unlike his TV persona. He was, for instance, known as an ardent eater, capable of side trips to the refrigerator during the course of a meal. There were hints of Norton in him as far back as grade school. Once, bored by standing in line, waiting to sharpen his pencil, young Art broke the tension by approaching a bust of Beethoven and blowing its nose. The school's principal, dismayed, concluded that "Art Carney will never amount to anything."

Carney was a perfect foil for Gleason's actions and reactions, whether in delivering lines or executing physical comedy. He was always in motion, even if he was only drumming his fingers on the kitchen table. Ron Powers has described Ed Norton as Ralph's "inadvertent agent of doom, a dissolving picket fence in a windstorm, his elbows and chin an arsenal of harpoons aimed unconsciously at his pal's righteous blubber."

Gleason had body English. Carney had body English. Gleason could do one ludicrous pinball routine with his arms and his head and his hips. Carney, without copying him, could do another. The simplest motion for Ralph was preposterous, with his weight. The most bizarre was effortless for Norton. It made sense for the scripts to reflect these situations.

Ralph moved. Norton moved. Alice, as we know, stood still.

"Actually," recalls Audrey Meadows, "the way I built the character was because of the way Jackie and Art worked. One of the reasons that I was never physical—you never see Alice waving her hand around or doing big takes—was because the two of them were very physical. I decided that even if I was off camera, if Ralph paced up and down, I wouldn't go to him. He'd have to come to me. The camera would be on me when it was time. I realized that the only way to develop something interesting was to be as quiet as possible physically. It worked very well. It kind of evolved."

Alice stood still, but her marriage to Ralph Kramden didn't. As Walter Stone describes it: "I think it was gradual. I'm trying to look into Gleason's thinking, too, on this. Gleason was basically a visual comedian, and it reached the point where he finally said, 'We're doing all these visual-type sketches like Reggie, the Poor Soul, Fenwick Babbitt, and the others. We need a talking sketch.' So it came down to where this was the logical talking sketch, a man and his wife. So I think it evolved possibly from his own feeling that he wasn't that happy as a talking comedian, because he was a physical comedian too. He had a tendency to exaggerate moves, and because he did, we wrote them that way.

"Now, I look at some of the old ones, and there's constant screaming. Both of them screaming. We gradually realized that you can't continue the screaming, people can't stand it. So it got into more of a normal relationship. There's that, and the fact that the early episodes, most of them, were short sketches. In those, you had to score quick, and the insults got laughs. But we couldn't have it reach the saturation point where you didn't like Kramden because he was doing it too much. With her too, you didn't want to find viewers disliking her because she was answering him in kind.''

As Neil Simon discovered when he tried to cast the female version of his endlessly popular *Odd Couple* in 1985, what a man can get away with, a woman sometimes can't. From playing Olive, the female Oscar Madison, Rita Moreno concluded that ''you'd be surprised how hard those lines are if you put them in the mouth of a woman.''

The same was true for Alice Kramden; the verbal contention was a highlight of *The Honeymooners,* but Alice could not, forever and unrelievedly, pick, pick, pick. This was another reason the Ralph–Norton relationship blossomed; it took some pressure off the Alice *vs.* Ralph fights.

According to Audrey's sister, Jayne Meadows Allen, in her first years as Alice, Audrey was disappointed that Jackie didn't give her the funny lines writers had given Pert. Though it wasn't the dialogue Audrey expected, it had nothing to do with Jackie playing favorites. It was, rather, a case of the story line broadening, and an old approach becoming something new.

It must, if nothing else, be remembered that husband-and-wife humor—in real life, and on television—has changed since 1951. In those days, if a man, in fury, said ''hell'' or ''damn'' to his wife, it was an outrage of major proportions. You wouldn't hear such words on TV. You wouldn't hear them in your home. Cursing wasn't perceived as merely venting steam. It was ugly business. Since a man couldn't show rage in four-letter words, he fell back on something that at the time was considered much softer. He'd threaten to wallop the woman. By today's standards, that is the ugly business; a woman would rather hear ''go to hell'' than have her lip split.

You might argue that anyone would prefer a swear word to physical assault. But consider the great *Gone With the Wind* controversy of 1939. Producer David O. Selznick had to fight for permission to end the film with Rhett Butler's unforgettable ''Frankly, my dear, I don't give a damn,'' which was considered extremely scandalous. The fact that, midway through the movie, Rhett chased wife Scarlett up the staircase and forced himself on her—in gratitude for which, she woke up the next morning with a wide smile on her face—never fazed either public or censors. In that scene, he'd *only* attacked her. He hadn't gone so far as to say ''damn.''

All this goes to defend those early *Honeymooners* moments in which Ralph seemed almost capable of socking Alice. Not exactly *apt* to. Certainly not *prone* to. Nor would anyone watching have thought it desirable. But no one was actually shocked. In a few short years, things were different. Viewers knew that Ralph would never lay a hand on Alice in anger. It was played that way because everyone felt that way. "Pow, right in the kisser" had become an absolutely empty threat.

In other ways too, the marriage grew stronger. Because the Classic Thirty-nine episodes depict childless Kramdens, we assume them to be comfortable without children. This may well be the case, but we learn from the Lost Episodes that they would have liked to have children. From a writer's standpoint, there was no place for infant Kramdens. Babies would have altered the thrust of *The Honeymooners*. But from a psychological perspective, the fact that they came through a problem together, and resolved it in complete satisfaction with each other, indicates infinite love.

We've always known Ralph and Alice were crazy about each other. Even when it was Pert and Jackie, we knew that more than a wedding ceremony bound them together. But it deepened. In one Lost Episode, Ralph overhears Alice rehearsing a play, and concludes that she wants to kill him. "Why should she want to do this all of a sudden?" he asks Norton, who answers, "Yeah, you'd think she'd have done it years ago." As David Margolick wrote of this scene last year in the *New York Times*, "He is convinced that Alice is plotting to kill him, and, given the nature of their relationship, his fear does not seem all that far-fetched. . . . Though it hardly seems possible, viewers will now realize that the Kramdens' marriage apparently improved over the years."

What all these ingredients amounted to was a series of top-notch scripts. What the scripts amounted to were splendidly written documents that are sidesplitting to read and to envision performed. What they were, in fact, were springboards for the rehearsals and executions that followed. But, as Jackie Gleason has commented, "No matter who you have—you can have Laurence Olivier—four Laurence Oliviers—unless you have a script to bounce off of, nothing's going to happen."

Rehearsing "The Hypnotist."

RUN-THROUGH

It is not unusual for the star of an hour-long television
show to put in between 25 and 50 hours of rehearsal
beforehand. Gleason's program boasts the shortest
rehearsal schedule in the entire industry: two hours.
COLLIERS

W hen the Lost Episodes were originally presented on *The Jackie Gleason Show*, they were just one dish on the menu. And the chefs were up to their elbows in other pies, other stews. The master chef, Jackie Gleason, oversaw *everything* on the show, in addition to being the central figure in every trademark character sketch, whether Reggie Van Gleason, Rudy the Repairman, Fenwick Babbitt, Charlie Bratton, Stanley R. Sogg, Joe the Bartender, or the Poor Soul. Art Carney was second banana in *Reggie* (as Reggie's father, Sedgwick Van Gleason) and in *Charlie Bratton the Loudmouth* (as Charlie's milquetoast dupe, Clem Finch). Players like Zamah Cunningham (Mrs. Manicotti in *The Honeymooners*; Reggie's mother in the *Reggie* sketches) and Ethel Owen (Alice's mother and Aunt Ethel in *The Honeymooners*; a proper dowager in *Reggie* sketches) might also have other duties in the course of an hour show. So it was not, as later happened with the Classic Thirty-nine, a case of coming in to do one sketch for the week and then going home.

All these details had to be drawn together—along with production numbers and special guest stars—and none were done very far in advance. The only exceptions to this were the big-name guests, whose availability was determined by their schedules and when they were in town. Recalls Bullets Durgom "Don't forget that people didn't travel between the East and West Coast then as easily as they do now. Often we'd get calls from Hollywood stars when they hit New York. They'd say they were fans of Jackie's and really enjoying his show. He'd say, 'Why don't you come on and do one? We'll have some laughs.'"

Advance bookings of top stars were a plus from a promotional point of view. It would have been bad business to get Jack Benny or Red Skelton without mentioning them in the TV listings for Saturday night. Jackie Gleason, Jack Philbin, and Bullets Durgom were most involved in these bookings. If the star was going to participate in something besides his or her own routine, the writers would be advised.

One time, Jack Benny was going to be in New York. "Benny was a good

Gleason with director Frank Satenstein.

friend of Jackie's,'' says Jack Philbin. "And Jack was very fond of Benny. I mean, how could you not like Jack Benny? So we invited him on the show.'' The writers had enough notice to be able to use him as the Kramdens' tight-fisted landlord, who appears at the door in one Lost Episode. As a gag, Jackie had a special dressing room prepared for him—about the size of a shoebox. The furniture was more dilapidated than the Kramdens'. When Benny saw it, he immediately enthused, "This is *much* bigger than my dressing room in Hollywood.''

In all, some one hundred people might take an active part in presenting any *Jackie Gleason Show*. More than once this figure included a troop of boy scouts marching in a huge production number.

Each week on Monday, the June Taylor Dancers started on a new set of steps. Each week, the writers resumed writing, assuming approval. Art and Audrey siphoned off pages to study as fast as they got them. Jackie's pages were slid unceremoniously under his door. Joan Reichman typed up a whirlwind getting final pages off to staff members, sponsors, and network personnel.

Recalls Audrey Meadows, "I used to get my script Friday night. Sometimes, if I was lucky, I might get a script Friday afternoon. But I had a habit, when the script came, if it came before eleven o'clock, of not looking at it until after the TV news. The news then was only fifteen minutes, eleven to eleven-fifteen P.M. I'd learn the whole show, even when it was an hour show, in the fifteen minutes between the end of the news and the start of the late movie. I have pretty much of a photographic mind, but I've also discovered that when something is well written, you can memorize it in two seconds. When you have trouble memorizing it, there's something wrong with the way it's written.''

Each week, Peggy Morrison would have to establish players' dimensions, and the themes for the June Taylor Dancers' dances, in order to line up costumes. Of her many responsibilities, costuming *The Honeymooners* was the least of her worries.

Says Joyce Randolph (who met her husband through Peggy Morrison), "Well, Ralph mostly wore his uniform, or the outfit Jackie called his 'clam suit.' Norton only wore a few outfits, and after a while, only that same one outfit. Audrey wore those Pat Perkins rack dresses. I wore blouses, which were supplied, with skirts, which I supplied. And the Racoons wore those spiffed-up jackets and coonskin caps.

"I seem to remember, on one occasion, having to go out and buy my own front apron, or aprons. Then I got smart. Once I sold Peggy one of my coats for the show. The script called for Trixie to be in a coat, and I had one I was about to give to Goodwill or the cleaning lady, so I asked Peggy if she could use the coat. That way Peggy could save herself a shopping expedition. When she said yes, I asked her what the going rate was, so they more or less had to pay me. Then that became Trixie's coat for the rest of the season."

In other words, *Honeymooners* costumes hardly constitued a complex fashion statement.

By midweek, Stanley Poss was pulling things together for the entire hour variety show. Jack Hurdle was casting players for the various scripts. "It seems to me," says Gingr Jones, "that we'd get the call to play in a *Honeymooners* or a *Reggie* or what have you early in the week. We were pretty busy working in other jobs around New York City, television like *Playhouse 90* and *Kraft Theatre* or *The Edge of Night.* Or radio. Many of us were from radio." But sometimes players were called at the last minute, and only their quick minds enabled them to survive.

Frank Satenstein (left) *in black shirt; Stanley Ross kneeling; Jack Hurdle* (right) *behind Gleason.*

Working on a scene from "Kramden vs. Norton." Ralph's long johns look on.

On Saturday morning the troops would assemble, with the June Taylor Dancers arriving first. "Saturday! How did we do it?" June Taylor asks, amazed. "What we were up against was a real, constant thought of trying to top the previous week. I do the cheerleaders for the Miami Dolphins now, and I'll look over and see Don Shula pacing, and it reminds me of what we went through, every week. You had to have a cast-iron stomach. You did your best. You did the show. After the show, you collapsed. Then you had to get up the next day and think about the following week.

"On Saturday, we'd be in the theater by seven A.M. First I'd have an hour's dry run, then we'd go into camera rehearsal, which would be another hour. In those days, we used to do an opening number, usually a production number, at the start of the show. Then, many times, a finale. We got in our rehearsals early. When you're in a theater, there's no extra place to go off and rehearse, unless it's a real emergency; then we'd go into the lobby. As a rule, we didn't have to do any side rehearsal unless a girl sprained an ankle or a girl came down sick, because you see, we didn't have any extra girls. Though I remember when we were rehearsing one of the '50s black-and-white 'Trip to Europe' *Honeymooners*—the one where they go to Paris—we had two young men dancing, as chefs, with prop knives. They were doing a turn, and one of the knives went into the other boy's eye, and almost took his eye out. It could have been much worse. But whatever happened, we used to manage."

The live commercials spots were also rehearsed in the morning. Around ten A.M., Stanley Poss, with a stopwatch around his neck, and director Frank Satenstein would muster their legions. The place was loaded with people named Jack—Jack Hurdle, Jack Lescoulie, sometimes Jack Albertson. But Jackie Gleason and Jack Philbin would not yet have arrived. On Saturday morning, Jackie usually breakfasted with Philbin and learned his lines, taking perhaps three hours to master seventy-five pages or more.

The sketch performers would begin to arrive. Says Ethel Owen, "We'd come in and say hello to each other. Then we didn't see each other the rest of the day, except to rehearse, and then you only rehearsed your lines. There was no chitchat.

"I'd known Art ever since he was a very young boy, but I didn't know the rest of the cast before. But even with Art, we just said hello and how are you. Audrey would come in—this is why I think she was such a terrific actress—she would come into rehearsal and she looked like something out of *Vogue* or *Harper's Bazaar.* Her hair was well coiffed, she wore stunning Adrian suits. She was like a million dollars. And then, a few hours later, she was a downtrodden, beaten woman who had nothing, absolutely nothing, not even enough food. And you couldn't believe it. Even I couldn't believe it. It was a great piece of acting. It really was. Joyce was pretty much the same. She'd come in looking like a million dollars too, but as Trixie, she didn't have to look as awful as Alice. Alice was the bottom of the barrel.

"We each had our own dressing room, and we'd go to the dressing rooms and read our lines. I didn't have to work all day on what I had. But I stayed in my room, and I'd go over my lines, play solitaire, or read a book. We wouldn't hang around and relate to each other as Art, Audrey, Joyce, and Jackie; so that for me, when we hit the air, they were *The Honeymooners.*"

"My first impression of Gleason," says George Petrie (Freddie Muller, the hypnotist, the guy who elopes with Alice's sister, and countless other characters), "my first show wasn't *The Honeymooners.* It was a *Reggie Van Gleason* segment. The show they were doing had to do with Reggie Columbus, his ancestor. My part was less than spectacular. I was a native in knee britches. All I can remember is that the whole thing was awesome to me. Jackie was in charge. Jackie was in the pit. When the show was being rehearsed, he was in the pit. Even if he was in the scene, somebody would stand in for him, Stan Poss or Jack Hurdle, and they would be playing the scene and Jackie would be down front saying, 'No, no, I want you to—' Strong. That's the first impression I had of Gleason. The enormous—more than energy—the strength. The control. He had full control. All the time.

Rehearsing for "Kramden vs. Norton." Says Joyce, "I only learned that shot the day of the show. And I managed to make it on the air— but just barely!"

Breaking up at rehearsal.

Watching a rehearsal from the pit.

"Early on in my experience with the show, there was a one o'clock rehearsal. Sometimes we didn't get the script until we got there, though usually we did. We had a read-through. We would have it without wardrobe or anything. Jackie wouldn't attend. He'd watch it from his room or the pit. Jack Hurdle would read Jackie's lines."

Says Ethel Owen, "He'd read them the way you'd say 'Please—pass—the—butter,' or 'What's—that—I—see? He-ey?' but with less conviction. He couldn't read lines. He sounded awful. They sounded like nothing. But there was a method to his madness. If you laughed yourself silly at rehearsal, the material might have less oomph when you did the show. I'll never forget one line I had. I was sitting at the table facing the audience, in that awful kitchen of theirs, and Ralph comes through the door. My back is to him. And I just said very casually, 'Hullo, Ralph.' He said, 'How did you know it was me?' And I said, 'I could feel the floor sag.' We all laughed so hard at rehearsal, it took us a while getting started again. It was still a funny line when we did the show, and it got a big reaction. But for us, it wasn't as much of a surprise."

Remembers Eddie Hanley (telephone man, telegram man, television man, and Racoon), "You'd get a little description, you'd do a run-through, the producer would do Gleason's part. I'd walk onstage, install a TV set, and maybe my line would be, 'Gee, a hundred dollars!' It wasn't really anything I had to take home and study and come in the next day and say, 'I know my line.'"

The sketch performers had their work cut out for them but rarely spelled out. Jackie, the sun around which other planets revolved, knew exactly what he wanted, but hated to have to dissect it. More than anything, he hated to rehearse.

Ethel Owen: "About that walk-through. Walk through what? On that set, there weren't many places to stand. There was a sink and a stove and a table. You seldom sat in a chair. There weren't that many chairs. If anybody sat in a chair, it was Alice's mother, me.

"I also remember what we would call in the business a line rehearsal, in place of a dress rehearsal, with Mr. Gleason. About an hour before we hit the air, we went to his dressing room and he was on a lounging chair with his eyes closed, resting. And we stood around him, saying our lines with no inflection, and he did the same. You didn't know where the laughs were. The show sounded like nothing. I left thinking the show would never come off."

"His eyes would be closed," says Frank Marth (Grogan the cop and a few dozen more roles), "but he was thinking, or visualizing the script."

"Jackie would show up for the dress rehearsal," says George Petrie. "I had a scene once, with him, which Jack Hurdle had staged. I was doing the dress rehearsal the way we had set it up, and Jackie went stage left while I walked stage right. Jackie said, 'Hey, pal, where are you going?' I said, 'Well, I was—' and he said, 'Hey, pal, if you want them to see you on camera, stay with me.' I learned very early, if he's pacing, forget what you did in the walk-through and just pace right behind him."

"To be fair," says Frank Marth, "if you were doing a scene, Jackie would never start something ten feet away. He'd wait, because he was very aware of the camera, and wanted to be sure it focused on whatever the important thing was that was happening."

Jackie might change the lines, too, either during rehearsal, or later, live. He might change a line if an actor wanted it changed. "He was very open to those things," says Anne Seymour (Mrs. Stevens, Miss Lawrence and other roles). "If he liked the line, you stayed with it. If the line was wrong, he'd fix it. But *he'd* fix it. He's a genius that way."

"The important thing to him," explains George Petrie, "was that you should be comfortable with your lines. Be comfortable. It's more real. If you're fighting words, you're fighting your character. So Jackie was open to modifications. But really, the writers knew the characters completely."

The writers themselves had little or no interaction with the players. According to Boris Aplon (Northside Mob boss Barney Hackett), "They never talked to the actors. They talked to Jackie." According to Walter Stone, "As far as dealing with the actors, we seldom did. With actors other than Jackie, Art, Audrey, and Joyce, we never knew who we were going to use." Says Ethel Owen, "The only reason I knew writer Marvin Marx was because one day he introduced himself to me on the street."

The story goes that at one line rehearsal, Jackie wrapped up before the end of the script. Writer Marvin Marx asked why. Jackie said the rest would take care of itself. Marx moaned. Jackie registered surprise: "But Marv, we *said* all the lines up to there."

There were few rehearsals when scripts were drastically changed, although, when major alterations were made—in those prephotocopy days—secretaries, showgirls, and people's sisters were recruited to type and circulate pages. There were occasions when complications in setting up a sketch left no time to rehearse it.

"One time," recalls Jack Philbin, "I think we threw out a whole script. Instead, we did a highlight show. I don't remember which one we threw out, or why. Generally, when Jackie threw something out, it was because something mechanical in it didn't work. I mean, sometimes there would be a funny sight gag that required mechanics and special effects, and sometimes they wouldn't work. Or Jackie was assured that they would work, but because of time or some unknown factor, he hadn't been able to see the things in advance. He always demanded to see things beforehand. But sometimes the delays were unavoidable. Then, on show day, in would come this thing, and it would be entirely wrong from what his concept had been. It would have to go. But he always had the confidence that we could come up with something."

"One time, we wrote an impossible routine," says Leonard Stern. "It was for a very gifted actor who later became a star, Jack Albertson. We had written him in, we had gotten him the part, so he really made an effort to do it. It was a drunk climbing a ladder while it was lying on the stage, flat on the floor, and he thought he was climbing up a building. We didn't realize it required an acrobat. Jack struggled with the bit. His pants had cuffs. His moves ripped the cuffs off his pants. Jackie called us and said, 'Who wrote this?' We said, 'We did.' He said, 'Then you must know how to direct this. Come over here.' We saw that he was right. It was impossible. We went upstairs to rewrite it, and when we came down, it was like *The Twilight Zone*. The theater was dark. There was nobody there. Everyone forgot they'd sent us upstairs to rewrite. We knew we hadn't been upstairs that long. It turned out that he'd canceled the show, if I remember correctly, because he found out the network was monitoring it.

"What had happened was, those days, Gleason's rehearsals were private because of all the tension. He had to learn some seventy or eighty pages in the course of a day, staging, blocking, choreography. I suppose there were a few expletives on this day, and the director, Frank Satenstein, said, 'Jackie, watch your language. A CBS executive might hear you.' Gleason said, 'How? Where's any CBS executive?' Frank explained that there was a monitor in the executive's home, and he was watching the rehearsal that way. It was the first time Gleason heard about this. Gleason said, 'He's watching now?' Frank said yes. Gleason said, 'Attention, Mr.'—I forget his name. Let's call him Mr. X. 'Attention, Mr.

Backstage.

Gleason rehearsing with a broken leg.

X, no show tonight. Everybody go home.'

"Eventually, cooler heads prevailed, and by six-thirty they'd talked him into going back on. Now everybody was reassembled, and we had the new scene, which no one had read, and didn't have time to rehearse. They had June Taylor Dancers, anyone who could type, typing pages for everybody. Between scenes, as the show was unfolding, they kept passing the script back and forth to whoever was about to go on stage."

Says Jackie, "The general rule was that once we started rehearsals, we were pretty committed to the scripts. I would have turned the scripts down earlier if I didn't like them."

By the time Jackie came down to join the dress rehearsals, cast and crew would be running through the entire hour variety show. As *jackie gleason enterprises,* he was responsible for all of it. "I am directly responsible for everything concerned with this show. I can't relax. I don't sleep well . . ." He

Rehearsing, probably for a Charlie Bratton sketch.

might put the dancers through step after step. Over and over. Or the orchestra. Or anyone else. Although his concern with the sponsors' scripts was minimal. "One time they were getting too ambitious. Nescafé wanted a hundred coffee cups on-stage. It would have taken about four or five stage hands. We had to make a scene change while the commercial was on, so I told them they just couldn't do this. They agreed. They were very nice about it."

Just when people thought there was no time left for revisions, Jackie would be suggesting some. "Jackie's instincts are phenomenal, far-seeing things," remarks Jack Philbin. "You have no reason to believe that he knows what he's talking about, and so you don't believe him, really, most of the time, but he turns out to be right many, many times."

Anyone not rehearsing would be in the general vicinity. You never knew what crisis might arise the moment you turned your back. Says Nescafé announcer Bill Nimmo, "We couldn't go home, obviously. We had to hang around the theater. We'd do such things as—for instance, Art Carney and I would sit down at the piano and pretend to do a little radio show. Answering letters: 'Here's a lady, Art, from Council Bluffs, Iowa, and she's sent you this recipe'—and we'd kid around, or play four-handed piano."

Toward evening, each woman on the program would receive a flower from Jackie Gleason. An hour or two before air time, anyone not enmeshed in a debacle or catastrophe was free to break for dinner. At that hour, even later, Gleason might still be waiting for, or deciding on, monologue jokes. The writers might be tossing lines at him: "How about saying Ray Bloch is writing a new song? 'Grandma, don't bother washing your neck. You haven't got a chance with Gregory Peck?'" And Gleason might run his fingers, Ralph-like, through his hair.

Inexorably, air time would arrive. Ready or not. Live. Of these Lost Episode years, Gleason remembers "working as hard and as long on them as we ever did later. If someone had told me back then that we'd be in syndication thirty years later, it wouldn't have made any sense, but we wouldn't have worked any harder. We really gave everything we had on those things. Not that we rehearsed a great deal, but when we were performing them, we gave the best we could. And I'm glad of that, because otherwise, now, I could be very embarrassed.''

Birthday party on the Honeymooners *set.*

Closing credits of The Jackie Gleason Show.

LIVE, ON STAGE

*The Jackie Gleason Show... a revue which is far
and away the most expensive entertainment ever
devised in TV history.*
CORONET (1953)

Even though the Lost Episodes have been found and released for
broadcast, the rest of the show they were part of is still as good as lost
today. The miracle of the Lost Episodes is that they're strong enough
to function as independent entities. But the truth remains that, unlike
the later Classic Thirty-nine, the Lost Episodes were never intended
to stand alone.

These live episodes were only one facet of a grand, flashy jewel called *The
Jackie Gleason Show*, and not always the most sparkling on a particular Saturday
night. According to a 1953 *Cosmopolitan,* "In the single year since Jackie
Gleason burst into big-time TV, he has become video's most relentlessly imitated
comedian." And when Jackie was imitated by kids on the street or grownups at
parties, they weren't just doing Ralph's "One of these days..." They were
doing Jackie's "Away we go" and Reggie's "Mmmmm-boy, are you fat," at
least as often.

So although a Lost Episode can stand by its lonesome, next time you watch
one, try to imagine it within the framework for which it was styled. In other
words, imagine, if you will—

Along about 7:55 P.M. on Saturday, with cameras about to go on, Jack
Lescoulie, on stage, warms up the audience. He tells them jokes, and shows them
how to make their applause sound louder, by cupping their hands. No applause
sign will signal them to clap. Their spontaneous reactions are taken for granted.
With total justification. This is network nirvana. Of course they're going to clap.

Production people enter the video booth, known as the Submarine because
about fourteen people sit there, with room for maybe eight. Frank Satenstein is
one of them, choosing which of the live camera views will be broadcast at a given
instant. He communicates with the floor staff by phone and mike.

In the audio booth sit fewer people in ampler space—Jack Hurdle, Bullets

Durgom, and the sound engineer. They're hooked up by phone to Jack Philbin (video booth) and Stan Poss (backstage).

Now Gleason heads down the stairs from his dressing room, through the crowds backstage, to the curtain. Stan Poss says anything from "Stretch the monologue to eight minutes," to "Think you can cut it to three?"

The Jackie Gleason Show is on the air.

A series of Portrettes announce that it's *The Jackie Gleason Show,* starring Jackie Gleason. Music swells. Other stars and guests are enumerated.

The June Taylor Dancers open the show. The overhead camera captures their kaleidoscopic patterns. They conclude, like Rockettes, with stunning precision kicks. The audience thunders applause. The dancers part, like a human curtain. Gleason strides toward the audience like he's parting the Red Sea.

As described by June Taylor, "No one had an opening of a show like Jackie, and it was his idea. We really opened with a bang. And when he walked out, to deafening applause that built as he entered, it was sensational. It's funny, but after we'd been on the air a while, he'd gotten a lot of mail. He called me in one day, and said, 'June, look, I've gotten some mail from people who feel I'm stepping on your applause.' I said, 'Jack, that doesn't matter. That's not what's important.' He said, 'No, let's do this. Let the girls finish their number and get their applause. Then let me walk out.' I said, 'Okay, if you want to try it, but it's not going to work.' Sure enough, we got our applause. When our applause died down, he walked out, and the applause started up again. But it was anticlimactic. Because, you see, when we finished the object was *bang/applause.* And he'd walk out— *crescendo/applause.* And it was all one. Tied together. So we went back to the old way after that."

To the roll of the continuing ovation, Gleason assumes command at stage front and center. In the first years of the show, Gleason enters to join the high-steppers in song and dance,

Jack Lescoulie with Jackie Gleason.

The monologue.

punctuating the closing bars with one of his earliest trademark phrases, "Hey, you kids, get offa the roof." In later shows, he switches to monologues. The curtain closes behind him—a hand-woven curtain sporting the gigantic away-we-go stick figure designed by Gleason himself. Gleason acknowledges, or makes fun of, "the flower of the musical world," conductor Ray Bloch. Since no cue cards prompt him, neither for the monologue nor for anything else, he may have to ad-lib if he forgets a line. He begins with "Ladies and gentmun," because no one put three syllables in "gentlemen" in the Golden Age of Television. Gleason does his monologue, half the time making fun of the fact that it isn't funnier. Sometimes it leads to physical comedy.

"There were a few shows where, at the beginning of the monologue, I did a weigh-in. How that came about was that I'd told the audience I was going to lose weight, and I said, 'To prove it to you, I'm going to have a scale here every week and I'm going to weigh myself.' After about the third week, I got on the scale, I saw that I didn't lose anything. So I hit the scale with a chair."

To close the monologue, Gleason strikes his away-we-go pose, calls for "a little traveling music," and travels across the stage.

A guest star may follow, maybe Robert Merrill singing an aria, or Patti Page singing her latest golden record. Or Jackie, June Taylor, and her sister Marilyn Taylor (now Mrs. Jackie Gleason) doing a soft shoe. Or—once—Audrey Meadows and her sister Jayne doing the song they recorded, "Hot Potato Mambo." Or Jack Benny outsmarting children to earn a quick dime.

June Taylor and Audrey Meadows do a song-and-dance routine for The Jackie Gleason Show.

"There was one," says Jack Philbin, "with Jack Benny and the Hines boys from Hines, Hines and Dad. I knew the Hines act, so we cooked up this contest where the prize was something like twenty dollars. The Hines kids came out and danced up a storm. Then Benny came out in a little-boy suit and played the violin. Benny wins the money, and the kids are looking at him like he just beat up on Santa Claus. And finally, Benny says, 'Oh, wellll, here,' and gives them the prize money. It was a funny, funny bit."

Music might be next, conducted by orchestra leader Ray Bloch. Music, whether for the June Taylor Dancers or any other reason, is a consuming interest of Jackie's. Though he can't read a note of music, Jackie's compositions and LPs of mood music are number-one chart busters, and his theme song, "Melancholy Serenade," is a million-seller. It's what he calls "plain vanilla music . . . it's for a guy with his girl. Maybe they got a couple of bottles of beer and they're feeling sentimental. Well, why should I stand in nature's way?

"Actually, it all happened because of Clark Gable. I saw Gable in a picture, and he was dressed in tails, looked great. And he was doing the dialogue. Then he sat down on the couch with the girl, and the music snuck in. And everything he said was magnified a thousand percent. So I figured, if Gable needed music, a guy in Brooklyn must be *desperate*."

Jackie stuns viewers with "Lovers' Rhapsody," his own composition, which he conducts. He has fifty-five musicians onstage. The dancers are onstage too, up on a platform twelve feet high. The lighting is striking, artistic. The dancers are superb and, because of the lighting, not entirely sure where the platform ends and the twelve-foot drop begins. Deems Taylor, the dean of American music commentators, introduces the offering: vignettes of romance, in haunting song and dance, with a cameo by the Poor Soul.

"Tawny,"—Gleason's tone poem and ballet in four parts, is presented by the June Taylor Dancers in 1953. This twenty minutes of genuine audiovisual breakthrough wins sweeping praise from *New York Times* critic Jack Gould: "Bravo for Gleason. One of the most exciting hits of the video season."

Another number, an absolute knockout, has the sort of repercussion that's synonymous with live TV.

"It's forever burned into my memory," says June Taylor. "Jackie was in the hospital, so we had to meet there. He asked, 'What do you want to do as the production number next week?' and I said, 'Well, I have this idea for a fire number. I'll have the girls dressed as fire nymphs. I'd like platforms, ramps, and I'd like to use de Falla's "Ritual Dance of Fire." So he looked at me, because I realized he wasn't sure what the music was at the time. He said, 'All right, that sounds exciting. Go ahead.'

"We rehearsed. I was happy with it. Jackie came to the theater. This was going to be a big show, and I felt it needed a production number in the middle. Jackie watched the number and listened to the music, and when it was through, he said, 'That's sensational. But I tell you what, June, we're going to wait until next week to do it.' I looked at him, and said, 'What are you talking about? What do you mean, next week? What do I do this week? Don't you like the number?' He said, 'It's great. But wait till next week because it's going to be even better next week. I'll meet with you and we'll talk about it.' Well, I was ready to cry, because I'd worked very hard on this.

"So we went into a meeting on Monday morning, and CBS had hired for us a very special special-effects man, who had won the Academy Award for the locust scene in the movie *The Good Earth*. Jackie proceeded to lay out what he felt I should do with this fire dance. And he said, 'I'll tell you what, we'll have the ramp, and we'll have the platforms, but we've got to have some special effects. We must have fog coming down from the ceiling. And we've got to have shots of fire going up in the air.' And he's going on, and I'm looking at him in utter vacant disbelief, and then he says, 'But we need even more exciting music. The damnation music from *Faust*.'

"I said, '*How* are we going to do this?' The special effects man did too, he said he wasn't sure we could pull it off. I mean, these were the days we worked with Scotch tape, spit, and string. But they rigged up this idea. This was before the advent of fog machines. Across the top of backstage there was a string of let's say thirty buckets, and the thirty buckets had little springs in them, heaters to keep the water hot. When the number started, every other bucket had chips of dry ice dropped into the bucket. When you put dry ice into hot water, it gives out a fog. Because there was air conditioning in the theater, the dry ice only lasted half the number. So halfway through, we had a rope to trigger the rest of the pails, to continue with the fog. We had it so that the fog hung down like a water fall.

"Also, behind our ramps, where you couldn't see them, were Sterno cans shooting flames up in the air. And Jackie had wanted to get the sort of elevator they have on the backs of garbage trucks, used to lift garbage from the ground to truck level. He wanted one for the devil, Peter Gladke, with a cape, to come up out of the flames.

"Showtime, the girls came dancing down these ramps. Flames. Fog. Effects. Quite a number. For the finish, the girls went running up the ramps to jump into the flames as though they were being devoured. The devil jumped in too. One of the Sterno cans tipped over. A fire started. They almost had to pull the asbestos pad down. This was, mind you, live, it happened while people were watching from the audience and in their homes.

"We managed to put the fire out. But the fire department came, found the special-effects man who had won the Academy Award, and put him in jail. No one knew about it. We didn't know about it until Monday. The poor man spent the weekend in jail.

"That was Saturday night. On Monday, at our meeting, Jackie turned to me and said, 'June, do you know how much *your* production number cost? $55,000!' He was kidding. But do you believe it? We still laugh about what lengths he went to."

Between segments, while Jackie is backstage changing costumes, is announcer Jack Lescoulie. Lescoulie knows what he has to convey, but has no script whatsoever. He ad-libs everything. Stan Poss is giving him signals to stretch his

Jack Lescoulie.

chatter or compress it. "We'd just say to stretch it," explains Jack Philbin, "and he'd go into some 'Another thing Jackie said to me this morning...' He was terrific. Tremendous radio experience, and very personable. A very talented man."

"We had a thing going," says Gleason, "that if a change was very difficult for me to make and I didn't make it by the time I was supposed to, Jack Lescoulie would go into a public-service announcement for the March of Dimes. We had more March of Dimes spots than any program in the world."

Jackie comes on in costume. Perhaps he's Rudy the Repairman, attempting to fix a sink. "One day," says Ethel Owen, "I got a call from Jack Philbin to do the show. I was told not to wear anything I was too fond of. That should have warned me. But I got busy and forgot, and wore a very nice Saks Fifth Avenue suit. In the sketch, I played a society woman who called this man and his helper to fix the plumbing. Jackie says to me, 'Lady, would you get in the sink and hold this?' The other goon is under the sink. I climb into the sink. I wasn't in it more than two seconds, and I was a human fountain. My hair, which I'd had fixed immaculately because I was playing a society woman, was hanging down my face. I was sopping wet clear through to my girdle.

"I still had lines to do, so I stepped out of the sink. Before I got the lines out, my rayon suit started to shrink. It had a bolero jacket. It was starting to look like a scarf around my neck. The skirt was going up and up and up. I was as good as standing there in my black slip.

"When I got offstage, Jack Philbin said, 'That was an expensive dress, wasn't it?' He asked how much it cost and I told him, and he said, 'You'll have your check in the mail.' I thanked him, but I said I really wasn't worried about the dress. I was just so embarrassed. He said, 'Well, it was funny as hell.'"

Interspersed between sketches and numbers are, naturally, commercials. The Sheaffer pen commercials, generally on film, demonstrate such heart-stopping features as the Sheaffer snorkel tip fountain pen. It operates so easily, you can refill it while wearing your best white evening gloves.

The Nescafé instant-coffee commercials are most often live, with Jimmy Blaine doing the pitch. Remember, these are the days when you use fountain pens and own white evening gloves. Do you dare make coffee from a jar of powder? Half of what Jimmy Blaine has to convey is that nice people *do*. He does this by drinking it and telling the waiting world, "Mmmm-mmmm, that's real coffee flavor." Or by comparing its price against the cost of ground. For this, he might use props like ticker tape and a blackboard.

The Nescafé sponsor also, on occasion, manages to set a jar of Nescafé instant on the Kramden table in a *Honeymooners* sketch. Alice offers to make people coffee "in an instant." Says Gleason, "It happened, but I'll tell you this. If a Nescafé jar was put on the table or the icebox, they didn't mention it to me. And you can bet they didn't have it there during rehearsal."

Sheaffer magazine ads from 1953 and 1954.

Nescafé instant coffee promotion, 1953.

Note sponsor's jar placed prominently on the table.

Later, Old Gold is one of the sponsors, and in "Manager of the Baseball Team" (1957), Ralph does offer Old Golds by name to Norton, one of the features that distinguishes the episode from its earlier (1953) version, made before Old Gold came aboard.

Bill Nimmo is the spokesman for Schick electric shavers. Like Jimmy Blaine, he has to pitch the concept as much as the product. Yes, you *can* get a close shave with something that looks like a space-age gadget. He proves this by having a beautiful woman rub her cheek against his before and after a shave with Schick, after which she tells him which experience she prefers. Sometimes he ex-

Announcer Bill Nimmo.

tends special offers, perhaps ten dollars if you buy now. Then he holds up a hand-lettered sign reading $10 OFF.

Says Nimmo, "We had a lot of people on commercials that were quite well known. I did a Christmas commercial one night with Hope Sansberry, who played the colonel's wife on the *Bilko* program. She was a fine actress, but toward the end of the commercial, she was supposed to say, 'In that case, I'll take two'—then look into the camera and continue—'one for my husband, and one for my son.' But when we did it live, she turned to me, looked into the camera, and froze. I put my arm around her and said, 'I'm sure in that case you want two. One for your husband, one for your son.' She stammered, 'Ye-s-s,' and I kissed her on the cheek. The audience went mad. We got mail. Hundreds of letters. If everything had gone right, we'd never have heard about. It sounds like it would have been a botched commercial, but the beauty of live TV was that this little incident made it a success."

Sometimes Jackie assays a commercial. The audience loves it. He could love it more. As Leonard Stern remembers, "There was one—Jackie was supposed to say, 'When you walk into the store, ask for a Schick razor.' But he went blank on the name of the sponsor, and since there were no cue cards, he had to wing it. So he held up the razor and said, 'When you walk into the store, ask for a razor just like this one. Be sure and say *this* is the razor I want.' He never did say Schick. There were two advertising men in the back of the theater. I overheard one ask the other, 'Do you think we should talk to Gleason about this after the show?' The other answered, 'I don't know. He got most of it right.'"

"Speaking of sponsors, there was one time," says Walter Stone, "a magazine, I think it was *TV Guide,* ran an article about Jackie. It was accompanied by photos, and one shot had him shaving with a straight razor. Maybe a Gillette. When the sponsors saw it, they said, 'You know, we don't mind your not using it, but do you have to get your picture in a magazine not using it?'"

But the simple fact is that any sponsor on the Gleason show is getting too handsome a deal to complain. Gleason is king. Gleason sells. He wants me to buy that stuff? Gladly. In that case, I'll take two.

Though he labors like a serf, Jackie Gleason *is* king. He does his regular character sketches. Sometimes he does other things. On January 30, 1954, the June Taylor Dancers do a number on bicycles. Rosin is used on the floorboards to keep the bikes from slipping. Following this is a Little Lord Fauntleroy bit, a spoof of the silent film *The Wedding.* Seltzer hits the stage and mixes with the rosin. Gleason hits the blend of goo and skids as he exits. Boris Aplon, backstage, breaks Gleason's fall—"The impact nearly flattened me"—and Gleason sustains a dislocated foot and broken leg. The audience laughs uproariously, thinking the spill is deliberate. With Gleason disabled, Art Carney has to close the show.

Bullets Durgom remembers, "The night he broke his leg was very interesting. I'd just gotten married, about a month earlier. I told Jackie I was going to take a honeymoon, a long weekend, and he said, 'You can't leave. You're needed here.' But I set everything up, and arranged it so that I could finish the week with him, then be back before the next Saturday's show. There was a midnight plane. I have a limousine at the stage door. I have my bags waiting backstage.

"That night I said, 'Jackie, I'm leaving after the show.' He said, 'Naw, pal, you're not.' The show goes on the air. I'm in the booth. We're into the closing minutes. There's Art Carney saying goodnight instead of Gleason. So I run to Jackie, who I see is on the floor with a broken leg. We call the doctor, send for the ambulance. I said, 'Jackie, the ambulance is on its way.'

"He looks up at me and says, 'Didn't I tell you, pal?' And he was right. When this happened, I couldn't leave, I had to stay."

"There's another irony with his breaking his leg," says Leonard Stern. "That was a sketch he wrote. I remember because every once in a while he'd say we weren't capturing the characters. Then he'd come up with something. And he came up with this. Broke his leg. I remember, as he was going out—they were carrying him on a stretcher—he looked at me and said, 'Don't say anything.'"

Over the next few weeks, guest hosts sub for Gleason. With Gleason not there to do Gleason sketches, other bits have to be devised. In one priceless offering, Art Carney and Zamah Cunningham play the parents of Edward L. Norton of Chauncey Street. As Ed Norton Senior, Carney holds forth about being a sewer worker, in the tradition of his father before him. Ed Senior looks and dresses like Ed Junior, except that he wears a bowler hat. Ed Senior has a personality like a village coot.

Instead of a Rudy, or in addition to, Jackie segues into Reggie Van Gleason III, Joe the Bartender, the Poor Soul, or another popular character. Not quite weekly, he is Ralph Kramden in *The Honeymooners*. An assemblage of players take their places on stage. No cue cards. Barely rehearsed. Stepping out into Lost Episodes immortality. Strains of Irving Berlin's "Always" open the scene.

"And then I knew," says Ethel Owen, "why we weren't more rehearsed. There would be the music. And then the script would start. It was all you could do to keep from laughing. That was a real problem. The laughs were sensational. You had no idea what Mr. Gleason was going to do, because he hadn't done it at rehearsal. He would not let anybody see what he was going to do. I don't think he knew himself until he hit the airwaves. I think it was all spontaneous. But he knew exactly what we were going to do because he'd sat in the audience or watched from his room during rehearsal. Of course, you had to be on your toes. You couldn't deviate from the script.

"I'd worked for some comedians who were overbearing fanatics, and they rehearsed you to death. By the time you were onstage, you were just going through the motions. But Mr. Gleason had a way of getting all that you could give him. Including spontaneity. And if you don't have spontaneity in a comedy script, you don't have anything.

"Not that spontaneity meant ad-libbing if you thought of something funny to say. Gosh no. You wouldn't just take it upon yourself to change the script."

Of course, Gleason could ad-lib at will, and did. In "Teamwork Beat the

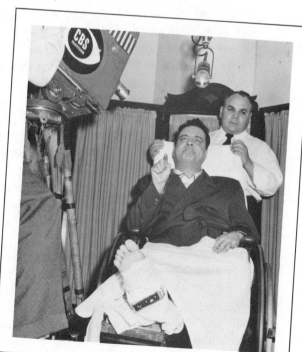

Gleason does the last five minutes of the February 6, 1954, show from his hospital room after breaking his leg on the previous week's show. With him is valet and longtime friend Tony Amico.

Clock,'' Norton is supposed to break balloons by accident, and Kramden is supposed to holler, ''I knew it! I knew somehow you'd ruin everything!'' Instead, Kramden snaps, ''You and your hangnails!''—to cast and crew's complete surprise.

Says Audrey Meadows, ''The scripts were written very, very well. We had very powerful, great writers. The only time we would really ad-lib or change anything, because the show was done live, was if somebody forgot a line. You had to fill in and make something up until you got back on the track again.''

According to writer Herb Finn, ''At first, Carney knew every word. But then he got in the habit of not knowing everyone's lines. And there was Audrey, who always knew how to pull them back to the right lines. We had shows where Gleason suddenly came up with a line that belonged to the next act. You can imagine working a live show with someone who does that. But Audrey always knew how to pull Ralph and Ed back to their lines. She knew the whole script.''

Finn continues, ''You know the very effective manner Ralph had of saying, 'You think I don't know what you're doing, Alice? You think I don't know what you're doing? You *think* I don't *know* what you're doing?' This was Gleason's very effective way of stalling while he groped for a line. It became part of Ralph's character. Perhaps he did it deliberately after a while, when he found out that it worked.''

Anne Seymour remembers a forgotten line during a seance scene. ''I was playing a fortune teller ('The Fortune Teller,' April 1955, of which only half has been found to date). He had a long speech, and he went up higher than a kite. And I thought, 'Golly, can I help him?' Then I thought, 'I will not help him. This is his show, and he can get out of this as best he can.' And he paced. That's what he always did when he didn't know what exactly he was going to do. So he paced like mad, and he got himself around, and out of it. When we came off, he said, 'Anne, thanks. You're a pro.' I knew I was right in not trying to push into it, to let him do it himself. He respects that.''

Says Walter Stone, ''Because Jackie didn't like to rehearse, long speeches could be tricky, even though he had a photographic memory. In the adoption episode, we had a scene with Ralph getting sentimental about the baby in the crib. He can't take his eyes off the crib. People have told me what a touching scene it is. But you know what he was doing? He was looking into the crib because there was a script there. When he first saw the script, he said, 'Hey, this is great. I don't have to learn this part. I'll just look in there and read it.' But he's such a great actor, he was believable. He conveyed real emotion in that scene.''

Sometimes everyone knows their lines, but a prop doesn't work. Gingr Jones remembers ''sitting at a counter having coffee in a scene, and Jackie came in. The phone was supposed to ring, and Carney was supposed to come in. The phone didn't ring. We didn't know what was going on. So I knocked a spoon off the counter and ducked down to pick it up. At the same time, Jackie went for the spoon. We had a slight discussion behind the counter about what was going to happen in the scene.''

One time, Norton is supposed to come into Kramden's apartment and talk to Alice. Norton tries the door. The door doesn't open. It doesn't budge. He tries again. Nothing. Finally, he climbs through the window. Since there's no glass in the window, he forgets to open the sash. He just steps right through. The audience howls. Carney ad-libs, completely in character, "There's more than one way to skin a cat." A Wester Union messenger knocks at the door. By now, it's common knowledge that the door is a lost cause. Norton says, "Good luck, pal." But the door has been repaired. The messenger breezes in. The audience goes wild.

"There was one," says George Petrie, "in the episode where Alice's sister is eloping with this schnook who runs the projector at the local theater. My wife, Patti Pope, is the sister. I'm the schnook. Ralph is helping the sister elope. At rehearsal, the scene presented problems so we had to rewrite. We got our new lines when we came back from dinner. I remember Patti and I, sitting on the steps, learning our lines. It was a good-sized scene.

"Well, the show goes on, and everything plays fine up until the last. Now, it starts. Patti's coming out of the window. She's got one leg out, to step onto this ladder Ralph has against the building. She's handing things out to him. The ladder starts shaking. He says, 'Go back, go back.' She doesn't know what he means. This isn't in the script."

Says Patti, "I didn't see why I should go back. You know, I wasn't standing inside the Kramden apartment. I was standing up on a ladder behind a piece of scenery, hanging out of a hole cut into the scenery, not a real window. The ladder I was standing on wasn't the Rock of Gibraltar."

George: "I'm down there. Finally, she goes down her ladder and comes out the front door. We go into the dialogue. I happen to look at Jackie. Then I grab Patti and head offstage. She's resisting. She's muttering, 'I've got lines and I'm going to do them.' But I get her offstage and tell her I'd noticed Jackie jerk his head as a signal for us to get off. Then Jackie reels off the material that was supposed to be covered during her descent down the ladder. Then he signals us back on, and we finish the scene."

Whatever happens, the cast plays the script straight through. If a line is missed, someone ad-libs in character. If a prop doesn't work, ditto. This is true of the live *Honeymooners*. It's equally true of the Electronicam *Honeymooners*.

Only once is it not true. As Gleason revealed on the New Year's Day 1986 edition of *P.M. Magazine,* "Strangely, in all the times, of all the shows we've done, variety shows and *Honeymooners*, we only stopped once. And that's because the whole wall fell down. We had to stop for that because Carney had his head through the scenery. This flat came down, and he looked up to see what the grating noise was, and the scenery fell on him and his head came through the scenery. He wasn't hurt. He was laughing, and he had the scenery around his

Musical number—probably "Song of the Sewer"—with production crew members as sewer workers.

head. We were hysterical. That's the only time we ever stopped.''

Generally, the largest cast on a *Honeymooners* set is a meeting of Racoons. There are occasional exceptions. There's a racetrack scene, by the betting windows, with every familiar Gleason extra in a walk-on. "But," says Jack Philbin, "you wouldn't do that too many times. That's where I was supposed to come in and say, 'Keep the costs down.' The number of people was always a consideration, but we always stretched the budget as far as it had to go. We didn't cheat the public.''

Explains Walter Stone, "We'd seldom use crowds of people because Jackie had a theory about too many people standing around to do what he called, 'catching flies.' You can't do a joke or anything with distractions onstage. If we did a street scene, like in 'Santa and the Bookies,' we had people crossing in the beginning, then the street cleared when Kramden and Norton did their dialogue. Maybe a dancer crossed with Sammy Birch or Eddie Hanley. Then they disappeared. They got out of the way.''

In a New Year's Eve episode, the Kramdens and Nortons go to a posh New York hotel to see Tommy and Jimmy Dorsey perform. "That," says Walter Stone, "violated all the rules, in a way. We had many, many more than the usual number of people onstage. The Kramdens and Nortons were just part of the group watching at the club. But this was a case where we wanted to devote the last twenty minutes of the program to sort of a Tommy and Jimmy Dorsey segment, so we tied it in with a *Honeymooners* plot.''

What is fascinating about the scene is how little it looks like live TV, and how much like documentary insert photography. ''But it wasn't,'' says Jack Philbin. ''We never had insert photography in our shows, because we always felt that the audience in the theater would be cheated by something we shot outside. That was one of Jackie's rules, and it was a good one.''

''It was live, all right,'' adds Jackie. ''We had everybody in the show sitting at tables. We had stage hands, husbands, wives, everybody. And it looked just like it was in a night club.''

The Honeymooners, as a general rule, concludes with a few bars of George and Ira Gershwin's ''Our Love Is Here to Stay.'' *The Jackie Gleason Show,* for several years running, wraps up each season with a finale featuring cast, crew, producers, writers, and the rest of the gang onstage.

As the clock approaches nine P.M., Stan Poss goes into his signals. Gleason starts cutting lines, or stretching them, on his feet. ''One time,'' says George Petrie, ''Stan signaled 'out of time' and Jackie, completely in character, said, 'You all listen to me,' then he did everyone's parts.''

Recalls Audrey Meadows, ''Jackie had an uncanny sense of timing. I used to think he had a time clock in his head. When he sensed we were running too long, he'd come up with a line from pages ahead in the script. Art and I would pick it up. I've seen other actors go white when he did it. It always seemed to work, though, with few exceptions.''

The foremost exception is ''Stand In for Murder'' of April 17, 1954. Gleason plays the double role of a mob boss and his look-alike, Ralph Kramden. The convoluted twists and switches—and prolonged audience laughter—eat up the clock. It ends abruptly, with Alice holding a gun on the gangsters. It's nine P.M. before the story's over. The theater audience sees the rest of the show. The TV audience is stopped short by the CBS Eye—station identification—end of the Gleason show.

The next day, each of New York's major dailies has stories speculating about how the story was to have ended. The following week, Gleason's monologue, perhaps his most successful ever, reveals the ending. This time the monologue runs so long that *The Jackie Gleason Show* runs over again.

The show generally closes with Gleason, sweating, often in a dressing gown like a boxer after a fight, delivering a few words of wrap-up. If Poss signals ''Go long,'' he says a lot of whatever comes into his mind. If Poss waves goodbye, he gives a quick good night. There's no anticipating what he'll have to say, so it's all ad-libbed. When time is really short, there's not even a chance for closing credits.

Gleason returns to his dressing room. A crowd has gathered to jump him. He passes someone who asked him, earlier in the day, about an idea for a bit. "Hey, pal," he calls, "That idea you had. I was thinking about it during the broadcast . . ."

Next time you watch a Lost Episode, try to imagine that framework. That *Jackie Gleason Show.* Better yet, go to New York's Museum of Broadcasting on Fifty-third just east of Fifth Avenue. You can see one with monologue, commercials, announcers, dancers, and guests, essentially intact.

You can see the show as the '50s saw it. And why those were the good old days. "They *were* the good old days," sighs Bill Nimmo, "when we were not old, and we were pretty good."

Curtain call on The Jackie Gleason Show.

DEJA-VU

*There was some of the vaudeville sense that a good
idea deserved repeating. And sometimes, look, we were
doing a live show. Sometimes we got stuck.*
WALTER STONE

With the syndication of the Lost Episodes, viewers can be expected to bang the sides of their television sets (or their heads), intoning "What? Wasn't this in color the last time I saw it? And how can it be a lost anything from the '50s, when I know I saw it in 1966?"

These are nifty gestures, but unjustified.

The explanation is simply this. Not only was Jackie Gleason reluctant to refuse a script; if he liked one, it stood a good chance of being recycled. There was never a stated strategy, never an unwritten law about it. It was just the way things happened, and an entirely sensible way for them to happen at the time.

Says Jack Philbin, "It was a terrible drain to keep coming up with material. You always figured that if you had another day, maybe you'd be funnier, maybe more interesting, or maybe something. And of course to a writer, everything he writes is the best thing he ever did. And somewhere between is the answer. Then, too, the demands on the writers and on the cast were such that many times it would help a little to know the material in front."

There was another factor as well. Initially, the *Cavalcade of Stars Honeymooners* were live, meaning that each was seen only once—and also of DuMont vintage, meaning that most viewers never even saw them once. So when *The Honeymooners* moved to CBS, it hardly seemed like repetition to recycle a few plots or premises. Besides, as *The Honeymooners* grew from a ten-minute sketch to a longer story, a premise that had been a one-line joke could be fleshed out into something more substantial.

One of the earliest examples of recycling is "Honeymooners Christmas Party," with Gleason using a Christmas fete to bring the Poor Soul, Joe the Bartender, Reggie Van Gleason, and the others to the Kramden apartment. It was originally presented as a long DuMont sketch. Essentially the same sketch was redone on CBS in 1953. It opens with Ralph coming through the door, and Alice sending him right back out for food—exactly as the first ever *Honeymooners* began, and with dialogue reminiscent of that one. It continues with Gleason making a series of quick changes into his repertory of characters. This has

Cavalcade Honeymooners Christmas-party antecedents, as well as roots in another *Cavalcade* predecessor that also starred Gleason, in which he did a series of quick changes to play all the roles in a Dickens tale. And, just as this episode was inspired by past efforts, it became the inspiration for later ones.

There were even instances of direct reprise in the early CBS years. "Halloween Party" (1954) was "Halloween Party" (1953), with relatively minor changes in dialogue and costuming. "What's Her Name?" (1953) returned as "What's the Name?" in 1954, the main difference being the addition of the song "One of These Days, Pow."

By 1955, when *The Honeymooners* was being done as a half-hour sitcom, it was again reasoned that all the previous shows, live shows, had been seen only once and therefore were largely forgotten. So, as before, some of the scripts were reshaped and redeveloped for the new half-hour format. "A Matter of Life and Death," the arterial monochromia episode, had its roots in *Cavalcade*'s "Six Months To Live" (a favorite of Gleason's because of the writing), where Ralph's canine malady was cerebral monochromia. Bits from "A Promotion" showed up, expanded, in "Pardon My Glove" ("What a surpri—") and "Please Leave the Premises" (everyone freezing in the Kramden apartment). "Pardon My Glove," in turn, had roots in a DuMont sketch (the jealousy routine and the attempt to get Ralph to go out for the night). Alice's "Not every woman has a husband who's still jealous... after fifteen years of married life" has its roots in the same DuMont sketch ("...after twelve years of married life"). There are definite echoes of "Boys and Girls Together" in "Alice and the Blonde." Ralph getting Alice a box made from two thousand matches glued together, then someone else giving her one first, was recycled from "The Anniversary Gift" to "'Twas the Night Before Christmas." "'Twas the Night Before Chrsitmas" also used the device—echoing "Honeymooners Christmas Party"—of Ralph giving Alice what Ed gave Trixie, a juice squeezer resembling Napoleon.

Then there was the case of "Funny Money," with Ralph finding counterfeit money on the bus. Observes Walter Stone, "Remember the adoption episode? We'd already done some where Ralph thought Alice was going to have a baby, so we thought maybe we could get a baby quick some way and see what happens. So he finds a baby on the bus. Later we did it with the money he found. Money, baby, I was working on a canary. . . . "

In 1956, when Gleason canceled his contract for half-hour *Honeymooners*, he went back to the varied-length approach. By February 1957, he was striking out in an entirely fresh *Honeymooners* direction: musicals by the songwriting team of Lyn Duddy and Jerry Bresler. These musicals, the *Trip To Europe* segments, involved Ralph's winning the opportunity to go bumbling across Europe and into Africa with Alice and the Nortons. In these episodes, the June Taylor Dancers danced up a storm, and the Kramdens and Nortons sang their hearts out. "There was so much new material to learn for each one," says Joyce Randolph. "Songs

"'Twas the Night Before Christmas," 1955, *expands on favorite lines and scenes from previous Christmas shows.*

and dance routines as well as considerable dialogue. Fortunately, we all had musical backgrounds, we didn't have to go out and learn to sing. But it was really hard work making them. That's why Jackie curtailed them. At one point he just said, 'No more countries. That's the end of this. We're going back to Brooklyn.'"

The traveling episodes covered previously untrodden ground, though the kick-off, in which Ralph enters the breakfast-cereal contest, draws on the earlier "Boxtop Kid."

At the end of the 1956–57 season, Art Carney left the Gleason show to pursue other interests, such as *The Art Carney Show* series of specials on NBC (1959–'60) and, later, winning the Academy Awards for Best Actor in 1974 for *Harry and Tonto*. With his departure, Gleason dropped *The Honeymooners* altogether.

As the years rolled on, Gleason's credits mounted. In the early '60s, his show was called *The American Scene Magazine*. When Art was available for a few shows, *The Honeymooners* resumed. Since this show originated from Miami, and neither Audrey Meadows nor Joyce Randolph wanted to relocate to Florida, Sue Ane Langdon (Alice) and Patricia Wilson (Trixie) played the wives.

This early Poor Soul sketch reemerged with few changes in the Classic Thirty-nine Honeymooners *episode entitled "Young At Heart."*

In January 1966, Audrey Meadows became briefly available again, as was Art Carney, so a musical *Honeymooners* special was made. The reunion, after so many years, was an exciting, emotional event, and the story chosen was just as exciting and emotional: "The Adoption," a classic that had been seen only once before, live, and which was recycled for the memorable occasion.

By late 1966, Art was prepared to spend more time on what was once more entitled *The Jackie Gleason Show*. *The Honeymooners* re-emerged, this time with Sheila MacRae as Alice and Jane Kean as Trixie. Many of the earlier stories were used—the logic being, in part, that these *Honeymooners* were in glorious color where the others had been black-and-white. Also, the scripts that were recycled were the ones that hadn't been rerun, including with updates and revisions—along with Duddy-Bresler numbers and June Taylor Dancers—the *Trip to Europe* series. With forty new songs and 2,100 pages of dialogue to learn for the season, the cast was anything but complaining if a thing or two smacked of the familiar.

This series, later syndicated in multiple markets, consisted of:

TITLE: *"In Twenty-Five Words or Less"*
DATE: *September 17, 1966*

Ralph wins the Flakey Wakey trip to Europe for four.

TITLE: *"Ship of Fools"*
DATE: *October 1, 1966*

The Kramdens and Nortons sail to Europe.

TITLE: *"The Poor People of Paris"*
DATE: *October 8, 1966*

Ralph and Ed get a great exchange rate—on counterfeit money.

TITLE: *"Confusion Italian Style"*
DATE: *October 15, 1966*

Ralph is jealous of Alice's guide, not knowing the guide is a little boy.

TITLE: *"The Curse of the Kramdens"*
DATE: *October 29, 1966*

Ralph and Ed have to spend the night in the ancestral Kramden castle, which has its very own ghost.

TITLE: *"The Honeymooners in England"*
DATE: *November 12, 1966*

Ralph appears in a Flakey Wakey commercial on an English TV show.

"Pardon My Glove" echoes earlier gags from CBS and DuMont Gleason shows.

TITLE: *"You're in the Picture"*
DATE: *November 19, 1966*

Blackmailers fake a hanky-panky photo of Ralph in Madrid, and for a change, Alice is jealous.

TITLE: *"We Spy"*
DATE: *December 3, 1966*

Ralph and Ed wander onto a Russian firing range while visiting Germany.

TITLE: *"Petticoat Jungle"*
DATE: *December 10, 1966*

The Kramdens and Nortons go on a safari.

TITLE: *"King of the Castle"*
DATE: *January 7, 1967*

Back from Europe, Ralph advises Ed to stand up to Trixie—and, suddenly, Alice moves in with Trixie and Ed is living with Ralph.

The other Gleason-Carney-MacRae-Kean *Honeymooners*, those not in the *Trip to Europe* group, found Ralph as a sidewalk Santa and Norton as his elf . . . Norton winning a door prize with a ticket Ralph bought him . . . Ralph duped into playing the double of a notorious mob boss . . . and so on. When people saw these episodes in the '60s, perhaps they experienced some vague déjà-vu, some little voice saying "Remember when you watched me on your Motorola ten years ago?"

Today, as people watch the Lost Episodes, it may be just the reverse, with the little voice whispering, "Remember? Remember when you watched me in color, in 1967, twenty years ago?"

Of course, all this recycling occurred long before there was any thought of finding the Lost Episodes—before anyone dreamed that two similar episodes might one day be viewed side by side. There's no telling, twenty years from now, what the little voice will be saying, because there's no knowing, for certain, which of the found episodes will still be running. Or which of the still-lost episodes might, by then, have been found.

STILL LOST

I wanted to be sure they [the thirty-nine] had run their course before I brought out the new ones. I'll let these run about thirty years, and then we've got a few left.
JACKIE GLEASON

With the end of the *Jackie Gleason Show* from Miami in 1970, Gleason went on to other things. He made more movies—he already had *The Hustler, Soldier in the Rain,* and *Gigot,* to name a few, under his belt. ("Inside a master jester, there is a masterful actor"—*Time,* 1961). He did more theater, such as *Sly Fox,* a triumph in the tradition of his Tony-winning performance in *Take Me Along.* He played more golf—his Jackie Gleason Inverrary Classic was the richest seventy-two-hole golf tournament in the country. More everything—everything except *The Honeymooners.*

There was the occasional special, reuniting Gleason, Carney, and Meadows, with Jane Kean in the Trixie role. Since specials don't fit the half-hour rerun mold, these shows aren't seen today, unless by people who a decade ago owned VCRs and taped them. (Anyone reading this book in the year 2000 should please note that in the late '70s relatively few people owned VCRs). These specials were:

TITLE: *"The Second Honeymoon"*
DATE: *February 2, 1976*

The Kramdens plan to renew their vows for their silver wedding anniversary. Ralph and Ed get smashed on grape juice. Ed warms up at the keyboard with "Swanee River." Ralph thinks Alice is expecting, and she is—her mother.

TITLE: *"The Honeymooners Christmas Special"*
DATE: *November 26, 1977*

Ralph stages Dickens's *A Christmas Carol* for the Gotham Bus Company. Ed plays two parts, Scrooge and Tiny Tim, and has trouble with quick changes.

TITLE: *"The Honeymooners Valentine Special"*
DATE: *February 13, 1978*

Ralph is going to surprise Alice with an all-modern kitchen. Alice is going to

The role that brought Gleason a nomination for the Best Supporting Actor Academy Award—Minnesota Fats in The Hustler (1961), with Paul Newman.

In a serious role, in the CBS dramatic special The Million Dollar Incident, with Peter Falk and Jack Klugman (1961).

In the movie Gigot, 1962.

Jane Kean, Art Carney, Jackie Gleason, and Audrey Meadows in "The Honeymooners *Valentine Special" (1978).*

surprise him with a custom-tailored suit. He immediately concludes she wants to kill him, so he and Norton dress as women to expose her dastardly scheme.

TITLE: *"Jackie Gleason* Honeymooners *Christmas"*
DATE: *December 10, 1978*

Ralph is the victim of a "Transylvanian blessing," which leads him—and the people he convinces, like Norton and Alice's mother—to invest money in buying hundreds of lottery tickets.

These specials are, for all practical purposes, lost. For that matter, the 1966 *Trip to Europe* series, though it was in syndication in the '70s, is presently unavailable except to people who taped it when it was on.

Another episode lost—also because it was a special—is the 1966 adoption show, the much-heralded Gleason-Carney-Meadows reunion. Likewise, the episodes done in 1962 for the *American Scene Magazine*, with the Gleason-Carney-Langdon-Wilson cast, are on the scene no longer.

There are some lost episodes brought forth from Gleason's vault, episodes from the CBS years, that had deteriorated too badly to be salvaged. There were some held back (a later "Manager of the Baseball Team," an earlier "Vacation/Fred's Landing") because they are too similar to others in the package to be released. There are some CBS lost episodes that to date are unavailable on television but available on MPI videocassette. At press time, the breakdown is:

"Halloween Party" (10/30/54): lost
"Manager of the Baseball Team" (6/1/57): MPI has released
"Easter Hats" (4/4/53): lost
"Alice's Birthday" (5/16/53): lost
"Missing Pants" (12/6/52): lost
"The Turkey" (9/27/52): lost
"Lost Baby" (10/11/52): lost
"Quiz Show" (10/18/52): lost
"Question Mark" (10/25/52): lost
"Christmas Party" (12/52): one reel found; MPI may release
"Fortune Teller" (4/3/53): half of show available; MPI may release
"Vacation at Fred's Landing" (6/53): MPI will release
"What's the Name?" (5/15/54): MPI will release
"Law Suit" (3/27/54): MPI will release
"One Big Happy Family" (4/9/55): MPI will release

Ralph stages "A Christmas Carol" for charity in "The Honeymooners Christmas Special," November 1977. With Jane Kean, Audrey Meadows, Jackie Gleason, and Art Carney.

All these are significant. But the bulk of the still-lost episodes falls into two categories: those from the Du-Mont years, and the black-and-white Gleason-Carney-Meadows-Randolph *Trip to Europe* musicals. The latter, because of their similarity to the 1966 series, suffer the stigma of being redundant—which doesn't seem to be hurting the Lost Episodes—and somehow inferior because they're not in color.

The question of color, an issue any student of Woody Allen would happily debate, may one day go the way of the who-wants-to-watch-kinescopes argument. As Jack Philbin has said, "Jackie always believed, and he sort of taught me to believe, that you didn't need color for comedy, which is very true." Sid Caesar once went so far as to state, "I think color detracts from com-

This appears to be a scene from the still lost "The Turkey" of September 27, 1952.

edy. You get too distracted by colors, unless you have something that directly deals with color. When you have black and white, it doesn't detract. You just see the comedy." When it comes to *The Honeymooners* a further point can be raised, which is that we've come to believe the Kramden's apartment *is* black-and-white, even to the jar of jellybeans he brings home.

Any hope of recovering the earlier, and very rough kinescopic, black-and-white DuMont material seems slim. Reports suggest that DuMont's archives went up in flames, were sold for scrap, or were erased and reused a long time ago. In fact, DuMont's disregard for kinescopes was what led to Jackie Gleason's starting a vault in the first place.

According to Jack Philbin, "When I was first working with him, he was having a problem. The one thing he had told me was that they had discovered, through accident I guess, that all the kinescopes they had had at DuMont had been destroyed by DuMont as an economy measure, for space. So we made up our minds right then and there that we wouldn't repeat the mistake. We kept all our kinescopes. That's what the Lost Episodes are. The result of 16mm kinescopes."

In addition to the above still-lost sagas are a number of quasi-*Honeymooners* saga-ettes. There are the wraparounds filmed for the specials launching the Lost

Ralph and Ed enter the Flakey Wakey contest, 1966. Alice (Sheila MacRae) doubts their sanity.

Episodes re-release. It's unlikely these will return again in quite this form. There was a *20/20* tribute to Gleason and *The Honeymooners* in 1981, celebrating Jackie's 65th birthday. There are sketches that spring from nowhere when they're least expected, but infrequently enough to be virtually lost. Among them are a *Honeymooners* sketch starring Gleason and Carney that was done for *The Ed Sullivan Show* which can still be caught, however rarely, on a *Best of Sullivan* compilation; a sketch starring Audrey Meadows as Alice, Jack Benny as Ralph, and Dennis Day as Norton, done for the *Jack Benny Show;* a sketch done for *The Hollywood Palace* with Audrey playing Alice and Ray Bolger as Ralph; an episode of *The Lucy Show* in which Gleason appears as a bus driver named Kramden, and Jack Benny appears as Jack Benny.

As lost as anything can be are the never-televised live stage shows: the tour that introduced Gleason and *The Honeymooners* to the nation in 1952; a similar stage show, with the CBS cast and the June Taylor Dancers, presented at the Paramount Theatre in 1954; a "Thanksgiving with Jackie Gleason" *Honeymooners* of 1978, at Resorts International's Superstar Theater in Atlantic City.

Lost, and related to *The Honeymooners*, are the sketches and variety numbers by which the live *Honeymooners* were framed. At the moment, only the "*Honeymooners* Christmas Party" preserves the '50s Gleason gallery of characters and the June Taylor Dancers. But the best moments of either, while contained in the footage found in Gleason's vault, haven't yet been re-released. Therefore, missing is a twenty-fifth-anniversary-in-show-business special program of the Loudmouth, the Poor Soul, Reggie Van Gleason III, Joe the Bartender, and Ralph. At present, only a Gleason compilation series, culled from the *American Scene Magazine* and featuring some of these characters, continues to run in syndication on some local stations.

Some people will insist that the made-for-TV movie *Izzy and Moe* is *Honeymooners*-related. It is, in the sense that it reunited Jackie Gleason and Art Carney, in 1985, for the first time in many years. It is, in the sense that a few flourishes and gestures echo Norton and Ralph. But it is not, in the sense that it certainly wasn't supposed to be. Said Gleason, "People will say we weren't as funny in it as we were in *The Honeymooners*. Well, on those terms, I don't think we could do anything that would be comparable with *The Honeymooners*. I'd like to work with Art again, but it would have to be a strictly dramatic script. Then we're sure of not being compared with *The Honeymooners*."

There were rumors circulating that Gleason and Carney were teaming up for a TV movie about two retired gents who win a cruise and then have to masquerade as a married couple. This was an idea, but the project never got far.

Art Carney has said he'd like to do another *Honeymooners*, this time situated in Florida, with the Kramdens and Nortons retired. It's safe to say that the idea hasn't been ruled out.

Gleason as Joe the Bartender with Frank Fontaine as Crazy Guggenheim, from Miami.

Honeymooners *tie-ins released in the '50s.*

RALPH KRAMDEN, INC.

Get the bag!
RALPH KRAMDEN

O n screen, the Honeymooners always went full circle. Ralph started each episode poor, and no matter what luck came his way in the course of the episode, no matter what good fortune he seemed to encounter, he always started the next episode poor. Back to the same kitchen. Back to the same icebox. Not one of his schemes ever bailed him out of his poverty. Not the Handy Housewife Helper. Not the KramNor. Not betting on Cigar Box or Happy Feet. If only he'd thought of selling his personal effects to *Honeymooners* fans . . .

Because *The Honeymooners* as a media phenomenon has achieved the success Ralph always dreamed of. It's gone from square one to the moon. And now people are making money by planting his likeness on T-shirts, board games, figurines, and dozens more items.

Of course, there was memorabilia in the '50s—an "Away we go" button, a tin bus, comic books, a paper doll book, a "Story Stage" game, fanzines, and other items. And any that haven't been lost, or junked by a mother cleaning out a closet, are worth saving. They were yesterday's throwaways, but they're collectors' gold today.

The more recent memorabilia, made possible through the deal Viacom struck with Gleason, which includes merchandising rights, is just beginning to surface. Calendars from Crabwalk, Inc. Novelty sunglasses, fans, and postcards from American Postcards. Sleepwear from A.J. Schneierson. T-shirts from Changes. Statues from Esco Products. Board games from T.S.R. From Effanbee Doll Corporation, as the first two celebrities in their "Great Moments in Television" series, come painstakingly crafted Ralph Kramden and Ed Norton dolls. These collectibles, each 16½ inches tall, retail in the neighborhood of seventy-five

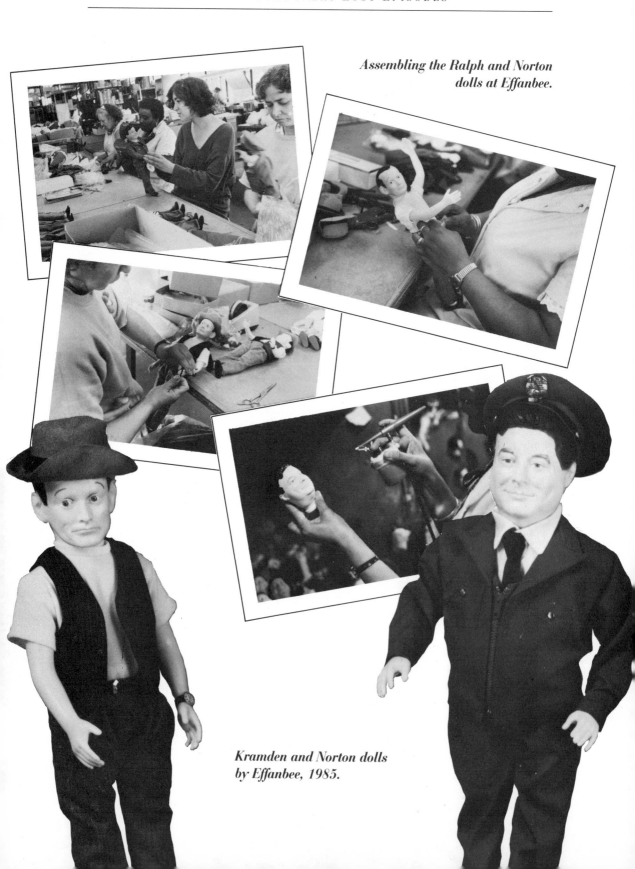

Assembling the Ralph and Norton dolls at Effanbee.

Kramden and Norton dolls by Effanbee, 1985.

dollars, which is more money than Kramden or Norton earned in a week.

Joe Piscopo's *Honeymooners Rap* of 1985 was nominated for, though didn't win, a Best Comedy Recording Grammy Award. The all-star LP album "It's *Honeymooners* Time!" was released in 1986. It combines past and present ditties like Art Carney's "Song of the Sewer" and "Va Va Va Voom"; Audrey and Jayne Meadows singing "Dear Ralph"; Jackie Gleason singing "One of These Days, Pow," and conducting "You're My Greatest Love"; Jesse Goldberg's "It's *Honeymooners* Time"; and Rose Maione and Jack Simmons's "I Want a Wife Like Alice Kramden."

If you buy any dolls or records or games or other memorabilia, don't lose them. And this time, don't let your mother throw them away.

Insights into memorabilia, old and new, are often found in newsletters available to members of RALPH (Royal Association for the Longevity and Preservation of the Honeymooners, C. W. Post Campus, Greenvale, New York, 11548), as is membership in the organization and convention updates. Conventions offer the chance to see new merchandise, visit with Gleason players, and view Alice's dress and apron—donated by Audrey Meadows—and Ralph's bus driver uniform, donated by the Great One himself. Conventions also mean you can eat pigs' knuckles and sauerkraut and dress like Fortune the parrot.

Prototype of "The Honeymooners Game," brought out by TSR in 1986.

RALPH events have made musical-entertainment history with the debut of Jesse Goldberg's "It's *Honeymooner* Time" and Jack Simmons and Rose Maione's "I Want a Wife Like Alice Kramden." They've made comedy history with the hucklebuck and bang-zoom lessons of husband-and-wife comedy team Ruth and Eddie Ayres. They've even made airborne history—no, not as in "to the moon"—when the Audio Digest earphones channel of Northwest Orient Airlines ran highlights of a 1985 RALPH convention.

Imagine what Ralph would think of all this. His eyes would bulge. He'd say "homina homina homina." He'd pirouette into a cartwheel faint. Then—well, you know Ralph—he'd probably recover and go back to Bensonhurst, to his black-and-white kitchen, because Ralph is Ralph. He's a full-circle sort of guy.

Justin Roy Bender, age one, dressed as Racoon Stanley Saxon at the May 1984 RALPH convention.

THE GLEASON PLAYERS

The Gleason Actor is the kind of guy who lets nothing bother him once he's on the air.
AUDREY MEADOWS

A Gleason Actor can do a show in the middle of the Civil War.
JACKIE GLEASON

At first blush, the *Honeymooners* cast is its principals. The Kramdens and Nortons could hardly have been portrayed by the first four fools who walked in off the street. Quite the contrary; *The Honeymooners* required nothing short of flawless cast chemistry. As the Lost Episodes reveal—even the early ones where the players were still finding their characters—the cast chemistry never failed.

From the first *Honeymooners* on, Gleason was as ready to define Ralph Kramden as any actor ever was for any role in the history of entertainment. He had the experience. He had the talent. When their time came, Art Carney, Audrey Meadows, and Joyce Randolph were ready too, with talent and experience in abundance. Art had done television (Morey Amsterdam's two programs) and radio (on *Report to the Nation,* he did the voices of leading political giants). He'd been an announcer with Horace Heidt's orchestra, and made a movie with Heidt. Audrey had done television (starring with Bob and Ray on *The Bob and Ray Show*), light opera, and Broadway. Joyce had done Broadway musicals and television (from Dean Martin and Jerry Lewis's show to detective mysteries).

Each was a skilled performer. Together, the four were perfection. "The thing you've got to remember," says Harry Crane, "why this show succeeded—and I tell this to everybody—a successful show has to have a stock company. If you haven't got the people, you can't make it. Gleason had the people."

Jackie . . . Art . . . Audrey . . . Joyce. Yes, Gleason did have great people. The greatest. But not all of them played characters named Ralph, Ed, Alice, or Trixie. Some played Racoons. Or doctors. Or cops. These were known as "Gleason Actors," who could get their scripts at the last minute and know not only their cues, but everybody else's.

George Petrie and Art Carney rehearsing.

The Gleason Actor so often seen in *The Honeymooners* that he could almost be a fifth principal is George Petrie. In recent years, Petrie has been seen on *Cagney and Lacey, Maude,* and, in the regular role of the Ewings' lawyer, Harve Smithfield, on *Dallas.* In the '50s, George could be seen in *The Edge of Night,* and as a hypnotist, bad guy, bus dispatcher, and relative on *The Honeymooners.* "Gleason would tell me to wear a goatee, or a scar," says Petrie, "so that I wouldn't look like the same man every week. We never expected these things to go into zillions of reruns where it would be this obvious."

Petrie remembers the instant he became a Gleason Actor. "It was a Reggie Van Gleason sketch, a gymnasium scene, and someone was massaging a corpse. In comes Reggie Van Gleason to solve the mystery. Gleason and I are exchanging lines, and suddenly he's gone blank. In those days, I learned the whole script. Everyone's lines. I didn't try to, but lines stuck with me, so I knew his. I said, 'Mr. Van Gleason, don't you—? Wasn't there—?' He said, 'Yeah, and I'll tell you something else,' and we got back into the script and finished fine. We walked offstage, and he patted me on the back, and said, 'Thanks, pal.' That was very nice. Then I got a call from the producer, Jack Hurdle, over the weekend. He said, 'You're in very good shape. Jackie said, "Any time that Petrie guy is right for a role, use him. We work good together."' I was lucky, because something came up that I could handle."

Boris Aplon (Barney Hackett in "Stand In for Murder") was known as the biggest villain of all time on *Captain Midnight* ("I was the master of disguise and dialects. Every thirteen weeks I'd jump off a cliff or something and be thought dead, then come back as a Chinese potentate and ingratiate myself with Captain Midnight"). He was a meanie on both television and radio, to the point that this sort of role was being called a "Boris Aplon part." But this menacing mien only partly accounted for his popularity with Gleason for a wide range of sketches. "George is right. I think that's why he used so many of us over and over again. There were times when a line would be missed, and it would be a line leading up to a very expensive gag that the writers had done that would be lost. Most of us were quick enough to put it back on track. That's all Gleason needed. To be put back. And of course, there were times when other actors went off, and Gleason brought them back by doing their lines.''

Most of the Gleason Actors were recruited by producer Jack Hurdle, whose extensive radio experience had introduced him to hundreds of players. George Petrie and Boris Aplon were both called in by Jack Hurdle. So was Petrie's wife, Patti Pope Petrie, whose previous theatrical credits ranged from *Kraft Theatre* and *Studio One* to the part of Carole Landis's sister in the original *One Million B.C.* and the ingénue lead in the play *Cordelia,* which also had in its cast a young Nancy Davis (now Nancy Davis Reagan). Patti's brush with ''rewrite-on-your-feet,'' in ''Game Called On Account of Marriage,'' was so unsettling that she vowed she'd never do the show again. (But she weakened, and did.)

Humphrey Davis (train conductor in the Classic Thirty-nine ''Unconventional Behavior'') had been friendly with Walter Stone since the days when Stone

Humphrey Davis.

Patti Pope Petrie, who elopes in "Game Called on Account of Marriage."

was an actor, and he'd worked with Jack Hurdle in radio for years. On radio, it wasn't unusual for Humphrey to do two or three shows in a day, among them, with Hurdle, *Portia Faces Life.* On television, he appeared in everything from *Gangbusters* to *The Jack Benny Show* to *Omnibus* and *Kraft Television Theatre* (eighty times). On radio, Hurdle liked to use him as "a b-man, his term for bad man" but in the Lost Episodes he's generally a bus company biggie or Racoon officer. He describes one scene at the bus company in which "one of the actors had to drop out at rehearsal, so all the other actors there had to move up one rung. This left a very minor opening at the bottom rung. I'm pretty sure Stan Poss stepped in to fill it." As was so often the case with Gleason Actors, Humphrey's first association with the Gleason show had nothing to do with *The Honeymooners.* Rather, he appeared in a musical mood piece with the June Taylor Dancers, scored by Jackie Gleason.

Another of Hurdle's recruits was Anne Seymour (Miss Lawrence from the adoption agency). The first member of a seven-generation theatrical family to turn to radio, and radio's Mary Marlin *(The Story of Mary Marlin;* and for a while, Portia on *Portia Faces Life),* Anne Seymour recalls "working with Art Carney on *The Magnificent Montague* for three years. He played everything from Monty Wooley's father to a garbage man. Coincidentally, Pert Kelton played the maid, Agnes, and Agnes was a smart-mouthed gal from Brooklyn. On *The*

Ethel Owen as a society matron in a Reggie sketch.

Les Damon as FDR in the play Sun- rise at Campobello.

Gingr Jones.

Honeymooners, I remember doing a scene with Audrey and Jackie. I looked at Audrey and immediately forgot the line, but Audrey threw it to me. Then he picked up on it. It was done with such ease, such professionalism. It was recovered before the audience guessed a thing.

"Something else, now that I think about it, is that there weren't many women in the *Honeymooners* stories. I know Jackie likes women. It must have been the situations. You really wouldn't have women around the pool hall, the race tracks, the Racoon Lodge, the way you had extra men."

But one role a woman had to do was the role of Mrs. Gibson, Alice's mother. Ethel Owen was Mrs. Gibson many, many times. "Jack Hurdle was after me to do it. He knew me from Chicago radio. Then I came to New York, and did three Broadway shows, one after another. Each one ran a year. With the shows going on at eight P.M., I was out of commission for evening television all those years. Finally, he phoned and I wasn't involved in Broadway, so I did it. I did *The Honeymooners*, and other Gleason sketches too. One thing that stands out in my

Zamah Cunningham with Art Carney as Mr. and Mrs. Sedgwick Van Gleason, Reggie's parents.

mind about being Mrs. Gibson is that I had to wear a red wig. It was an audience show, and they wanted me to look as much like Alice as I could, because I was supposed to be her mother. Audrey had red hair, so I wore a miserable old red wig that matched her hair. And I wore padding, because I was supposed to be chunky, so that Ralph could insult my weight. And I seem to recall wearing more than one awful old dress.''

Les Damon (Frank in "Stand In for Murder") and his wife, Gingr Jones, were also called by Jack Hurdle. Les Damon, a popular New York television actor (*The Edge of Night, Search for Tomorrow, Playhouse 90*), was famous, too, as radio's Thin Man (in *The Thin Man*) and Falcon (in *The Falcon*). Gingr, who was Alice Kramden after Pert Kelton had to drop out of the 1952 live *Honeymooners* tour, also remembers "once or twice, early shows, perhaps on DuMont, where I played Norton's wife. I'm not sure the part was big enough to give me a name. It was more like talking furniture. But I remember it distinctly. Actually, I wasn't on that many *Honeymooners*, though I was on quite a few other Gleason sketches on CBS. My husband, Les, was in *Honeymooners* sketches all the time. His favorite *Honeymooners* show always was when they had the meeting of the Racoons. They wore those funny Racoon caps with the tails hanging down the back. Here were all the best actors in town, sitting there looking like a bunch of idiots.''

Some Gleason Actors were with *The Honeymooners* before CBS—including
Zamah Cunningham, Frank Marth, Eddie Hanley, and Sammy Birch. Joe Cates,
at DuMont, found Zamah Cunningham (Mrs. Manicotti, Mrs. Monahan, Mrs.
O'Leary), an accomplished actress with credits in vaudeville, Broadway, TV
dramatic series, and the movies (including work with early-cinema giant D. W.
Griffith). Along with her *Honeymooners* duties, she played Reggie Van Gleason
III's mother and the woman whose home was routinely laid waste by Rudy the
Repairman.

Frank Marth (recently seen in series like *Quincy* and *Dallas;* in *The Honeymooners,* the cop in "Stand In for Murder," "Honeymooners Christmas Party,"
"Santa and the Bookies," to name a few) was also called in by Joe Cates. "It was
for a sketch entitled 'The Last Mile and a Half.' A bunch of guys with broken
noses played cops. Clean-cut types like Art Carney and I played convicts. It was a
marvelous role. The very next week, Gleason needed a cop in a show and said,
'Get the kid who played the convict, Monk Meyers.' That's how it began."

Eddie Hanley and Sammy Birch had been friends of Jackie's since his
vaudeville days, and were brought to the show by him. (So was Jerry Bergen,
who played Rudy the Repairman's sidekick Whitey, and Gleason's tag team
partner on *Cavalcade.* Bergen appears with Rudy in "Honeymooners Christmas
Party".)

Gleason's ties to Sammy Birch go back to the Halsey Theater, where Birch
was his predecessor as emcee. When Gleason came to New York at the age of
nineteen, he stayed with Sammy Birch. On the night-club circuit, Birch had a hit
lip-synch act, considered to be comedy's first. On *The Honeymooners,* he was
everything from a Racoon to a denizen
of the underworld.

Eddie Hanley was a twenty-five-
year veteran of vaudeville when he
joined *The Honeymooners.* "Sammy
and I used to play pool with Gleason,
you know, socialize. And he had this
house up in Peekskill, New York. I
used to go there. He had an outdoor
barbecue—talk about extrava-
gance—he had a chimney made out
of Italian marble which was im-
ported. You know—a chimney!
Something smoke is supposed to
come out of. What the hell do you
need to import Italian marble for?
It was an experience.

"Well, what I did on *The*

Rehearsing with Frank Marth.

Honeymooners I also did on Milton Berle's show, and, later, on Phil Silvers's *Bilko*. If there were any lines to be spoken, any singing to be sung, or dancing to be danced, I was the handyman. I was on Broadway in *Top Banana* when he signed me. I was going to go on the road with it. If I had, instead of being in *Honeymooners* reruns, I'd probably have been in the movie version of *Top Banana*, and how many times is that shown now? So there's me, the Racoon taking minutes, or the guy on the fire escape, or the guy pushing the Chef of the Future on stage.''

At least two Gleason Players, not very well known in their *Honeymooners* days, subsequently achieved considerable fame. Robert Middleton (Mr. Marshall in "*Honeymooners* New Year's Eve Party") went on to distinction in movies like *The Desperate Hours, Friendly Persuasion,* and *Which Way to the Front?* Jack Albertson (a guy at the track, a guy playing cards) began his career as a straight man in burlesque. From there, he went on to *The Honeymooners*. From *The Honeymooners*, he went on to a starring TV role in *Chico and the Man,* and, for *The Subject Was Roses,* both a Tony award for his Broadway portrayal and an Oscar for the motion picture.

Two Gleason Actors, not regulars but not to be forgotten, were Martyn Green and Sandy Renda. Martyn Green, Gilbert and Sullivan star and veteran of the D'Oyly Carte Company, had the same role in both the 1957 and 1966 versions of the *Trip to Europe*. He was the mainstay in the "Coming to Paris" number both times. But there was a significant difference between the two. In 1959, he lost his leg in a garage elevator accident. He performed the 1966 show with an artificial limb. His philosophy was, "Take a lesson from a baby just learning to walk. He stumbles and falls, but he gets right up again and has another go."

Sandy Renda did only one *Honeymooners*, but it earned him unique status among Gleason Actors for learning the most lines in the shortest time at the youngest age. He was nine years old when he auditioned for the role of Tony, Alice's "boyfriend," in the Italian leg of the 1957 *Trip to Europe*. He won out over five-hundred boys, just two days before the show went on. In that time, he learned the lines, an original song, and a dance.

The first time Sandy Renda ever met Gleason was in front of a live audience. "He was never at rehearsals. I was nine years old, looking up at him, and it was like looking at an avalanche. And I was crazy about him, anyway, prior to this. A casting call had come through, because I'd done summer stock. For instance, I was a little Siamese kid in *The King and I*. When I auditioned, I sang "Getting To Know You" from *The King and I*. Then I had to read from the script. When I was finished, Stanley Poss said to wait outside.

"When he came out and told my mother they wanted me—if there had been a hole, she would have fallen through the floor. She got so excited, when they left for wardrobe, she forgot to take me. My mother went to tell my father downstairs. They got in the cab and drove away. They had to come back for me.

Frank Marth, Jackie Gleason, and Art Carney rehearse "The Hypnotist."

"In the show, I sang with Audrey, then we did a dance. At the end of the dance, the audience was very, very responsive. Their reaction was long, and loud, and it wasn't stopping. I'd always been taught, in the little things I'd done, to wait till the audience stops before continuing. Otherwise they won't hear you. But Audrey, in her smiling at the end, when the applause was running too long, was talking to me through her teeth. 'Okay, you can start now.' That was my cue. That really sticks out in my mind.

"I also remember that we could have purchased a kinescope of the show for $300 at the time. My parents didn't, whatever the reason. I was paid $500 gross. Net I think was $210, plus my father's losing a day from work. Maybe that was the reason."

Today, Sandy's still in the business with his own six-piece band, Sandy and the Wanderers. He's also author, with Joe Cinderella, of *Chord Playing For the Guitarist Musician,* just published.

Eddie Hodges had no lines and barely had to put one foot in front of the other when he appeared, at age six, in "Honeymooners Christmas Party." His

Sandy Renda "romanced" Alice in "When in Rome" (1957).

Page with Sandy Renda's notes from the "When in Rome" script. © 1986 by Jackie Gleason.

contribution was to sing "Walking My Baby Back Home," not as a Gleason Actor but as a guest star, since this episode used a *Honeymooners* premise to contain a variety show. This was Eddie's first appearance on national television. In short order, he was a contestant on *Name That Tune* (paired with Marine Corps Major John Glenn), and on Broadway as Winthrop Paroo in *The Music Man* (Pert Kelton was in it too, as his grandmother).

Another guest star in the guise of character, in the same *Honeymooners* episode, was Frances Langford. Langford—voted "No. 1 Girl of World War II" in a poll of G.I.s, picked "All American Girl" by radio editors in 1939, and radio's Blanche Bickerson on *The Bickersons*—was a frequent guest, as a vocalist and in comedy skits, on *Cavalcade* and *The Jackie Gleason Show*.

Tommy and Jimmy Dorsey, longtime pals of Jackie Gleason and Jack Philbin, played themselves, and invited the Kramdens and Nortons to watch them entertain, in "*Honeymooners* New Year's Eve Party." Bud Collyer and Roxanne played themselves—host and hostess of CBS' *Beat the Clock*—in "Teamwork

Beat the Clock." Since *Beat the Clock* was done from the same studio, the same day, as the Gleason show, in the 7:30–8:00 P.M. slot, Collyer and Roxanne's *Honeymooners* appearance was essentially a matter of not leaving the theater at the usual time. Jack Benny did a cameo, as a tight-fisted landlord, in "Principle of the Thing." Elisha Cook, Jr. (consummate worm in a string of gangster movies; Wilmer the gunsel in *The Maltese Falcon*) did a cameo, as Lefty, in "Santa and the Bookies." With both, when they were in town from Hollywood and seeing Gleason, he suggested it would be great fun to be on his show. Each gamely agreed.

It wasn't easy being a Gleason Actor. Scripts were late. At rehearsal, sneeze or blink and you'd had it. Jackie was somewhere on stage you didn't expect him to be. Nor was recognition quite what might be expected, either.

"When the show was finished," says Frank Marth, "people used to run around to the stage door to see Jackie, Art, Audrey, and Joyce. And this particular night I left the theater. Now at this point I'd been an actor about a year and a half, two years or something. So I'm walking out of the stage door, and a kid jams an autograph book in my kisser. 'May I have your autograph?' And I figure, hey, two years in the business and already I'm a star. So I start to sign my name. F-R-A-N-K. I get to M-A-R-. Somebody yells out, 'Here comes Gleason!' The kid rips the book out of my hand. It's an ego equalizer."

An ego equalizer *then*. Yet with the 1983 advent of RALPH, this score has been settled over and over again. No *Honeymooners* player escapes with less than a prolonged, resounding ovation. The Gleason Actor who tries to leave without signing a thousand autographs is flirting with disaster. When Frank Marth, even before stepping out on stage, said over the speakers, "I suppose I can put you down for the usual buck, Kramden"—the house went wild.

It's interesting to see actors getting accolades for the one job they never thought would win renown. Today, many of the top character actors in '50s radio and television—talents who did *Studio One* and *Kraft Television Theatre*—are resplendent on the TV screen in reruns of *The Honeymooners*. As much as you may want to, you can't see their brilliant Golden Age triumphs. You can't see Eddie Hanley in *Top Banana*. But you can see him shove Kramden into camera range in "Better Living Through TV." You can't see Les Damon and George Petrie on *The Edge of Night*. But you can see them flop their Racoon tails and go ooo-wooo.

If it doesn't seem like much, you're not paying attention. Wouldn't you settle for Abraham Lincoln doing comedy on *The Honeymooners*, if it meant a chance to see (1) Abraham Lincoln and (2) great comedy? Let us not shortchange immortality. Above all, let us never shortchange those wonderful Gleason Actors.

INDEX

PHOTO CREDITS